SEA TO SHINING SEA

SEA TO SHINING SEA

People • Travels • Places

Berton Roueché

AVON
PUBLISHERS OF BARD, CAMELOT, DISCUS AND FLARE BOOKS

Most of the contents of this book first appeared in *The New Yorker*.

AVON BOOKS
A division of
The Hearst Corporation
1790 Broadway
New York, New York 10019

Copyright © 1985 by Berton Roueché
Front cover photograph copyright © 1987 by Jim Markham
Published by arrangement with Truman Talley Books/E.P. Dutton, a
division of New American Library
Library of Congress Catalog Card Number: 85-20461
ISBN: 0-380-70265-7

The Truman Talley Books/E.P. Dutton edition contains the following Library of
Congress Cataloging in Publication Data:

Roueché, Berton, 1911–
  Sea to shining sea.

  "A Truman Talley book."
  1. Roueché, Berton, 1911– . 2. Voyages and travels—1951– . I. Title.
G465.R68   1985   910.4   85-20461

First Avon Printing: May 1987

To my travelling companion

"For my part, I travel not to go anywhere, but to go. I travel for travel's sake. The great affair is to move."

—R. L. STEVENSON
Travels with a Donkey
(1879)

Contents

1. On the Terrace: New York, Chicago, Seattle

I am lying in a swaying hammock, gently swaying in the sun. I am swaying and swinging. I am lightly bouncing, then suddenly rocking. I am rocking from side to side, from end to end. The hammock lifts and sinks. It lurches. It lifts again, it drops again, it jolts and pitches. I am falling. The ground comes arching up. There is a shuddering thump, a bump. It thumps me, bumps me, wrenches me awake. I open my eyes to darkness. I am lying sprawled on my back, entangled in sheets and blankets, in a clinking, clanking midnight dark. And the hammock—I'm not in a hammock. There is no hammock. I am lying in a lower berth in Bedroom C in Car 4901 of the Lake Shore Limited, en route from New York to Chicago on the first leg of an Amtrak journey to Seattle.

This was the third time in not quite twenty years that I had travelled from coast to coast by train. I made the first of these trips in the fall of 1961, when the American passenger train, at least in the West, was still almost as good as it had been at its impressive best: an extensive dining-car menu of well-prepared food; fresh flowers and linen napery; complimentary overnight shoeshines; convenient schedules; prompt, courteous, and efficient service. I made my second transcontinental trip in the fall of 1970, just before the advent of Amtrak, when train travel, even in the West, seemed almost designedly sleazy and uncomfortable: snack-bar food, unemptied ashtrays, torn sheets, no hot water, flat wheels, long halts on sidings to let a freight train pass. This third three-thousand-mile excursion was one of hopeful curiosity. I had been told that Amtrak had made a considerable effort to restore to its consortium of railroads much of the traditional pleasure of train travel. I had been told that the Lake Shore Limited was now composed of thoroughly refurbished cars and was manned by a reanimated staff, and that the Chicago-Seattle train, the Empire Builder, was an even more arresting accomplishment. It was, I was told, a brand-new train, an all-electric train, a train composed of newly designed equipment—new diners, new sleepers, new coaches. Last March, I thought I would see for myself.

I had seen a little already. The Lake Shore Limited, despite its name, is not an express. It leaves Grand Central at six-forty-five in the evening and is scheduled to reach Chicago at two-forty the following afternoon. It makes stops at Harmon, Poughkeepsie, Rhinecliff, Hudson, Albany (where it takes on a sleeping car and coaches from Boston), Schenectady, Utica, Syracuse, Rochester, Buffalo, Erie, Cleveland, Elyria, Toledo, Elkhart, South Bend, and Chicago. It is almost, if not quite, a local. It is, on the other hand, well patronized. When I got to the departure gate, at a cautious six-fifteen, a good fifty people—businessmen, couples of all ages and classes, students dressed as for a day of hard labor in the sugarbush—were already massed there, and another fifty quickly massed behind us. The gate opened, and we all filed through, and down the ramp and along the chilly, twilit, subterranean platform. Everything was much as I liked to remember it—the loom of stainless steel, the cluster of conductors and trainmen, the white-coated porters at their stations, the hisses and snorts, the endless tinkle of distant bells. I found my car, and the porter there took my bag. I followed him aboard and into the car ("Dining Car in Opposite Direction") and up a bustling corridor (every roomette and bedroom seemed to be occupied) to Bedroom C. The room was conspicuously clean, and the long settee that would open into my berth looked newly upholstered. There were coat hangers (old-fashioned, removable hangers) in the little closet, there were fresh towels and washcloths, soap, full dispensers of Kleenex and paper cups in the bathroom, even cold water from the tap marked "Ice Water." I made myself comfortable. The train gave a little stir, and began to move. I looked at my watch. It was exactly six-forty-five.

The dining car was almost full, but the steward found me an aisle chair at a table for four. The table appointments were reassuring: white tablecloths, cloth napkins, three yellow chrysanthemums in a vase. My companions had been served and were eating. They were a slender, freckle-faced girl in an enormous white sweater with a propped-up paperback book (*Père Goriot*) and an urban couple (business suit, tweed jacket) in their fifties. The man gave me a smile and a nod, the woman smiled, the girl gave me a glance (the kind of glance she would probably have given old Goriot) and went back to her book and her dinner. A waiter appeared with a menu. I ordered (onion soup, broiled Boston scrod, mixed vegetables, a half bottle of California white wine), and the waiter served me promptly and pleasantly. He opened the wine and poured some in my glass. He then recorked the bottle and set it tilted up on its side with the neck resting in the handle of a water pitcher. "That's just to be safe," he told me. "They've still got some bumps in the roadbed along this route. They're working on it, but we still get a certain amount of what the airlines call turbulence."

The wine was chilled. The food was hot, and good—good enough. The butter was sweet butter. The urban couple finished their meal, called for their check, and smiled and nodded and left. The girl read on. Our table was at the galley end of the car, and I could hear the kitchen crew at work. Only, it didn't sound like work. It sounded more like a cocktail party in the apartment down the hall. It was all smothered joyful shouts and muffled bursts of laughter, and the waiters seemed always to emerge from the galley smiling. There was a moment of turbulence. I reached to steady my wineglass, and my napkin slid off my lap. A waiter—not my waiter—standing ten feet away took three giant steps and swept it off the floor. But he didn't return it to me. Instead, he stepped into the galley, and came back with a crisp new napkin. He gave it to me with a little flourish. And smiled.

I lay in my berth in the chilled and clattering dark and bounced through another, less violent spell of turbulence. I was glad that the waiter had prepared me. The turbulence subsided into an easy, lulling rock—the incomparable cradling of sleep on a speeding train. I heard the sound of heavy footsteps in the corridor outside my door. A voice said, ". . . three above and snowing in Buffalo, with a windchill factor of . . ." I turned over and went back to my hammocky sleep.

I awoke to daylight and a slow-motion view of the wintry milltown outskirts of what I took to be Cleveland. It could have been any sooty, run-down Eastern city. I shaved and dressed to the leisurely passage of dumps and slushy crossings, then to quickening vacant lots and old frame houses, then to a racing open countryside carpeted with snow. I went in to breakfast. The diner was bright and shining and full of the good smell of freshly made coffee—the smell that is always better than the taste. I was given a table to myself, and a complimentary copy of the Cleveland *Plain Dealer*. The breakfast menu exhorted me to "Begin with a Bloody Mary or Screwdriver 1.75." I began with grapefruit juice. I was joined by a young couple and, a moment later, by an older woman in a camel's hair coat. She wore a man's gold pocket watch on a chain around her neck. The young man was dark, the young woman was fair. They both wore glasses and a look of happy excitement. He craned his neck around her and looked out at the snowy fields and bare-boned woodlots.

"Hey!" he said. "Wow! Isn't this great?"

"Oh, it is," the young woman said. "It's neat—really neat."

"I mean," he said, "I mean, here we are sitting here eating breakfast and looking out there at the scenery. I never knew it would be like this. I never knew it would be so great."

"It's just neat," she said.

The older woman turned to me. She, too, had a happy look. "It *is* neat," she said.

"I think so, too," I said.

"I've always loved trains," she said. "Ever since I was little. But especially the dining car. I've always thought it was more fun than even a plush restaurant. There's something about looking out the window while you eat. It's like a house with a terrace and a view that keeps changing all the time. It's so different from those boring, boring planes. It's even fun in bad weather."

The waiter had been pouring her coffee—and listening. He cleared his throat. "Yes, Ma'am," he said. "That's exactly what my dad used to say. He used to say bad weather wasn't all bad. He said it could be real nice to sit someplace where it's warm and dry and look out at it."

I spent the morning on my terrace, watching the changing view. I had a book I wanted to read, but my eyes kept lifting and shifting to the window. There was always something that seemed somehow worth seeing. I remembered my companions at breakfast. Train travel wasn't different only from those boring planes. Its sights were also different, and of a different quality, from those of high-way travel. Highway travel was either monotony or squalor. It was the landscaped Interstate or the strip—the filling stations, the body shops, the discount fabric centers, the motels, the drive-in movies, the Stuckey stores. A train moved through a different world. It was a world of change and surprise. It was a world of back doors, back roads, back country. It had a backstage intimacy. I looked out not on clouds, not on a riveting ribbon of highway. I sat and watched a bushy creek give way to a skeletal hillside apple orchard. Then a man in a grass-green jacket standing in a white pasture. Then an expanse of frozen water. Then the majestic ruin of a red brick Greek Revival house with a crow perched on one of its chimneys.

Then a dark and deep and gloomy Hansel-and-Gretel pine forest. Then children milling in a schoolyard framed by yellow buses. The train whistle blew. Farmland gave way to a treeless subdivision. An underpass yawned. The underpass gave way to a long retaining wall. Graffiti appeared: "Pot Smokers Do It Better." It began to snow. I went in to lunch.

His name, he told me, was Helsell—Charles Helsell. He looked to be in his early thirties, a tall, slender, partly bald man in a button-down-collar shirt and a tweed jacket. He took a bite of mostaccioli-and-meatballs and a swallow of Burgundy. He shook his head. "No," he told me, "I got on this morning—at Elyria. That's the stop for Oberlin College. I'm a museum man, and I've been down there looking at their museum. They've got a good one. I'm a curator at the University Gallery at the University of Minnesota, in Minneapolis. I do a lot of travelling, and I don't know how long it's been since I was on a plane, sitting there with my knees hunched up, eating off that little high-chair tray. I won't even mention the bus. I do my travelling by train. New York. Washington. Chicago. Denver. St. Louis. Cleveland. And all points in between. I figured out the other day that I've covered at least ten thousand miles by train in the last two years. As a matter of fact, I belong to the National Association of Railroad Passengers. No, no—we're not railroad buffs. Quite the opposite. We're concerned with today and tomorrow. We're consumer activists. There are ten thousand of us, and I think we can take some credit for the big improvement in Amtrak. We've certainly helped in getting the passenger train a priority over freight. And also with the on-time record. But that doesn't mean so much to me. I'm seldom in that big a hurry. I like to ride the train. I like to sit back and relax. I like the lounge car and the dining car and the coaches. I like to wander around and meet people. And talk. Like now."

I sat at my window and looked out at the blowing snow. I read my book. I dozed.

There was a knock at the door. It was the porter. "Coming into Chicago," he said. "You want to give me your grip?"

I got up and got into my overcoat and looked at my watch. It said two-fifteen.

"It's only two-fifteen," I said. "I didn't think we were due in until two-forty."

"That's right," he said. "But we're running ahead of time. Seems like we usually do these days."

"That's pretty good on a day like this," I said. "It looks like a blizzard out there."

"Sure does," he said. "They tell me that out at O'Hare they only got two runways open."

I was ahead of time, too. The Empire Builder wasn't scheduled to leave for Seattle until eleven-thirty the following morning. But I had friends in Chicago, and I had planned it that way. I spent the night at the Palmer House. The cabdriver who drove me there was a black man in his twenties with a little goatee, and he (and the cab) smelled to high heaven of grape chewing gum. He sat while I handled my bag and got in, he sat while I handled my bag and got out. When I asked him the amount of the fare, he pointed to the meter. He did, however, accept a tip.

The cabdriver who drove me back to Union Station the next morning was old and bald and wizened up and also black. He grabbed my bag and opened the door and all but helped me in. "Union Station, eh?" he said. "Well, it's a good day to get out of town. Paper says more snow. But there's one sure thing. It ain't going to snow forever. It never has. I been around long enough to know that. I got this grandson. And you know what I told him? I said to him, 'Vernon, I got the advantage of you. I know what it's like to be young. But you don't know what it's like to be old.'"

The new (Superliner) Empire Builder is a two-decker train. All its passenger cars—diner, coaches, sleepers—stand two stories high, sixteen feet from rail to roof, with the floor of the upper level a good ten feet from the ground. Through Gate 16, the train rose up along the platform like a great red-and-blue-and-silvery ship moored alongside a pier. The sleeping car came first, at the rear of the train. Beyond it was the diner, then three coaches, a baggage car, a mail car, and two electric locomotives. There was the usual cluster of conductors and trainmen, the usual rumble of luggage carts, the usual surge of passengers, the usual wailing baby. The sleeping-car porter was stationed at an open doorway halfway down the car. That was the entrance—the only entrance. He took my bag and looked at my ticket.

"Yes, sir," he said. "Up the stairs, turn to the left, fourth door, Bedroom B."

I walked into a kind of foyer the width of the car, with another door in the opposite wall and central corridors running fore and aft.

The corridors were lined with doors—roomettes, I presumed—and surging with people. The foyer was carpeted—wall-to-wall and floor-to-ceiling—in some sand-colored fabric. So were the stairs. They led up, in two sharp turns, to another carpeted foyer. The rear half of the second level was given over to more roomettes, and more people. The bedrooms were in the front half. There were five of them, opening on a windowed aisle. The three I passed on the way to my room were occupied. Mine, the fourth, was softly lighted and agreeably warm. There was a deep sofa, convertible into a berth, along the front wall. There was a built-in washbasin (with a three-sided mirror) to the left of the door. A swivel armchair faced the window end of the sofa. A door to the right of the armchair opened on an ingenious combination of toilet and shower bath: there was a raised doorsill, a drain in the floor, a shower head in the ceiling. The chair and the sofa were upholstered in a nubbly burnt-orange tweed, and there were matching curtains on the window. The window ran the length of the outer wall—a good five feet—and it offered a commanding view. I stood there, looking down, watching the platform suddenly sliding away, watching a broadening sweep of tracks and sidings, the burst of daylight, a spread of warehouses in the distance. The Superliner was indeed a new train. If my window on the Lake Shore Limited had been a terrace, my window here was a balcony, a gallery, a roof garden.

I found a little fold-out table in a slot between the armchair and the sofa, and that decided me. I had had a late breakfast, and I decided to lunch in the shoes-off comfort of my room. The porter brought my lunch (a baked-ham sandwich and a bottle of beer), and with it a timetable and a route map. Today was Sunday. We were scheduled to reach Seattle at eight-fifty-five on Tuesday morning. There were many scheduled stops along the way. The first was Milwaukee. Among the other important stops were Minneapolis; Fargo, North Dakota; Havre, Montana; and Spokane. We would cross the Rockies at East Glacier, Montana, in Glacier National Park, and cross the Cascades a few miles east of Seattle. Our route was due north to Milwaukee, then northwest to Minot, North Dakota, then west along the Canadian border. It was the most northerly, the most wintry, railroad route in the country. I ate my sandwich and drank my cold beer, and looked out at an empty, rolling countryside glazed with pristine snow. We were only in southern Wisconsin. But it already looked like Siberia.

* * *

I remember Milwaukee as a dark and crowded station platform, and a bustle in the corridor outside my door, and a man's voice: "... just terrific. I feel relaxed and lazy already." And then acres and acres of crowded sidetracks. I looked down from my eminence on a desolation of bent and battered coaches and freight cars and stranded, rusting locomotives. These were the discards of the railroad world, the wrecks. There were bashed-in sides and rear ends crushed into accordion pleats and missing wheels and boxcar doors spilled out on the ground. It was a vanished world, a nineteenth-century world of corporate indifference or innocence, or both. I wondered how it would feel at an airport to taxi out for takeoff past rows of crashed and broken and abandoned planes.

The other innocence—the innocence of the countryside—returned. It was abrupt and almost metaphorically emphatic. We moved slowly through the ultimate outskirts—the last industrial vacant lots—and the first fields and pastures appeared. Something burst into the air overhead. It was a bird—a big, gaudy, purple-and-red-and-golden bird. It came sailing down past my window. It landed in a bristle of fencerow brush and scurried out of sight. The Empire Builder had somehow flushed a cock pheasant.

I sat in my swivel armchair and watched the passing scene. The track curved slightly, and I could see the locomotives, the mail car, the baggage car, a coach. And then the black mouth of a tunnel. It loomed and engulfed us. I sat in an absolute, an impenetrable, an almost palpable dark. There was only a sense of motion and the clickety, clackety, click of iron on iron. I thought of Agatha Christie. I thought of Graham Greene. I thought of *The Lady Vanishes*. I had never felt so completely alone on a train. A minute passed—a long, long minute. Then daylight flooded back. I hardly dared look at the sofa. There was almost certainly a body sprawling there with a knife thrust deep in its back.

The dining car was the first car ahead of the sleeper, and the restaurant occupied the whole of the upper deck. The kitchen was below. The food was passed up by dumbwaiter to a serving pantry in the middle of the car. There were eighteen tables for four, and they were laid with pale beige tablecloths and dark-brown napkins, and each had a vase of fresh yellow chrysanthemums. The china was white and delicately ringed around the rim in burnt orange and black. It was also delicately made—as thin as the china one would expect to find in a first-class restaurant. The seats were upholstered in a rust-colored tweed and trimmed with dark-brown leather, and they were wide and comfortable. The diner had, I thought as the steward led me up the aisle, almost the look and feel of a club.

My companions at table were a bald, hawk-nosed man of around fifty and a heavyset couple in their forties. The menu offered stuffed breast of chicken, roast prime ribs of beef, baked rainbow trout with crabmeat stuffing, grilled ham steak with pineapple ring, and ten-ounce New York strip steak with mushroom caps. I ordered the rainbow trout, and it was good—very good. And it was modestly priced: $5.95. Before it, I had a dry Martini ($1.75) and with it I had a half bottle of rosé ($2.50). The couple across the table were of a kind I had often seen in restaurants. They sat together in amity, but they never exchanged a word. They ate and drank (three Scotches each, rare prime ribs of beef, two half bottles of wine, pecan pie, and coffee) in silence, a concentrated, ravenous silence. They had just been served their first Scotch when I sat down, and they were finished and up and gone before I had taken two bites of fish.

The man beside me was eating steak and drinking beer. He watched the waiter bring me my drink. He watched me take a swallow. He leaned forward. "Going far?"

I told him yes, all the way to Seattle.

He nodded. "I live in St. Paul," he said. He took a quick bite and gave me a friendly stare. "I could have been home five hours ago by jet. But what the hell! I mean this thing about speed. I played three rubbers of bridge with some folks that got off at Milwaukee. I read *Milling & Baking News* from cover to cover. I worked a crossword puzzle. I even stretched out and took a little nap. And now I'm having a nice, quiet dinner with plenty of room for my legs. I'm enjoying myself. There used to be a slogan: 'Getting there is half the fun.' That always made me laugh."

"Laugh?" I said.

"It was an airline slogan," he said. It wasn't, of course; it was a steamship slogan. But I let it pass. I liked it better his way.

I woke up, as I often do, in what felt like the middle of the night. I looked at my watch: twenty minutes past three. I lay for a moment in the sensual grip of pure comfort. The sheets were soft, the pillow was just firm enough, and it was difficult to believe that I was lying in a berth. It was six and a half feet long, and at least as wide as my twin bed at home. I rolled over to settle into sleep again—and smelled something. It was faint, but explicit, and familiar. It was deeply, nostalgically familiar. It was, incredibly, the smell of skunk.

When I awakened again, it was morning. The light between the curtains at the window looked like early morning, but my watch said almost eight o'clock. I crawled over to the window and looked out at a world of gray and white. It was snowing—snowing hard, and blowing. There was nothing to see but snow on the ground and snow in the air and a lowering pale-gray sky. And then a spot of color appeared, a moving spot of yellow. It was a school bus. I watched the bus moving serenely through the driving, drifting snow, and wondered. I marvelled. This wasn't Siberia; it was somewhere in North Dakota. But it was truly another country. In all the years I had lived in the East, in the New York metropolitan area, I had never seen a school bus venture out in anything more threatening than a couple of inches of snow.

The waiter came swinging up the aisle with a big, silvery pot of coffee. We were experiencing a period of turbulence, and he moved with the balanced grace of a dancer. He stopped at my table, swung into position, tilted the pot, and nicely, cleanly, filled my cup. I thanked him for an impressive performance.

"Thank you," he said. "But it's just a little knack you get used to. The only trouble I ever have is when I'm home in my home in Minneapolis. I have a real hard time pouring out my coffee with that kitchen table standing there so still."

The diner was full this morning, with people waiting for seats. None of the faces looked familiar. About half of them looked like college students. The other half looked like their grandparents. A young man up the aisle from me wore a Buffalo Bill mustache and a flat-crowned cowboy hat pinned up in front like a Pony Express rider's. But his breakfast was a toasted Danish pastry and a Coke.

I shared my table with a somewhat collegiate-looking couple in their fifties. They were, the man told me, from Michigan—from Ann Arbor. I mentioned the university. "No," he said, "I'm not an academic, but we do lead a university life. I have a dry-cleaning establishment near the campus, and the business lives and breathes with the students. When it's spring vacation at the university, it's spring vacation for us. We've tried a lot of things, a lot of different places, and we've sort of settled for the train. We travel just for pleasure. There's nothing like a train for recharging the battery. We eat and sleep and read and play cards and enjoy the scenery. Especially eat. I'm not much of a glutton, but the minute I get on the train I'm hungry. I'm always waiting for the next meal. I don't know—there's always something interesting going on. Last year, we had dinner one night with an Americana historian. A fascinating man. He told us the whole story of Chief Joseph. But I'm also satisfied to just enjoy the sights. There's always something to see. Or to—Let me tell you something strange. I woke up in the middle of last night, and it was the damnedest thing! It was really weird. I smelled a skunk!"

I stayed on alone at the breakfast table for another cup of coffee, and I was presently joined by a young Amtrak official named Gary Erford—the manager of Amtrak's Onboard Services in Seattle. Erford was wearing the Amtrak uniform: navy-blue suit, yellow shirt, blue necktie. "I'm not really working," he told me. "I've been back in Chicago for a visit with my dad. My dad is an old railroad man—he was with the Burlington Northern—and I guess he's probably why I took up railroading. It didn't look too promising when I started out. I think we're definitely part of the future now. Anyway—I don't want to sound like your captain speaking, but I thought you might be interested in a few things. You may be wondering why we picked this particular route—it's the Great Northern route, you know—to inaugurate our new Superliner series. Well, the reason is this. It's the toughest route in the country. If an all-electric train will stand up to midwinter in North Dakota and Montana and through the Rockies, it will stand up to anything. This isn't the coldest day of the year, but"—he nodded toward the window—"the temperature out there half an hour ago was five below, with a windchill factor bringing it down to almost minus twenty. In summer, it's the other extreme. A high of one hundred and fifteen is nothing. We've got a big investment here, so we want to make sure. The sleeping car you're in is brand-new. It just came out of the Pullman plant, and it carries a price tag of three-quarters of a million dollars. This diner is also on its maiden run. It was designed by airline engineers, and it cost almost a million. But our galley isn't an airline galley. It's a real restaurant kitchen. Maybe you'd like to go down and meet the chef and take a look around."

A narrow, winding staircase led down to the kitchen from a corner of the pantry. The rear half of the kitchen was storage room and scullery, and two white-coated men were working there. The other half was the kitchen proper. The chef was a big, pale, raw-boned man in his early fifties named Parlin Nienhaus. He was standing at a complexity of ranges, drinking a cup of coffee. "That's right," he told me. "We're all-electric here—electric grill, microwave oven, four convection ovens. That makes a big difference. I'm old enough to have seen it all. I started out in 1944, cooking with soft coal, charcoal, and paper. Then, in 1946, we moved up to gas. We cooked with gas till 1972, and then they switched us to pressed sawdust—what they called Pres-To-Logs. Electric is better, cleaner, quicker. The only thing that hasn't changed is our approach to cooking. All the meat we serve comes into this kitchen raw. You'll never get a precooked steak or roast on this train. I've been a chef since 1949. Those are my cooks down there cleaning up. One of them is fry cook and baker. The other is vegetable man. My department is soups and meats. Except when I'm at home. My wife does the cooking there. That's one thing we never argue about. She cooks it and I eat it. I've never had any cause for complaint."

He swallowed the last of his coffee and set the cup down on a counter. Erford picked it up.

"We're new in almost every direction," he said. "I suppose you've noticed our china."

I said I had. I said I thought it was unusually handsome, unusually elegant.

Erford nodded. "I think so, too," he said. "But it's also something else . . ." He slammed the cup against the edge of the metal counter. "It's also practically unbreakable. Corning developed it. It's some special kind of glass ceramic."

When I got back to my room, I found the porter there, making up my berth. I sat down in the chair by the window. The snow had almost stopped, and the sky had lightened and lifted. But the countryside looked, if anything, even more desolate than before—a rolling emptiness of snowy fields, an occasional skeleton tree, a half-buried barbed-wire fence.

"It looks pretty grim out there," I said.

The porter shoved the berth into its daytime metamorphosis and smiled. "Well," he said. "I'll tell you what they say around here. They say when a crow wants to fly through this country he's got to pack a lunch."

Half awake, half dreaming, my book half open on my lap, I sat stretched out at the window like a clubman in his favorite easy chair. I felt a stir of appetite, and thought of the man from Ann Arbor. It was almost time for lunch. Almost, but not quite. I took up my book and read a page, and put it down. It was snowing again, and blowing. A patch of blue emerged in the white. It was a house, a barn, a crossroads garage—standing alone and deep in the drifted snow, and painted a pale but thrusting shade of blue. I stared at it in a state of startlement, with a sense of visitation—a sense, almost, of déjà vu. I had seen it before, and more than once, but only in my imagination, only in my mind. It was the blue hotel of Stephen Crane's story: "The Palace Hotel at Fort Romper was painted a light blue, a shade that is on the legs of a kind of heron, causing the bird to declare its position against any background. The Palace Hotel, then, was always screaming and howling in . . . the dazzling winter landscape of Nebraska." It gave me a funny feeling. I went in to lunch remembering old Scully and the Easterner and the cowboy, and the doomed and disdainful Swede jabbing out "harpoon-fashion with his fork to pinion a biscuit." It was as if at last I had actually seen them.

There was a knock on my bedroom door. It was the porter. He said we were coming into Havre. He pronounced it, in the local fashion, "Haver." "Havre is a twenty-five-minute stop," he said. "I thought you might like to get out and stretch your legs. See the sights. But don't forget your coat."

I got into my coat and went up the corridor and down the stairs and out onto a wide promenade platform recently cleared of snow. The air was crisp, and it was snowing a thin, dry pellety snow. There were people with luggage coming off the train and people with luggage heading toward the coaches. I looked at the station— a two-story building of red and yellow brick. A main street, with a handful of angle-parked cars, paralleled the platform. It seemed to be lined with bars and cafés. Around the corner was a more imposing building: "Downtowner Serv-Ur-Self Furniture." Beyond the town, a mile or so to the south, I could see the bulge of big, round, treeless hills. Those were the sights. I saw the couple from Ann Arbor. I saw the heavyset couple from Sunday night, strolling together in silence. I saw the young man in the Pony Express hat. Parlin Nienhaus, pale-faced and wearing only his thin white cotton coat, nodded to me from the open door of his kitchen. "Feels good, doesn't it?" he said. "Better than a nap." A string of boys and girls with skis and bulging rucksacks trooped by. Gary Erford appeared at my elbow. "Interesting, isn't it?" he said. "All these people. That's something I meant to tell you. Amtrak is a winter lifeline up here in the high plains. This has been a mild winter. But most years the roads are blocked for days at a time by ten- and fifteen-foot drifts. And, of course, you can never count on landing a plane. We move the folks from town to town." The whistle blew twice. Erford moved off at a trot toward the coaches. I walked back to the sleeper. The porter was standing in the lower foyer.

"Enjoy yourself?" he said. "Didn't freeze nothing?"

I said I hadn't really noticed the cold.

"That's the trouble," he said. "You don't, right off. But the temperature out there is seven above; and with this wind it's probably ten below. But you know something? The people who live out here in this country, they love it. Wouldn't live anywhere else. Or so they like to tell me."

The rounded hills to the south grew higher, climbing and tumblig and piling up on the far horizon, and their summits were hazy with spindrift snow. We passed through Shelby (bars, cafés, and the Rainbow Hotel), and through a wandering, fenceless range, where a herd of twenty or thirty shaggy horses grazed in knee-deep snow, and through the town of Cut Bank (bars, cafés, and the Glacier Motor Hotel), and under a hilltop obelisk (a ten-foot pillar of orange-colored stone honoring a regional hero), and then the hills were no longer hills but merely foothills, and we were in the mountains. We were twisting and turning and crawling through snowshed tunnels, and I was looking dizzily down from my suddenly acrophobic terrace into sheer and bottomless chasms and up through a precipitous forest of pine and fir to naked rock and a fading sunset sky. It was almost six o'clock, almost time for dinner. We would be in the mountains, still creeping from ledge to ledge, until the smallest hours of the night. I rang for the porter, and ordered a double Martini.

"It's easy to see that you're not from this neck of the woods," the man across the table told me. I was dining (on an excellent slice of Parlin Nienhaus's rare roast beef) with a couple named Johnson and a business associate of theirs. They were all from Fargo, and were on their way to a meeting in Seattle. "The Johnsons are the Smiths and Joneses of North Dakota," Johnson went on. "The same for Minnesota. I'm one of I don't know how many thousand." He gave his friend an ambiguous glance. "There was this buddy I knew in Korea. He came to Fargo and called me up, and we got together, and he said it seemed to him that everybody he'd met since he got into town was named Johnson. How come? I said, 'Look out the window. Over there across the street. That sign on that big building right there.' So he looked. The sign said 'The Johnson Manufacturing Company.' And he said, 'Oh—I see what you mean.'"

Johnson's friend gave me a look. "You never heard that story before?" he said.

I shook my head.

"Then I've got another good one for you," he said. "These two guys met, and the first one said, 'Hey—who was that lady I seen you with last night?' And the other guy said . . ."

We were still winding our way through the mountains when I woke up and looked out the next morning. The mountains were, the time-table showed me, the Cascades, in western Washington. They looked much the same as last night's Rockies—fir and pine, snow and ice, canyons, misty peaks. But they somehow seemed less eerily acrophobic. Perhaps it was the cheerier light of morning. Something up ahead caught my eye. It looked like a herd of horses. I got a closer look. They weren't horses—they were elk. There were seven of them—five adults and two that I took to be year-lings. I looked down on the big, brown backs, the delicate, deerlike heads, as we passed. They stood there in a ragged row, regarding the train with a kind of bored attention. They might have been a crew of trackmen interrupted in their work, waiting stolidly for the train to pass.

The talk at my table at breakfast was of snowmobiles. I went back to my room with the understanding that the snowmobile was indis-pensable to life in the high plains in winter. After the past two days, I thought it might even be true. We were due to arrive in Seattle in less than half an hour. I locked my bag and got out my coat and sat down at the window to wait. We had still been in the mountains, still deep in winter, at breakfast, but now the season was changing. We were coming down from the heights, and the snow was thinning and melting away in patches. The patches of snow became puddles. The puddles dried into mud and weedy yellow grass. The grass began to green. The sun came out. The sky was blue. We passed the first of dozens of Boeing plants, a Boeing landing field, a sta-dium. The Seattle railroad station—the King Street Station—came distantly, imposingly, into view. It soared in all its red brick, battle-mented, bell-towered Victorian grandeur, and around it lay an or-dered landscape of driveways and walkways and rich green lawns and flower beds ablaze with the red of rhododendrons and the blues and purples and whites and yellows of crocuses and hyacinths and daffodils. I picked up my bag and hung my coat over my arm and walked away from winter and into the verdancy of spring.

[1980]

2. First Boat to King Island: The Bering Sea

The Eskimos were waiting for us on the beach just beyond the boulder breakwater on the eastern outskirts of Nome. It was six o'clock in the evening, but the June sun was still high in the sky and the air was almost warm. Offshore a mile or two, the ice that had moved out in the night was white and clear on the horizon. We said goodbye to the friend who had driven us out from town, and unloaded our gear—boxes of food, seabags, sleeping bags, a portable Coleman stove, some photographic equipment—and carried it across the road and down the embankment and onto the beach. The beach was steep and stony, with dirty snow in the hollows and a heavy crust of ice at the edge of the water. The *umiak* was moored to the ice. It was an open dory made of walrus hide stretched over a wooden frame, and it looked to be about thirty feet long. The Eskimos—three men, three women, and three teen-age boys—were loading the boat from a pile of boxes and bundles and gasoline tins and oil drums and oars and ice lances and boat hooks and rifles. I counted a dozen rifles in the pile, and there were others already stacked in the bow of the boat. The Eskimos were King Island Eskimos. Their native place was a little island in the Bering Sea about a hundred miles northwest of Nome. They had spent the winter in Nome, and now that the ice was breaking up they were going back to King Island to take supplies to their friends and relatives there, to hunt for seal and walrus, and to collect for sale on the mainland the walrus-ivory carvings that the islanders had made during the winter. My companions—John Fuller, a teacher in a school for Eskimo children run by the Bureau of Indian Affairs, and Joseph Rychetnik, an outdoor photographer and a former Alaska state trooper—and I had arranged to go with them. Their boat would be the first to visit King Island since the ice had closed in last fall.

The Eskimos watched us coming down the beach. Some of them smiled, and one of the men waved. They all wore parkas with the hoods thrown back and dungarees, and most of them wore sealskin mukluk boots. The women wore flowered-cotton Mother Hubbards over their parkas. Two of the women, two of the boys, and one of the men wore glasses. The man who had waved came up to meet us. He was the boat captain, and his name was Vincent Kunnuk.

"No more to do," he said. "Everything is ready. We only wait for the old man."

Fuller nodded. He seemed to know what Kunnuk meant.

Kunnuk looked at me. "The old man has the experience," he said. "There is always an old man on a boat. He knows the weather and everything about the ice."

"I'm glad to hear it," Rychetnik said. "I made one patrol to King Island when I was on the police, and I got stuck there for over a week."

"I wonder if I know the old man," Fuller said.

"May be," Kunnuk said. "He is Pikongganna—Aloysius Pikongganna."

"Aloysius, eh?" Fuller said. "Good. Real good."

Kunnuk went back to the boat. We followed him down with our gear, and he showed us where to stow it. The boat was powered by two outboard motors—one at the stern and the other hung in a well a few feet forward. Two motors were no more than enough. They would have a lot of weight to move. The boat held nothing yet except gear, but it already sat low in the water. There wasn't much more than a foot of freeboard left.

A car stopped up on the road. The door opened and a little man on crutches got out. He had a rifle slung across his back. He called out something in Eskimo—a string of purrs and a sudden bark— and laughed and swung himself down the embankment.

"Now we go," Kunnuk said. "The old man is here. He goes on crutches all his life, but it makes no difference. He does everything a man can do."

The sea was a deep, translucent green and as flat as a village pond. We moved slowly away from the beach with only the stern motor working. Kunnuk sat at the helm. He kept the motor throttled down until we were clear of the shoals and shallows along the shore. Then he nodded to the man at the well, and the second motor coughed and stuttered and came alive, and the shore began to slide away. I watched the beach flatten out and the tumbledown houses across the road shrink down behind the embankment and the big brown mountainous hills rise up in the distance. Snow still lay on the tops of the hills and in their sheltered folds. The boat cut heavily away to the right, heading generally west, between the shore and the ice floes out to sea. I felt a breath of cooler air.

Aloysius Pikonganna sat in the bow on a plank laid across the gunwales. He had a pair of binoculars on a strap around his neck and a toothpick between his teeth. Below him, huddled in the shelter of a canvas windbreak, were the three women and the youngest boy. The boy wore a little pale-blue souvenir fedora, and on the front of the crown was a crayon scribble: "I want to hold your hand." The other boys were packed in the stern with Kunnuk and the other men. Fuller, Rychetnik, and I sat amidships with the jumble of gear. I had a few inches of thwart to sit on and the iron curve of a fifty-gallon oil drum to rest my back against. Fuller was perched on the corner of an open box of pots and pans, and Rychetnik was sunk among his photographic equipment. But we were thickly padded with clothes. Rychetnik and I had on Bean hunting boots and two pairs of socks and Air Force survival pants and Eddie Bauer down-lined jackets over two heavy shirts and thermal underwear. Fuller wore an Eskimo uniform—fur parka, fur pants, and mukluk boots. He shifted on his box, and looked at me.

"Comfortable?" he asked.

"I'm fine," I said.

"I hope so," he said. "We've got at least fourteen hours of this ahead of us, you know."

"How about you?" I said.

"I'm OK," he said. "Besides, I'm used to it. This is just the way these cats are. They've always got room for one more."

"Just relax and enjoy it," Rychetnik said. "Be like me."

Pikonganna looked over his shoulder and raised a warning hand. There were ice floes in the sea ahead. The boat slowed down. Kunnuk stood up in the stern with his hand on the tiller and watched the drifting ice. Some of the floes were eight or ten feet in diameter, and some were twenty or thirty or fifty or more. All of them were four or five feet thick, but their edges were deeply undercut and they all were raddled with pools and puddles. We picked our way among them. A file of big black-and-white eider ducks came over the horizon. I watched them beating slowly along just clear of the water—and a dark shape moved on a floe far off to the left. It could only be a seal. One of the Eskimos let out a yell and grabbed up a rifle. But the seal was already gone. The Eskimo laughed and pulled the trigger anyway. The bullet whined away across the ice.

We came out from among the drifting floes and into a stretch of green open water. The boat began to move again. But after about ten minutes Pikonganna held up his hand again. There was more ice ahead. Everything in front of us was ice. The sea was a plain of shifting floes for as far as I could see. Kunnuk cut the motors, and we drifted up to the flank of one of the big floes. One of the men took a lance and chipped away the treacherous overhang and then jumped out on the floe. Pikonganna tossed him a line, and he stuck his lance in the ice and knotted the line around it. Another Eskimo followed him and secured the stern of the boat with another line and lance. Kunnuk came forward.

"Now we wait," he said. "But the ice is moving. It will open up pretty soon." He stepped on the gunwale and onto the ice. "The women will make us some tea."

The women were already at work. They uncovered a Coleman stove and handed it out and set it up on the ice not far from the boat. While two of them got the stove started, the other woman got a teakettle and went off across the floe to a pool of melted ice. Rychetnik and Fuller and I stood on the ice, stamping the circulation back into our feet, and watched her fill the kettle from the pool.

"Do they make tea out of that?" I asked.

"Relax," Rychetnik said. "Saltwater ice isn't salty. The salt is expelled when salt water freezes. That's good water in that pool. I mean, it's fresh."

"It's potable," Fuller said. "Let's take a look at the ice. But be careful where you step. This rotten ice is full of potholes."

We walked down the floe. The ice was plainly moving. There was a lead of open water just ahead, and I could see that it was getting wider. The farther floe was pulling away in the grip of the tide. But the lead was still far from wide enough. I looked at my watch. It was twenty minutes past nine. Though the brightness had gone out of the sky, it was still full light. Everything was still fully visible—the hills and mountains on the mainland, a bread-loaf island in the distance, the drifting floes through which we had come. But the sun had moved down behind the mountains in the north, and it was only there that the sky had color. Overhead, it was dirty white, like a snowstorm sky, and the sky on the southern horizon was a cold, slaty blue. The mountains stood against a glory of pink and green and yellow.

When we got back to the boat, the Eskimos were gathered around a tarpaulin in front of the stove. The tarpaulin was spread with food—a box of pilot crackers, a tin of butter, and a big square of whale blubber. The blubber looked like a block of cheese—pale pink cheese with a thick black rind. We stopped at the boat and got a bag of sandwiches out of one of our boxes, and then joined the circle of Eskimos.

"It's moving, Vince," Fuller said. "It's opening up over there real fast."

"I know," Kunnuk said, and took a swallow of tea. "But we wait awhile. Have some tea." He spoke to the women in Eskimo, and picked up a fan-shaped knife with an ivory grip and cut off a slice of blubber. "Have some *muktuk?*"

Rychetnik smiled and shook his head.

"No, thanks, Vince," Fuller said. "Not right now."

Kunnuk laughed and looked at me. "This is the best *muktuk*—from the bullhead whale. Black *muktuk.*"

I took the slice of *muktuk*. I sat down on the ice, and one of the women passed me a plastic cup of dark, steaming tea. I looked at the *muktuk*. The blubber didn't look like fat. It had a softer, more gelatinous look. I took a bite of it. It was very tender and almost tasteless. The only flavor was a very faint sweetness. There was one more bite of *muktuk* left. I ate it and washed it down with a gulp of tea. Then I opened my sandwich.

It was almost eleven o'clock when we finally left the floe. The sky was still bright pink behind the mountains. We moved along a crooked lead of open water on one throttled-down motor. The floe on the left was piled with shattered slabs of pressure ice, sometimes to a height of four or five feet. Every now and then, the ice would give a kind of moan, and a big slab would slide into the water and the boat would lurch. Two of the Eskimos stood at the gunwales with lances and pushed the floating ice away. Pikonganna was standing at his lookout post. He looked at his watch, and turned and said something to one of the women. She reached under a pile of quilts and brought out a little plastic radio. It came alive with a thunder of Russian. Then a screech of static. Then a voice said, " . . . and partly cloudy tonight with widely scattered showers. Cloudy tomorrow. The present temperature in Nome is forty-two degrees." There was a moment of whistling silence, and then came the sound of guitars and a sob of Hawaiian music. The woman turned the radio off.

The lead began to broaden, and we were back in open water. The only big expanse of ice in sight was a shelf of anchored ice that stretched between the mainland and the distant bread-loaf island. Kunnuk came forward across the gear. He stepped over us and over the women and joined Pikonganna at the bow. They talked softly together for a couple of minutes. Then Kunnuk laughed and started back. He stopped where we sat, and balanced himself on the gunwale.

"The old man says we go around Sledge Island," he said. That was the bread-loaf island in the distance. "But after that—no sweat. No more ice."

I came out of a dull, uncomfortable doze. I was hunched against the flank of the oil drum, and I was stiff and cramped and cold. I sat up—and there was Sledge Island. It loomed hugely up no more than three hundred yards off the bow. There was a fringe of ice, a field of soggy snow, a rubble of boulders, and a brown grassy slope rising steeply to a brown grassy summit. My watch said five minutes to two. The sun was up from behind the mountains, but the sky was gray with cloud. We seemed to be making directly for the island. I looked at Fuller. Rychetnik was asleep face down between a seabag and a metal camera case, but Fuller was awake. He was sitting under the spread of his big parka hood, smoking a pipe.

"It looks like we're going to land," I said.

Fuller took the pipe out of his mouth. "Boat trouble," he said. "Vince says there's something wrong with one of the motors. He wants to stop and take a look at it."

Rychetnik sat up as we scraped alongside the shelf of anchored ice. "Hey," he said. "Where are we?"

"Sledge Island," I said.

"Sledge Island?" he said. "We're only at Sledge Island?"

"Relax," I said. "Relax and enjoy it."

When the boat was made fast, Kunnuk and one of the other men lifted the motor out of the well and began to take it apart. The trouble seemed to be in the feed line. I watched them for a minute. Then I followed the others through the field of snow to a ledge among the boulders, where the women had set up their stove. I sat down on a rock and gazed at them. They were boiling down snow for tea. I felt more than tired. I felt disoriented. The midnight daylight was confusing. After my sleep, it should have been morning. It gave me a very strange feeling.

Rychetnik touched me on the arm.

"Let's take our tea down the line a ways," he said. "Jack and I think it's time for a little depressant."

The idea of a drink at half past two in the morning was no stranger than anything else. I got up, and we sloshed through the snow to the sheltering lee of a boulder. Rychetnik handed each of us a little two-ounce bottle of Scotch, and we emptied them into our tea.

"It's better not to drink in front of the Eskimos," Rychetnik said. "It doesn't seem right unless you're going to pass the bottle around. And this is no place to do that."

"Good God, no," Fuller said. "I've lived and worked with Eskimos for quite a few years. As a matter of fact, I'm a first sergeant in the Eskimo Scouts. I know them and I love them. I really love them. Those cats have to have something to survive in this environment, and they've got it. They've got every virtue. They're honest —they're completely honest—and they're loyal and they're generous and they're brave and they're always in good spirits. Nothing bothers them. But they can't drink. When they do, they get drunk. And when they get drunk, they go wild—they go absolutely wild."

We left Sledge Island with both motors working. I settled back in my oil-drum seat and listened to their steady, synchronized growl. The sea beyond the island was all open water. The only ice was off to the north, along the mainland shore. But the weather had also changed. The overcast was heavier now, and the breeze had sharpened, and the sea had faded from green to gray. I felt a drop of rain.

One of the women turned and caught my eye and smiled. She pointed toward the shore, and held up four fingers.

"Four years ago, we stay there one week," she said. "Bad weather. Then we stay three days at Sledge Island. More bad weather." She smiled again. "Was very bad trip."

"It sounds bad," I said.

She pointed again toward the shore. "Is called Pinguk," she said, and turned away.

I felt more drops of rain. There was a raincoat with a hood in my seabag. I felt around and found it and put it on and tied the hood under my chin. In the pocket was a pair of wool-lined rubber gloves, and I put them on, too. The rain burst into a spitting shower and then sank down to a long, cold drizzle. Rychetnik was asleep and snoring among his photographic gear, and Fuller sat humped on his box. Pikonganna stood on watch at the bow in a shiny translucent raincoat made of walrus intestines. I pulled up my legs and turned on my side and tried to fit myself against the curve of the oil drum. It wasn't very comfortable, but I was out of the wind and warm and dry. The last thing I remember was the rattle of the rain on my raincoat hood.

* * *

The boat was reeling and rolling, and it lurched me wide awake. It was almost six o'clock. I sat up and hung on to the thwart. We were rolling in a heavy chop. Rychetnik was also sitting up. He sat with one hand on the gunwale, bracing himself. It was still raining, and everything looked strangely dark. But it wasn't the darkness of night. Then I realized—it was fog. The boat gave a sickening roll. We were running broadside to the wind and wallowing in the trough of the waves. Rychetnik looked at me and smiled and shook his head.

"This is getting kind of hairy," he said.

"What's the matter?" I said.

"Aloysius says it's too rough to go on," he said. "Too rough and too foggy. We're turning around and heading in to shore."

Fuller leaned over my shoulder. "Too rough and too foggy and only one motor," he said. "That motor conked out again."

"I wonder where we are," I said.

Fuller shrugged. "I don't know," he said. "My guess is somewhere off Cape Woolley."

"Where is that?" I said.

"Nowhere," he said. "It's just a name on the map."

"I know Cape Woolley," Rychetnik said. "I was up along there on my first assignment as a trooper. It was right around this time of year, too. I flew up from Nome with a bush pilot. As a matter of fact, it was Gene Farland. Three Eskimos had got drunk in Nome and gone out fishing in a skin boat and never came back. My job was to try to find them. Somebody said they had headed up this coast, so we took off. We flew along just above the beach—and pretty soon there was the boat. It was hanging up there in the driftwood. Then, a little farther on, we found the bodies. They weren't ten feet apart."

"What happened?" I said.

"There was a storm and they were drunk and the boat capsized and they went into the water," he said. "This is the Bering Sea. When you go into the water up here, that's the end of the story. You've had it."

"I don't know whether you've noticed," Fuller said, "but there aren't any life preservers on this boat."

The boat began to come around. It rocked and slipped and lumbered into the wind. Now that we were out of the trough, the heavy rolling stopped, and the boat sat a little steadier, but the head wind held us down to a bumpy crawl. We bumped through the chop for about an hour. It was a queer, empty twilit hour. There was nothing to see but the boat and the blowing rain and a few hundred feet of wild gray water vanishing into fog. It gave me an uneasy feeling. It was frightening to think that only half an inch of walrus hide lay between us and the clutch of that glacial water. But I was too tired and cramped and cold to really think about it.

A sheet of white ice emerged from the fog. It was shore ice anchored to a point of land. We moved along the flank of the ice, and the fog began to thin. The wind was blowing in offshore gusts, and it tore the thinning fog away in sudden streaks and patches. Land appeared beyond the ice. There was a narrow beach piled high with driftwood, a low embankment, and then a misty reach of tundra. A rhythmic whistling sounded overhead. I twisted my head and looked. It was a string of twenty or thirty big, dark-headed ducks swinging out to sea. Their size and the whistling made them goldeneyes. They dropped and braked and settled down on the water.

Kunnuk and Pikonganna exchanged a couple of shouts, and we edged closer in to shore. The shore ice shelf was deeply undercut, and its surface was ravaged with cracks and potholes. But apparently it would do—or would have to do. We came alongside, lifting and falling in the chop, and two of the men leaned out and hacked away the flimsy overhang. Another man and one of the boys jumped out on the ice and held the boat fast with lines. Kunnuk came forward. His eyes were red, and his face looked drawn.

"Everybody out," he said. "This ice is no good. The old man says is too rotten to hold the boat. So we unload quick and get the boat up on the beach."

The man and the boy continued to hold the boat. The rest of us worked on the gear. We hauled the boxes and the bags and the cases and the rifles and the tins and the drums and the motors well up from the edge of the ice and covered them with some strips of tarpaulin. Then we went back to the boat and got a handhold on the bowline and dug in our heels. One of the women let out a wailing heave-ho yell, and we heaved. The bow of the boat lifted and hung, and then slid up on the ice. We braced ourselves, and the woman yelled again: "Hooooo-*huke!*" We heaved again. One of the Eskimos stepped through a pothole up to his thigh, and I slipped and sat down hard on the ice, but the boat came up another five or six feet. Another heave brought all but the stern of it clear of the water, and after that it was easier. With some of us pulling and the rest pushing, the boat slid over the soggy ice like a sled. There was no need now for the women to help. They got their stove and some other supplies and then went on across the ice and up the beach to the tundra. By the time we got there with the boat, the women had collected a supply of driftwood branches and logs, and even trees, and had a big fire going. We careened the boat a few feet from the fire and propped it up on its side with the oars and boat hooks. It made an excellent windbreak and a kind of shelter from the rain.

We stood around the fire and warmed ourselves and caught our breath. The wind tore at the fire, and the flames leaped and twisted and darted in all directions, and my face was scorched but my feet stayed cold. It was a hot and furious fire. It took a lot of driftwood to keep it going, and the wood that the women had collected went fast. It was the deadest driftwood I had ever seen. Years of weathering on this desert beach had dried it to papery husks, and it burned almost like paper. When the woodpile was down to a few sticks and branches, Rychetnik and I volunteered to bring in another supply. It was plentiful enough. There was driftwood heaped head high at the high-water mark along the beach as far as I could see. It must have been accumulating there forever. We made a dozen trips and brought back a dozen logs—big, barkless silver-gray logs that weighed practically nothing. As we dropped our last load, Fuller came struggling up from the ice with a box and a bag of perishables. The women had their stove set up, and they were making tea and boiling a pot of mush. Rychetnik looked at them and then at his watch.

"Hey," he said. "It's eight o'clock. What are *we* going to do about breakfast?"

"Whatever you say," Fuller said. "But I didn't get any sleep last night and I'm really not too hungry."

"Neither am I," I said.

"Besides," Fuller said, "I'm not real eager to break out the stove right now and do a lot of cooking and washing up and getting packed again. It wouldn't be worth the trouble. My guess is this weather is going to clear, and I know these cats. They'll be wanting to take right off."

"But what about breakfast?" Rychetnik said.

"I brought up the rest of the sandwiches," Fuller said. "And we've got some cans of chocolate milk."

Fuller was right about the weather. The rain had stopped by the time we finished breakfast, and the clouds were breaking up. There were patches of bright sky overhead, and the air was bright and clear. Even the wind had dropped. It looked like a beautiful day, but we wouldn't be leaving soon. The sea was still running high and white. Fuller dragged himself away from the fire and lay down in the shelter of the boat. Almost at once, he was snoring. I was tired, but the change in the weather made me restless. Rychetnik was engrossed in his cameras. I got up and walked around the boat and out onto the tundra.

The tundra stretched endlessly away to the north and south, and far to the east, a smoky gray on the blue horizon, were mountains. It was an enormous, empty plain. There were no trees, no bushes, no grass. There were only weedy hummocks and pockets of bog and trickling, icewater brooks. Some of the hollows were still drifted over with snow. I skirted a bog and stepped over a brook, and a bird flew up from almost under my foot. It was followed by another. They were tawny, long-billed birds—snipe. A few minutes later, I flushed a phalarope. The tundra wasn't as empty as it looked. There were shrieks and whistles and drumming wings at almost every step I took. I flushed more snipe and phalaropes, and also sandpipers and plovers and ptarmigan. The ptarmigan had a shabby look. Their plumage was still a confusion of winter white and summer brown. Once, in the distance, I saw a flight of sandhill cranes, and there were many strings of ducks and geese. The geese were mostly snow geese, but there were also emperor geese and brant. The sun came suddenly out. It blazed down like tropical sun. I unfastened my padded jacket, and then took it off. It was actually hot. I sat down on a hummock and folded my jacket into a pillow and lay back. The hummock was matted with lingenberry vines and tiny creeping willow, and it made a soft and springy bed. I closed my eyes and enjoyed the feel of the sun on my face.

I woke up cold and shivering. The sun was gone and the fog was back, and it took me a moment to remember where I was. I put on my jacket and started back to the camp. My head was still thick with sleep. I stopped at a brook and squatted down and splashed some water on my face. That finished waking me up. I went on, stepping and stretching and hopping from hummock to hummock. The fog made everything seem very still. The mountains had disappeared in the fog, but I could see the camp across the tundra. A small white tent now stood not far from the driftwood fire. Several men were gathered at the bow of the upturned boat. One of them was Rychetnik. I waved, and he came out to meet me. He was grinning.

"We'll never get off this beach," he said.

"Not with this fog," I said.

"I don't mean only the weather," he said.

"Now what?" I said.

"More boat trouble," he said. "One of the Eskimos was sacked out under the boat, and he happened to look up—and what do you think he saw?"

"What?" I said.

"Daylight," he said. "There was a hole in the bottom of the boat about the size of a dime. Vince and Sam Mogg are patching it up. They think it probably happened when we were dragging the boat up over the driftwood."

"What about that conked-out motor?" I said.

"I think they've finally got that fixed," he said. "But don't start getting any ideas. There's something wrong with the other motor now. It needs a shear pin on the propeller shaft. They're going to fix that this afternoon."

"Do you have any more of those little bottles you had last night?" I said.

Rychetnik laughed. "No," he said. "But I've got a big one."

I followed him around the boat and around the fire and around behind the Eskimo tent. Fuller was there, sitting on a log in front of our portable stove and searching through a box of groceries. He looked refreshed by his nap, and resigned to a stay on the beach. I filled a pan with water from the nearest snow-melt brook, and Fuller found some paper cups, and Rychetnik got out a fifth of Scotch. We sat around the stove and drank our drinks. The Scotch was good with the cold snow water, and it made the fog and the beach and the miles of tundra seem less bleak. Then Fuller cooked us a lunch of bacon and eggs. It was the first hot food I had eaten in almost twenty-four hours, and nothing ever tasted any better. We finished off with bread and butter and strawberry preserves and a pot of strong boiled coffee.

We spent the afternoon hauling driftwood for the fire. The Eskimo tent had been raised for the women, and we could hear them talking and laughing inside whenever we stopped at the fire to rest and warm ourselves. We also worked to the sound of shooting. The Eskimo boys roamed up and down the beach with .22 rifles, and they shot at anything that made a target—a driftwood stump, a raft of ducks far out to sea, a flight of mile-high geese. Kunnuk sat alone in the shelter of the upturned boat with a cigarette in his mouth and filed and shaped a nail into a new shear pin. When he finished, he walked down and stood on the edge of the beach and looked at the water. The next time I came back to the fire, he was sitting there with the portable radio in his lap. I sat down beside him. We listened to a snatch of Siberian Russian and the end of a talk about getting back to the Bible. A hillbilly tenor sang "Does He Love You Like I Do?" Then a voice said: "This is radio station

KICY, in Nome, Alaska. The time is six o'clock. Here is the weather forecast for Nome and vicinity: Fair and cold tonight. Fair and warmer tomorrow. The present temperature in Nome is thirty-three degrees."

Kunnuk turned off the radio. "Good weather coming," he said. "Maybe we leave soon. Maybe by midnight."

But the fog hung on. At nine o'clock, it looked thicker than ever. I doubted that we would be leaving by midnight, and I didn't care. I hardly cared if we ever left. Work and the weather and a drink of Scotch had given me a big appetite, and I had eaten a big dinner of reindeer steak, macaroni and cheese, canned peaches, cookies, and coffee. All I wanted to do was sleep. Someone would wake me before we left. If we left. I found a corner deep under the boat and took off my boots and my jacket and my heavy survival pants and unrolled my sleeping bag and crawled in. Something poked into the small of my back. There was a stick or something under my sleeping bag. I tried to squirm it away, and it moved an inch or two. That wasn't enough. I would have to climb out and move the bag. But instead I fell asleep.

I slept all night. I awoke to a crying and croaking and whistling of birds. It was half past five. There was frost on the ground, and the air was cold, but the sea looked calm, and the sun was shining in a wide blue sky. The fog was completely gone. I sat up. Kunnuk was propped on his elbow in a sleeping bag on my left.

"We make it today," he said. "Look!" He handed me a pair of binoculars and pointed out to sea. "You can see King Island."

I looked, but I couldn't see it.

"Maybe I know better where to look," he said. "I was born there."

I got into my clothes and rolled up my sleeping bag. Underneath it was the end of one of the boat lines. I stooped out from under the boat and into the bright sunlight. Most of the others were already up. The women were boiling another big pot of mush. I washed my face in the snow-melt brook. The water felt even colder than it had the day before. It was so cold it made my nose ache. I was starting back when Rychetnik came up to get some water for breakfast, and we walked back together. The stove was going, and Fuller, in a bright-red hunting shirt, was peeling bacon into a frying pan. Then, while Rychetnik got the coffee started and I got out some cups and plates and knives and forks and spoons, he stirred up a bowl of pancake batter. He fried the pancakes in the bacon pan, and we ate them with butter and strawberry preserves.

We finished breakfast at a little after six, and a few minutes later the Eskimos began to break camp. The women did the packing. Kunnuk called us over to help the men with the boat. We rolled it back on its keel and swung it around and dragged it down and across the ice and let it into the water. The glare of the sun on the frosty ice was dazzling. Two of the boys held the boat against the edge of the ice, and we went back and got out gear. The ground where the women's tent had been was littered with bones and cigarette butts. Aloysius Pikonganna directed the loading of the boat. The arrangement was somewhat different from that at Nome. It was planned for safe and easy shooting if we happened to get a shot at a seal. Rychetnik and Fuller and I shared the forward thwart again, but the gear was all piled amidships and the women and two of the boys were also settled there. The other boy and a man called Norbert took over the motors, with Norbert doing the steering. Kunnuk and Sam Mogg joined Pikonganna in the bow with the guns. We pushed away from the shore, and I looked over the side of the boat. The water was a yellowy green and so clear that I could see the bottom, five or six feet below. The bottom was stone—big slabs of granite worn smooth by grinding ice. It was as smooth and flat and bare as a pavement.

The motors started up, first the one at the stern and then the other, and the boat began to move. The women huddled closer together. They bowed their heads and made the sign of the cross, and their lips moved silently in prayer. Then they sat back, and two of them lighted cigarettes. We left the last of the shore ice and came out into open water and into an easy swell. Yesterday's chop had gone with the fog. An acre of rafting eider ducks exploded off to the right. I watched the big birds beating slowly in to shore. The shore looked just as it had when we saw it on Thursday morning. There was no sign that anyone had ever camped there. Kunnuk turned and looked back down the boat. He was smiling, with a cigarette in his mouth, and sparks of sunlight glinted on his glasses.

"Everybody sleep good?" he said.

The women nodded and the boys grinned and Norbert yelled something in Eskimo. Everybody laughed.

"Good," Kunnuk said. "Now we got good weather. Now we travel."

Sam Mogg caught my eye.

"We got Sears, Roebuck weather," he said.

"What?" I said.

"Sears, Roebuck weather," he said. "I ordered it."

The radio came suddenly on. A familiar voice said, " . . . seven o'clock, and the present temperature in Nome is forty-four degrees. The wind is northeast at fourteen. The forecast is for fair and warmer today, tonight, and tomorrow." In spite of the sun, it was cold on the water. I could feel the forecast wind. I zipped up my jacket and put on my gloves and listened to an operatic tenor singing "I Love to Laugh." He sounded very far away. When he laughed ("Ha-ha, hee-hee"), he sounded even remoter.

King Island came faintly into sight at about eight-thirty. It was just a cloud on the western horizon. I got out a pair of binoculars and fixed them on the cloud. The cloud became a bigger and darker cloud, but it was still no more than a cloud. Then it began to grow. It darkened and broadened and lifted against the sky. By nine o'clock, the cloud was visibly an island. It continued to grow, and to change. Through the binoculars I watched it shift from a little gray lift of land to a rocky mountain rising steeply from the sea.

The woman who had spoken to me before leaned forward. She was an elderly woman with a big, square face framed in her parka hood.

"King Island," she said. "You see?"

I nodded. "It looks like a mountain," I said.

"Ukivok is Eskimo name," she said. "Not King Island. Eskimo call it Ukivok. "

"Ukivok," I said. "What does that mean in Eskimo?"

"We go up on top Ukivok," she said. "We go high up and pick green flower. Many green flower grow on top Ukivok now."

"What is green flower?" I said.

"Is good," she said. "Is like salad."

Floating ice began to appear up ahead. A flight of murre swung low across our bow, and in the distance a kittiwake soared. King Island rose higher and higher. I watched it through the binoculars. It looked to be about two miles long, and it really was a mountain. Its sides were weathered into crags and pinnacles, and they rose abruptly from a beach of anchored ice to a saddle summit that was still partly covered with snow and at least a thousand feet high. It seemed impossible that anyone could live there.

I turned to the woman behind me. "Where do the people live on Ukivok?" I said. "Where is the village?"

"Ukivok is name of village," she said. "Island and village is same name."

"Where is Ukivok village?" I said.

She smiled and shook her head. "Not this side," she said. "Too much mountain. On other side."

Fuller gave me a nudge. "Walrus," he said, and pointed off to the left.

I put up the binoculars again. I saw them almost at once—a row of six or eight enormous creatures sitting erect on an isolated floe. They were reddish brown, with big sloping shoulders and little round heads and drooping two-foot tusks. They had a prehistoric look. They also looked strangely human.

"You see them, Vince?" Fuller said.

"I see them," Kunnuk said. "Good ivory, too. But we don't hunt walrus today. No room in the boat."

The shelf of anchored ice was wider than it had looked at first. We were still two or three miles from the island when we came in sight of its outer edge. But there were stretches of open water showing within it, and it seemed to be breaking up. Pikonganna stood balanced on his lookout plank surveying the ice. He said something to Kunnuk. Kunnuk nodded and looked back at Norbert and raised his hand in a signal. The boat cut away to the right. We moved northward along the edge of the shelf through a wash of broken floes. After ten or fifteen minutes, a break appeared in the anchored ice. We turned into a calm blue lead as broad as a boulevard.

We followed the lead for about a mile. It ran between two glittering shores of tossed and tumbled ice. Pikonganna held up his hand, and the motors slowed. There was a sudden bend just ahead. We moved slowly around the bend. Pikonganna raised his hand again, and the motors cut off. Fifty yards beyond the bend, the lead abruptly ended. We drifted up to the dead-end ice, and two of the boys jumped ashore and made the boat fast with lines and lances. Kunnuk stepped over the bow and stood and helped Pikonganna down, and Sam Mogg handed Pikonganna out his crutches. Kunnuk and Pikonganna moved off across the ice. I watched them climb to the top of a big ice ridge. They stood there studying the surrounding ice with binoculars for a moment, and then Kunnuk turned and waved.

Sam Mogg gave a grunt. "Time to eat," he said.

The women set up their stove at the foot of the ridge. They filled the teakettle with melted ice from a hollow in the floe and got out a bag of dried seal ribs. Rychetnik and Fuller and I sat down on a ledge of ice nearby and made an easy lunch of bread and butter and bologna and Swiss cheese and canned grapefruit juice and chocolate bars. From where we sat, King Island looked hardly a mile away. The cliffs that formed its northern tip loomed steeper than ever. Some of them were stained yellow with lichen, and the

air around them was alive with birds. Kunnuk came down from the
ridge. He stopped where we sat on his way to join the other Eskimos.

"Don't worry," he said. "We make it OK. The old man and I see
plenty other leads."

There was another blue lead about a hundred yards back down
the lead we were on. It was narrow and twisting, but it led in the
right direction. The King Island cliffs rose dead ahead. We went up
the lead, and after another hundred yards or so it opened into a kind
of lake with many islands of floating ice. The lake was a haven for
murre. There were murre stringing overhead and murre perched on
the ice and murre bobbing on the water. They were very tame, and
I got a good look at them. They were pretty birds with vivid pen-
guin plumage and long, sharp bills. Sitting erect on the ice, they
even looked like penguins.

Pikonganna suddenly stiffened and then sank slowly down on
his plank. It was an alerting movement. Everybody tensed.

"*Ooguruk,*" he said, and pointed.

About a hundred and fifty yards to the right, a big, silvery
bearded seal lay basking on a floating floe. It hadn't seen or heard
us yet. Norbert cut the motors and we drifted silently toward the
ice. Nobody spoke. The most accessible rifle of adequate caliber
was a Remington .30/06, and the man closest to it was Fuller. It
was Rychetnik's rifle, and he motioned to Fuller to take it. Nobody
moved. Fuller swung the gun to his shoulder, steadied himself, and
fired. A flight of murre veered loudly away. The seal gave a start,
and lay still.

The boat nudged up to the floe, and Kunnuk vaulted over the
gunwale and onto the ice. He had a revolver in his hand. Sam
Mogg and Fuller jumped ashore and trotted after Kunnuk. Rychetnik and I got out on the ice and watched them. Kunnuk was the first
to reach the seal. Apparently, it was still alive. He squatted down
and shot it in the head. He put the revolver away and took out a
hunting knife and cut two belt-loop slits in the skin just above the
eyes. Sam Mogg and Fuller came sliding up, and Mogg threw
Kunnuk a length of rope. Kunnuk threaded the rope through the
belt-loop slits and made it fast, and then he and Mogg and Fuller
dragged the seal across the floe to the boat. The seal was a young
female. It was about six feet long and it weighed at least four
hundred pounds, and Kunnuk and Fuller and Mogg were sweating
when they got it up to the boat. They were grinning, too. Everybody was grinning, and Mogg slapped Fuller on the back. When
Kunnuk and Fuller and Mogg had caught their breath, they rolled

the seal over on its back, and Kunnuk got out his knife again and gutted and cleaned it. Then they hoisted the carcass over the gunwale and into the bow. The fur looked suddenly different. The brilliant silver lustre had begun to fade. By the time we were ready to leave, it was a dingy, leaden gray.

We moved along the lakelike lead. The wind and the tide were shifting the ice, and the lead grew wider and more open. There was open water now all the way to the looming cliffs. I stood up. There was open water everywhere ahead. An open lagoon stretched for two or three hundred yards between the shelf of anchored ice and the foot of the cliffs, and it seemed to encircle the island. We moved across the open water and into the shadow of the cliffs. Then, at a signal from Kunnuk, Norbert swung the boat to the left. We headed down the eastern face of the island. I looked up at the towering crags and pinnacles. Every ledge was a rookery. The rocks were alive with perching murre and kittiwakes and gulls and auklets and cormorants and puffins and terns.

Kunnuk turned around. He had his revolver in his hand. "You like to see some birds?" he said, and pointed the revolver overhead. "Just watch—I show you something."

He fired two shots, and then a third. The revolver was only a .22, but against the sounding board of water and rock it sounded like a bomb. It sounded like a hundred bombs. The shots went echoing up and down the face of the island, and a cloud of birds came screaming off the cliffs. They flew screaming over our heads and across the lagoon to the outer ice and then veered around and came streaming back. They came off the cliffs and over the water in waves—hundreds, thousands, tens of thousands of birds. It was impossible to even guess at the number.

The elderly woman leaned over my shoulder. "Ukivok is good place for eggs," she said. "All kinds of eggs." She smiled at me. "Very good to eat."

We sailed down the lagoon in a turbulence of birds. Many of them were birds that had never seen a man or a boat or heard a shot before, and it took them a long time to settle down again. The lagoon was irregularly shaped. Because of the broken line of the shifting outer ice, it was sometimes as wide as a lake and sometimes no more than a river. We followed it across a lake and through a little river and into another lake. I heard the motors cut off and felt the boat begin to drift. Pikonganna and Kunnuk were standing together on the lookout plank, and Sam Mogg and Rychetnik and Fuller were on their feet. Even Norbert was standing. I stood up, too. The lake we were in was the end of the lagoon.

Kunnuk came down off the plank. "OK," he said. "We go back. We go round the other way."

We all sat down. The motors started up, and the boat swung around, and we headed back up the lagoon. The boat suddenly slowed. Kunnuk was back on the lookout plank with Pikonganna, and Mogg was standing below them peering out between their legs. I couldn't tell what they were looking at. I didn't see anything unusual. We were approaching the upper end of the lake, and it looked much like the other end. And then I realized. The outer ice was moving in on some shift of wind or tide, and the little riverlike passage through which we had come had almost disappeared. The passage was about two hundred feet long, and ten or fifteen minutes ago it had been a good hundred feet wide. It now was hardly twenty.

The boat began to move again. Pikonganna and Kunnuk had come to some decision. We made our way across the last of the lake to the head of the passage. The passage had an ugly look. There was a ten-foot embankment of glassy ice on the island side, and the outer ice was pitted with holes and piled with pressure ridges, and it was moving fast. I could see it closing in. Rychetnik gave a kind of grunt.

"I don't like this very much," he said. "I don't think I like it at all. You know what this boat is made out of. If we get caught between the ice in there . . ."

"I don't like it, either," I said. "But I guess there isn't much choice."

"These cats know what they're doing," Fuller said. "I've never seen them take a chance they didn't have to."

The boat edged into the passage. The water was thick with chips and chunks of floating ice. We moved carefully between the embankment of anchored ice and the moving floe on one throttled-down motor. Norbert kept the boat inching along just off the lip of the floe, away from the height and bulk of the ice embankment, but every time I looked, the ice seemed higher and closer. I could already feel the cold of its breath. Kunnuk reached out with an ice lance and jabbed at the edge of the floe. He jabbed again, hard, and a slab of ice came loose and slid slowly into the water. The boy at the stern with Norbert poked it safely past the boat with an oar. It was rotten ice. The whole rim of the floe was rotten ice.

Kunnuk said something in Eskimo, and stepped up on the gunwale and jumped out on the floe. Mogg and Fuller followed him over, and Rychetnik and the boy at the stern followed them. They all had lances or boat hooks, and they spread out along the floe and

began hacking at the rim of rotten ice. They worked just ahead of
the inching boat, and Pikonganna hung over the bow with an oar
and guided the slabs of floating ice to the island side of the passage.
I found another oar and kept the ice moving and clear of the boat.
Some of the slabs were the size of boulders, and it took all my
strength and weight hanging on the oar to push them off and away.
But I kept them moving, and the boat was also moving, and finally
I raised my head and looked out over Pikonganna's shoulder and
there was the end of the passage and a blue expanse of open water.
Norbert shouted, and the women gave a quavering wail. We were
through.

We went back up the eastern face of the island and around the
northern end and down the western side. Everybody was talking
and laughing. There was no ice anywhere on the western side except along the shore, but the island was the same. There were the
same gray cliffs, the same patches of yellow lichen, the same thousands of screaming birds. There was no sign of a village, and no
place where a village might even conceivably be built. So the village was down at the southern end of the island. We still had some
distance to go. I looked at my watch, and I could hardly believe it.
It had been nine hours since we stopped for lunch. It was almost
nine o'clock.

Rychetnik had been dozing in the evening sun. He sat up and
shook himself. "I'm getting kind of hungry," he said. "As a matter
of fact, I'm starved."

"I've been thinking about our dinner," Fuller said. "I thought
the first night on King Island we ought to have something real
special. Anybody got any suggestions?"

"I suggest we all go down to the Four Seasons," Rychetnik said.

"We've got a ham," Fuller said. "It's one of those Polish hams.
I guess we'll have that, and maybe some spaghetti."

"And a drink," I said.

"Don't worry about that," Rychetnik said.

The village was well around on the southern tip of the island. It
was built on the slope of a chute of landslidden rocks. It hung on
the slope about three hundred feet above a beach of ice and tumbled
boulders, and it consisted of eighteen or twenty houses. The houses
were wooden shacks with tarpaper roofs, and they were stepped out
from the slope on tall wooden stilts. Scaffolding walks and ladderlike steps connected the houses, and a long flight of steps led down
to the boulder beach.

"It looks even hairier closer up," Rychetnik said. "But I guess it's safe enough. The house we're going to stay in is the school-house—what used to be the schoolhouse. The teacher left about ten years ago. It's the house with all those windows up there at the head of the steps. That's where I stayed when I was here before. It isn't any Hilton, but it's got four walls and a roof and some chairs to sit on and a table. It won't be too bad."

The boat turned in toward the shore, and I watched the village coming clearer. It was hard to think of it as an Eskimo village. It looked remoter than that. It looked Tibetan. A man came out on the balcony of one of the upper houses. There was a green and red and purple patchwork quilt hung over the railing to air. The man watched us for a moment. Then he raised both hands high over his head and waved. Pikonganna waved back. He was grinning from ear to ear. He reached down and slapped Kunnuk on the back.

"Home sweet home, boy," he said. "There's no place like home."

Kunnuk smiled and nodded. "That's right," he said.

[1966]

3. A New Kind of City: Portland, Oregon

I went out to Portland, Oregon, not long ago, and spent five mild and mostly sunny days in a leisurely walking tour of its downtown streets, its many parks, and its garden riverfront. Portland was founded in 1845 and evolved in the course of the next hundred years or so into the usual hodgepodge American city; then, beginning around 1970, it was transformed in look and spirit and became, at least in its center, a city of some individuality and distinction. There are those who see in this transformation a model of urban development, a city that has returned itself to man, to a pedestrian way of life.

Portland is a city of nearly four hundred thousand, but it is also a town. It combines the intimacy of a town with the density and the richness of a city. This is to some extent a matter of topography. Portland has little space for urban sprawl. It lies in a valley cut by the Columbia River and its tributary, the Willamette (pronounced, visitors are quickly informed, Will-AM-ette), and it is all but surrounded by mountains: the Coast Range on the west and the Cascades (the setting of such eminences as Mt. Hood and Mt. St. Helens) on the east and north. The city itself is further affected by nature. The Willamette, flowing north toward its confluence with the Columbia, divides Portland more or less in half. Eastern Portland is a deepwater port and largely blue-collar residential area and industrial. Western Portland, or more particularly the southwest quarter, is the heart of the city—its business, its cultural, and, increasingly, its residential center. It is there that the new face of Portland—the closely controlled new building, the carefully monitored rehabilitation of worthy old buildings, the vigorous creation of open space—is most conspicuous.

* * *

I lived during my stay in Portland at the Heathman Hotel. The Heathman occupies a ten-story, Italianate building (with some two hundred suitelike rooms) on Broadway Avenue—the principal street (shops, hotels, theatres, restaurants) of southwest Portland—at Salmon Street. It is a recently renovated version of the New Heathman Hotel, which was built in 1927 (to replace an earlier Heathman Hotel), and is listed in the National Register of Historic Places. It is thus an acceptable representative of the Portland renaissance. I had my daylight introduction to Portland from the eighth floor of the Heathman. It, too, was representative. It showed me, across the roof of the Arlene Schnitzer Concert Hall (a recent gentrification of the Portland Paramount-Publix Theatre, and another member of the National Register of Historic Places), a steep and thickly wooded hillside called the West Hills—a barrier foothill of the Coast Range, no more than a mile away. A little later, on my way down to breakfast, I glanced out the window at the end of the hall. It gave me an opposite view—a broken view, through a skyline of buildings tall and low—of the Willamette shining in the morning sun. Breakfast at the Heathman provided another novelty. My waitress brought me along with a menu a little cordial glass containing an agreeable combination of fresh orange juice, lime juice, honey, whipped whole egg, and nutmeg. This, I found on inquiry, was an invention of Johnathan Robinette, the executive chef. "Our guests are mostly businessmen with work to do," Robinette told me. "My cordial is to wake them up, to knock off sleep. At first it also contained some rum. But then I was advised otherwise."

The streets of southwest Portland bear a teasing resemblance in name to those of Manhattan. The streets running north and south are avenues, and most of them are numbered, beginning on the east (after Front Avenue) with First Avenue. Broadway is paralleled on the east by Sixth Avenue. A block to the west is Park Avenue. Then Ninth Avenue appears, then Tenth, after which all signs of the renaissance tend to disappear. Beckoned by a glimpse of greenery, I walked up Salmon Street to Park. I found (as in New York) not one but two Park Avenues. But these Park Avenues flank a real, a substantial park—a park nearly half a block wide and twelve blocks long. It begins at Salmon and runs—gently climbs—to the rise of the West Hills. I turned in that direction, up a path furnished with occasional benches—benches that looked like park benches, not backless or back-breaking sculptural statements—and bordered by lawns and double rows of trees. I recognized the famous Douglas

fir and the cosmopolitan sycamore. A third was new to me. I asked
a young woman sitting on a bench with a book if she knew what it
was. "Me?" she said. "Trees?" She had a lovely smile. "You've got
to be kidding." A sycamore growing near the curb of the farther
Park Avenue caught my eye. It was a good fifty feet tall and of a
considerable girth—at least four feet in diameter. It was dignified
by a marble plaque. Commemorative plaques, though I didn't
know it then, are commonplace in Portland. This one read: "SYCA-
MORE TREE PLANTED BY SYLVESTER FARRELL, 1880." But I was
still curious about that unidentified tree. A man with a briefcase
approached. I asked him my question. He shook his head. "I'm
sorry," he said. "But I'm from out of town." The next man I
stopped kept going. I caught up with another briefcased businessman, a Chinese. "Oh, yes," he said. "It is elm." But what kind? He
gave a little laugh. "Maybe Chinese elm."

I walked on up the park. There was a statue in almost every
block. A double life-size Lincoln. An equestrian Theodore Roose-
velt in Rough Rider costume. Three lightly clad women with water
pitchers held aloft. There were beds of roses. Portland is called
"The City of Roses." The buildings that faced the park were all
substantial (churches, the Portland Art Museum, the Oregon Historical Society, a Masonic temple, apartment houses), but none was
overpowering. Most of the apartment buildings had the look of the
twenties and thirties (carved stone and polished brass), but there
were several that looked very new. The tallest was just six stories. I
came to a drinking fountain. I stopped for a drink, and stayed to
look and admire. It was no mere inverted tap. It was a work of
functional art: a heavy bronze base, a round and fluted bronze ped-
est ', four outward and upward branching arms, four little brass
basins, four sparkling jets of water. It was also, I came to know,
only one of many. There is a similar fountain on almost every
downtown corner, collectively the gift, on the eve of Prohibition, of
a philanthropic lumberman and bon vivant named Simon Benson,
and conceived (in his words) "to quench a frustrated thirst."

I followed the park, gently but steadily climbing, to its end. The
last two or three blocks are flanked by the buildings of Portland
State University and are integrated into its campus. Beyond the
park, to the south and west, the West Hills begin, and I could make
out houses clinging here and there along their wooded slopes.
There was no way to go but east, and I headed there, toward the
river, toward a residential complex called Portland Center. The
Park Avenue park was laid out around 1876, and Portland Center
continues in a contemporary mode that early appreciation of urban

breathing space. It rose in the first years of the Portland renaissance on a commanding slope some twenty blocks square that had once been a neighborhood of ramshackle single-family houses. I came into the Center at its summit by way of a wide and winding pedestrian promenade. A twenty-story condominium loomed on the left, loomed above a parking lot graced with laurel hedges and ivy-covered walls, and beyond was another condominium, a building architecturally compatible with the other but only three stories in height. Beyond that were other parking lots disguised as parks, a row of three-story buildings, then another high rise. On the right was a long one-story building occupied by shops purveying the essential goods and services of city life. I passed a liquor store, a travel agency, a hair stylist, a dry cleaner, a grocery store, a brokerage office, a café offering espresso and cappuccino. There were flowering planters and rose beds, there were rhododendron trees, there were benches with elderly people sunning themselves and young mothers with perambulators or toddlers. There were street lights with cast-iron standards and nineteenth-century globes. There was an almost bird's-eye view of the river and one of its several bridges and the chaotic beginnings of what looked like another Portland Center. An easy flight of steps led down to a paved plaza with trees and a fountain in the form of a mountain stream cascading down a rocky chute to a shallow pool. There were big stepping stones across the pool, and a young couple was leading a little boy—squeaking with fright or excitement—across. A row of two-story apartments faced the plaza on the north. The promenade continued past a ten-story condominium with shops and offices at street level. I came out into another, larger plaza with scattered groves of trees on artificial knolls and a centerpiece contemporary sculpture of painstakingly rusted metal. A young woman in a leather jacket was slouched on her spine on a bench, opening a battered package of cigarettes. I watched her extract what turned out to be the last cigarette, watched her crumple the pack, watched her stand and look around for a trash can. There was no trash can in sight. She sat back down, and stuffed the crumpled package in her pocket.

"Yes, I know," John E. Graham said to me at a reception following a concert at the Arlene Schnitzer Concert Hall that night. Graham is general manager of the Oregon Symphony Orchestra. "That's the way these people are. This is a clean city in just about every respect. The air is clean—cleaner than most, I'd say. Our power is mostly hydroelectric power. It's generated at the Bonneville Dam or at one of the others on the Columbia. They tell me the Willamette is practically unpolluted. And, as you may know, Oregon has the oldest bottle law in the country. But the main thing, I think, is civic pride. The people care about Portland. They feel it belongs to them. Our renewal program has practically unanimous support. I was born and raised on the East Coast, and when I arrived here, eleven years ago, I was stunned. I had never seen a really clean city before. Clean and orderly. I think they go together. You must have noticed how people stand and wait at traffic lights. Jaywalking is unheard of. But now I'm afraid I'm spoiled. If I come across one scrap of litter on my way to work, I almost fly into a rage."

A day or two later, while walking in a part of town less savory than Portland Center, I saw a weathered old man sitting in a doorway with a bottle in a paper bag, saw him tip it up and finish it off, saw him get creakingly up and shuffle a dozen steps to the corner and drop it in a trash can.

The tallest building in Portland is the First Interstate Bank Tower. It occupies a square block between Fourth and Fifth Avenues just below Portland Center and stands forty stories in height, with four stories below ground. There is a restaurant called the Loft on the twenty-eighth floor which has, the concierge at the Heathman told me, a view that is well worth viewing, and I went there one bright and sunny noon for lunch. The Loft is a spacious room with floor-to-ceiling windows on the north and east, and I was given a table facing east. I sat down and looked out—looked down and away— at a scatter of office buildings, at the river and its bridges, at a mighty wall of mountains rising to a mighty snow-topped pyramidal peak. Mt. Hood. I turned to the window on the north. Rooftops. The river. Another wall of mountains, rising to another snow-topped peak, but a different sort of peak—a flattened, truncated peak. Mt. St. Helens. The remains of Mt. St. Helens. I sat and looked from one to the other. It was, indeed, a view worth viewing. It was in my experience an urban view of views. I looked around at my fellow-lunchers—four businessmen with their heads together and their jackets hung over their chair backs a group of bantering officeworkers, some chattering shoppers, an ardent couple. I seemed to have the view to myself.

Portland is a city of greenery. It is blessed with a mild climate and an abundant rainfall that keep it green through much of the year. There are trees on almost every downtown street, and almost every office building has a terrace or a sunken garden bright with flower beds or ilex bushes or potted laurel trees. There are ten parks in the downtown area alone. With one notable exception, none of them is less than a block in size, and two—the riverfront park and the Park Avenue blocks—are, of course, many times larger. The riverfront park extends along the river for nearly two miles, and it is at some places a good two blocks wide. It is, moreover, just the beginning of the Willamette River Greenway, which eventually will extend the full hundred-and-twenty-mile length of the river. The park is otherwise, and perhaps uniquely, unusual. The land it covers was once—only a few years ago—a four-lane expressway, which, in the manner of most American cities, denied the riverfront to all but the speeding motorcar. I walked its pleasant length one afternoon, and there were fishermen here and there along the seawall. It could have been a stretch of the Seine. Except that there are actually edible fish to be caught in the Willamette. "All kinds of fish," one of the fishermen told me. "But what most of us are hoping for is sturgeon. Caviar, man!"

The smallest park in Portland is called Mill Ends Park, and it is also (I was told) the smallest park in the world. That would seem to be apodictic. It is roughly circular in shape, two feet in diameter, and it covers an area of four hundred and fifty-two square inches. It is situated, I was told, at the intersection of Front Avenue and Taylor Street, and although it took me some little time to find it, my directions were entirely correct. Mill Ends Park is situated in the *middle* of the intersection: a tiny island of concrete surrounding a round patch of earth (sprouting daffodils when I saw it) and two ornamental cast-iron posts. A bronze plaque on Taylor Street reads, FROM HIS OFFICE ON THE SECOND FLOOR OF THE OLD OREGON *JOURNAL*, JOURNALIST DICK FAGAN (1911-1969) PERIODICALLY GAZED DOWN ON THE BUSY FRONT AVENUE THOROUGHFARE. IT WAS HIS KEEN IMAGINATION THAT TURNED A UTILITY POLE HOLE, IN THE AVENUE MEDIA STRIP AT TAYLOR STREET, INTO MILL ENDS PARK." Fagan wrote a column called "Mill Ends." His park, one of the humblest fruits of the Portland renaissance, was dedicated into the Portland park system in 1976.

All of the Portland parks I saw have character, and most of them are interesting in nature or in origin. Emerging from the Third Avenue entrance to the Civic Auditorium (dedicated in 1968, but loosely Palladian in style), I found a park called Ira's Fountain (for a civic leader named Ira C. Keller), which is neither entirely a park nor merely a fountain. What it is is an enormous sculpture—a block-square cement sculpture in the form of a spread of waterfalls. The usual plaque relates the statistics: The lip of the falls is eighty feet wide, the highest fall is eighteen feet, and the water flows at a rate of thirteen thousand gallons per minute. The water emerges from a fountain, leaps into space, and drops to a system of pools and basins. There is a park with benches (all taken when I was there) and trees overlooking the fountain, and another park (whose benches also were taken) below. In summer, children jump through the screen of falling water and play in the pools behind, and the city provides a lifeguard to keep an eye on them. Ira's Fountain is a spectacular urban pleasantry, but it could easily be dwarfed and destroyed by the usual urban environment. The Civic Auditorium, however, is just three stories high, and the other buildings that surround the park are not much higher. There are no Wall Street canyons in Portland.

Two blocks north of Ira's Fountain I came to another green amenity. This is a three-block chain of parks, bounded on the east by Third Avenue and on the west by Fourth, which mark the governmental center of town. City Hall (circa 1895) is there, and so is the new (1983) Multnomah County Justice Center. The first of these parks is a peaceful amphitheatre of brick and lawn withdrawn behind a screen of trees and shrubs. It commemorates a former mayor, Terry D. Schrunk, who served from 1957-1973. It is also, like the riverfront park, an earnest of the Portland renaissance. Its site until recently was occupied by an office building; when it was decided that a park would be desirable there, the building was bought and razed. The two other parks in the chain are Lownsdale Square and Chapman Square, and they were laid out in 1852. A fountain and watering trough of the period, surmounted by a great bronze statue of a bull elk (in memory of a local behemoth of pioneer days), rises from the middle of the street that separates them. Through much of the nineteenth century, Lownsdale Square was frequented exclusively by men. Women gathered in Chapman. They are both conventional city parks with paths and benches and shade trees. Several of these were another species new to me. I asked a passerby if he knew what they were. "Sure," he said. "They're ginkgoes. They come from China."

Visitors to Portland are all but required to take a meal at an eating place called the Dan & Louis Oyster Bar. Dan & Louis is one of the oldest restaurants in Portland (est. 1907), and it is situated at the northern edge of the downtown center in the oldest part of the city. The building it occupies (and owns) was once the City Hall. I came there for lunch one day by way of a circle through the immediate neighborhood, through streets of nineteenth-century buildings of rosy brick and cast-iron that had survived the middle years of the twentieth century by reason of community indifference and are now revered as Historic Landmarks. I loitered in Skidmore Plaza, an agreeable square paved with cobblestones that arrived in Portland as ship's ballast. In its center is the city's oldest work of public art—a sculptured bronze-and-granite fountain with facilities for both human beings and horses. I inspected an elegant cast-iron building that was once the leading theatre and is now an enclave of shops and cafés. I passed the Salvation Army's Harbor Light Mission, and was offered a drink by a mixed gathering of jovial derelicts out front. Dan & Louis is across the street (Ankeny Street) from a musical café called the Chocolate Moose. I was shown to a place at a long communal table that looked capable of seating thirty. The walls were hung—were encrusted—with souvenir plates, with framed photographs and newspaper clippings, with marine artifacts. I ordered, at the command of a matronly waitress, a specialty of the house: Yaquina Bay oysters, no bigger than white grapes (from Dan & Louis' own beds), in a cocktail sauce; fresh Columbia River silver salmon with French-fried potatoes; a salad of tiny shrimp; and iced tea. Dan & Louis does not serve alcohol. I had a dish of orange sherbet for dessert. My bill was just over eight dollars. That included tip but not tax. There is no sales tax in Oregon.

The most esteemed survival of nineteenth-century Portland is a three-story (with cupola) Palladian building (with Greek pediments) now known as the Pioneer Courthouse. It occupies, with its lawns and trees and other plantings, a block between Fifth and Sixth Avenues not far from City Hall. It was built in 1868 and was the first United States courthouse in the Far West. It was rescued from mindless demolition in 1968 and restored to its full original glory in 1973. This glory is not immediately apparent. The main (Sixth Avenue) entrance and foyer have been converted into a branch post office. But beyond that, the nineteenth century—the opulence of nineteenth-century public buildings—awaits. I was shown all this by a friendly, or perhaps just lonely, security guard whom I found at a desk in a corridor served by a Fifth Avenue entrance.

"Well, no," he told me. "This is a National Historic Landmark building, but I wouldn't call it a museum. It's very much in use. The two upper floors are still courtrooms. The United States Court of Appeals sits there, and the Bankruptcy Branch of the U.S. District Court. These offices along here are the offices of the various court officials. And, of course, Senator Hatfield has an office here.

Most of the panelling here is the original panelling. It's ash. Now, if you're interested, I'll show you all the rest. These stairs are the original stairs, the original bannisters and all. I won't show you all the courtrooms. But I think you'll be interested in this one here. That woodwork is all old oak. You don't see that kind of wood anymore. The furnishings are partly original and partly of the period but acquired from other old courthouses. Those bench lamps came from Chicago. The benches for the public were found in St. Paul. The same for the hat and umbrella rack and the counsel tables and lectern—they came from all over. The fireplace is the original fireplace, and I guess that was all the heat they had in the old days." He looked at his watch. "I've got to get back in a minute, but I want you to see the cupola."

We climbed another staircase, curved and carved and darkly glowing, and passed another panelled courtroom. The guard opened an inconspicuous door. We climbed a flight of ladderlike steps. We came out in an octagonal room with windows all around. "This is where they used to bring the visiting dignitaries," the guard said. "It gave them a view of the whole city. You can still see the river. Mt. Hood is somewhere behind that building there. And that one there cuts off Mt. St. Helens. But the way they're doing the city over, you never know. They may be planning to restore this view. What you see down there in front is something new. They call it Pioneer Courthouse Square. That block used to be the old Portland Hotel. President Taft got stuck in a bathtub there. They razed the old hotel in 1950 and turned the block into a parking lot. They tore up the parking lot and built the square in 1983. They use it for all kinds of things—art exhibits, concerts, every sort of gathering. I guess that's why it's paved. It was built largely by public subscription. Everybody who paid fifteen dollars got his name inscribed on one of the paving bricks. There's supposed to be like sixty thousand bricks down there. I've got one myself, if I could ever find it. I don't know what those two big rows of pillars are for. I don't know why, with all that red brick, they used all that purple and lavender tile. That cavelike opening at the far end is a fountain, but it's also the entrance to some municipal offices. They're underground. I don't know why the square has all those steps and all those different levels. I don't know why there aren't any trees. There's been a lot of talk about Pioneer Square. Some people think it's a little weird. But a lot of people use it. As you can see."

I took a turn around the square to see it closer up. It looked a little less weird than it had from the cupola, and very much larger. It was indeed in use. I joined a crowd and watched a man and a dog playing with a Frisbee. I passed a red-faced man praying at the top of his voice. I stopped to hear a girl guitarist who was wearing golf-ball earrings and what looked like a fez. I passed a dozen embracing couples. I passed a vender selling daffodils. I passed three young men in running clothes handing around a marijuana cigarette. I squatted down and deciphered a couple of bricks: Frank Fifer, Gretchen D. Spence, Elinor Langer. I started up a wide and shallow flight of steps, and saw a man in a dark business suit standing above with an upraised open umbrella. I climbed the rest of the steps, and looked again. It wasn't a man. It was a statue. That is, the man was a statue, but everything else appeared to be real. His shoes were real shoes, his suit and shirt and necktie were real. So was his umbrella. Real but sprayed with some sort of preservative. There was a bronze plaque. It read, "GIFT OF HARRU H. SCHWARTZ, NEW YORK CITY, 1983."

There was a story in the Portland *Oregonian* one morning about the continuing aims and concerns of the renaissance. One of the planners quoted was Patrick Tillett, head of the planning-and-urban-design unit of the architectural firm Zimmer Gunsel Frasca Partnership. "Downtown development depends on weaning people away from their automobiles," he said. That effort would seem to be well underway. Traffic in Portland is neither heavy nor notably light. I was reminded of the traffic in midtown Manhattan on a Saturday afternoon. One reason, I was told, for this moderate flow is a recent regulation known as a "parking lid." The lid limits the number of downtown parking spaces, both metered street parking and space in parking lots and garages. There are no cruising cabs in Portland. All the cabs I saw were either parked in designated cabstands or working. Twelve midtown blocks of two major streets—Fifth and Sixth Avenues—have been redesigned and largely restricted to pedestrians, buses, and emergency vehicles. Both of them—Fifth Avenue running one-way south and Sixth running one-way north—have been reduced to two lanes, and the sidewalks proportionately widened. I paced at random a Fifth Avenue walk and got an approximate width of twenty-seven feet. The sidewalks are variously paved, with much red brick laid in different geometrical designs. There are plane and sycamore trees and stone planters and Benson drinking fountains and benches at intervals, and there is a glass-roofed shelter at every bus stop. The buses are frequent, and they are free to all within an area of three hundred downtown blocks. The streets that flank Pioneer Square and the Pioneer Courthouse (Yamhill Street and Morrison Street) were torn up for several blocks at the time of my visit and closed to all traffic. I assumed that this was for the usual mysterious metropolitan reasons. That was a faulty assumption. "You haven't heard?" an acquaintance at the bar at the Heathman told me one evening. "They're laying track. Portland has reinvented the streetcar. The route will be a loop from East Side Portland across the river and on to somewhere here on the West Side, and then circle around and return. They call it a light-rail system."

I had lunch and a bottle of Oregon wine (an Adelsheim Chardonnay) one afternoon with Steven Lowenstein, a native New Yorker and a graduate of the Yale Law School, who serves as executive assistant to Mike Lindberg, the Commissioner of Public Affairs for the Portland City Council. "My wife and I came here in 1970," he told me. "Our son was just a year old, and Portland seemed like a nice place, a safe place, for him to grow up. As it turned out, 1970 was just about the time the big excitement here began. The first stirrings. There were and are a great many people involved in the renewal program. You could say that everybody, the whole citizenry, was involved. The quality of the environment has always been important in Oregon. But the real leadership was provided by Neil Goldschmidt, who came in as mayor in 1973. As you may remember, he later served as Secretary of Transportation under Jimmy Carter. He saw, as we all do, that the automobile is the problem. We need it, but we don't want to be owned by it. He was concerned that it would be the death of downtown, as it has been in so many cities. He was afraid that the freeways would dominate the city. He was afraid that development would proceed with no concern for the people. And he thought the problem was urgent. Portland was growing fast in the seventies. Well, things began to get turned around. We began to see a new kind of city. We got rid of the freeway on this side of the river. We put through a comprehensive plan for the humanized development of downtown. All but two or three of the big buildings downtown here have come up under the new planning. We're making progress against the automobile. But, of course, that's only part of the problem. If we're going to have a downtown that is central to the area, it must have something to attract the people there. We've concentrated on that. All our new buildings are planned with the human element in mind. We have a height limitation, and the tallest buildings must be well back from the river. We try to preserve air and space. We're proud of our new buildings, and we want them to be seen and enjoyed. When buildings are crowded together, architecture doesn't matter. We have no rules about architectural style. Our new buildings are of all shapes and kinds and materials. The Portland Building, which was designed by Michael Graves and has won all kinds of awards, is probably the only one of its kind in the world. But we do have basic rules. I mentioned height. We also control bulk, through setbacks and limits on floor area. We think blank walls at street level dehumanize a building and a neighborhood, so we require that every new building provide space at street level for retail businesses—for shops and cafés. We think public art humanizes a city, so we require that one percent of the total cost of every public building be spent on some sort of art. We think downtown should be the cultural center of a city and the entertainment center. When I came here, there were no more than three or four real restaurants downtown. Now we have at least forty. We have the new Arlene Schnitzer Concert Hall, and that work going on next door to it will be our new Center for the Performing Arts. There are plans for a new theatre complex just across the street. Everything is in walking distance. That was the aim of the master plan. One of its goals is 'Provide for a pleasant, rich, and diverse pedestrian experience.' Downtown used to be deserted at night. Now it's full of people— people walking around enjoying themselves. My office is in City Hall, and I live down northwest. I walk to work every morning. It takes me about thirty minutes. Bud Clark, our mayor, lives a little farther on. He rides a bicycle to work. We have thousands of people living within walking distance of their work. People all over the country are running and jogging. We're getting them to walk."

My last meal in Portland, like my first, was breakfast. The waitress who served me was the one who had served me most mornings during my stay. She brought my morning cordial, and waited for me to order. "I hope you've enjoyed yourself," she told me. "I'm afraid everything's kind of torn up here downtown. All the new building that's going on, and the streetcar line and all. I guess we're in what they call a transition. I think it's a lot like letting your hair grow out. It's going to be beautiful. You just have to accept that middle-growth period."

[1985]

4. The Grower's Shadow: Canyon County, Idaho

It is four o'clock on a warm spring afternoon, and I am sitting at the counter of the Mobil Cafe in the crossroads hamlet of Wilder, Idaho, in the Canyon County flats of the Snake River Valley, some thirty miles west of Boise. I am sitting with the chief Canyon County agent. He is a big, easy, weathered man of fifty-four named Merle R. Samson, and we have stopped here for a cup of coffee after a day in an air-conditioned pickup truck, poking around a dusty countryside of farms and orchards and distant mountains. The Cafe is full of farmers in bib overalls and pointed boots. Samson is known to many of them, and they nod and call him by name. Most of the farmers are white, but two are Japanese and one is a dark-skinned Mexican. They are drinking the watery café coffee and talking in voices that would carry across a feedlot.

" . . . malathion."

"Yes, sir. I mean number one Idaho bakers."

"No, by God. What it turned out to be was the *web*worm."

"That's right. Sixty cents a hundredweight to the grower."

"You want to know what I think of malathion? I'd sooner *pee* on my alfalfa."

"Well, two days later he was down at Salt Lake City, and he walked into the Safeway store, and son of a bitch—they were selling the same potatoes there at the equivalent of thirteen dollars a hundredweight."

"And now the bastards say I can't use dieldrin. I say we ought to dump some dieldrin on the goddam ecologists."

"It's all those sons of bitches in between. They got their hand in *everybody's* pocket."

* * *

A county agent is the representative, at the barnyard level, of the Coöperative (state and federal) Agricultural Extension Service. It is he who brings to the farmer the fully ripened fruits of agronomical research. The county served by Samson and four other agents—an entomologist and three specialists in crops and cattle—plus two home economists, is an exemplar of that service. Canyon is the leading agricultural county in Idaho, and, with an annual farm income of more than seventy-eight million dollars, derived from a cornucopia of crops—sugar beets, apples, sweet-corn seed, hops, potatoes, alfalfa seed, cattle, peppermint, red-clover seed, wheat, onions, lima-bean seed, cherries, milk, prunes, barley, alfalfa hay, spinach, peaches, popcorn—it is one of the most productive counties in the nation. That was why I was there.

The office of the Canyon County agent is in Caldwell (pop. 14,219), the Canyon County seat. It is situated on the lumberyard-and-warehouse side of the Union Pacific tracks, and occupies a nest of low-ceilinged rooms on the second floor of a two-story stucco building that was once a garage. The ground floor houses the A-Gem Supply Company. A long flight of steps at one end of the building leads steeply up to a labyrinthine corridor lined with open doors and racks of United States Department of Agriculture publications: "Controlling the Mexican Bean Beetle," "Diseases of Mint," "A Career for Me in Agriculture," "Growing Carrot Seed in Idaho." I had climbed those steps for the first time at around nine o'clock that morning. Samson's room was the first open door on the left. He was there, at his desk, talking on the telephone. He looked up and smiled and pointed to a chair. I removed a pile of papers and an apple—a big, red, shiny Delicious apple—to the top of a filing cabinet and sat down. Through the window there was a view of a warehouse roof, and above the roof was an immensity of sky—the wide blue sky of the mountain West.

"And how about the leaves?" Samson was saying on the telephone. "Right. It looks a lot like wild parsley. Or wild carrot. And the root is very often mistaken for wild parsnip. . . . Well, that's what it sounds like to me. I think you've got yourself some poison hemlock there. . . . No, you sure don't. . . . You bet it is—it's very toxic. What I think you better do is fence that area off and treat it with a chemical weed killer, like maybe 2,4-D. . . . Right. And the sooner the better."

Samson hung up and swung around in his chair. His face was lined and deeply tanned. "Well," he said, and lighted a cigarette. "I'll tell you the truth. That's the only thing I don't much like about this job. I mean the telephone. I'm a county agent that likes to be out in the county. But I guess it could be worse. I know it could. I quit the Service back in 1951 and tried it out in the world. I went into the feed-and-grain business. I stayed out there for three years, and that was enough. I was more than ready to come back. County agents don't often get rich, but they get a lot of real job satisfaction—they're giving instead of taking. And they don't have to sit at a desk all day. At least, not every day."

The telephone rang. Samson swung back to his desk. He answered and listened and brightened. "Right," he said. "You bet I do—I was down there a couple of days ago. But it depends on what you want. You've got a good location there. The conditions are very good. If you want to try a legume, I'll have to suggest alfalfa. You might try mixing alfalfa and orchard grass. . . . You bet. It makes a real fine permanent pasture. . . . Oh, I don't know—I guess forty-sixty would be about the best proportion. Or you could try just a sprinkling of alfalfa and the rest grass. Or all grass. . . . Right. And, of course, grass is a good soil builder. But if you're going to broadcast it, I'd increase that just a little—maybe ten pounds to the acre. . . . Well, sure. And with an all-grass pasture you don't have to worry about bloat in your cows. . . . You bet."

Samson hung up. He sat for a moment, rubbing his left ear. "I guess I've been pretty lucky," he said. "I know what I want, and I've got it. I was born and raised in Idaho, and, except for the Navy Air Corps in the Second World War, I've never had to leave it. I got my B.S. at the University, up at Moscow. I've worked up there, in Latah County, and I've worked in the east, around Pocatello. I've been all over the state. And Canyon County here is the best of Idaho. They call this Treasure Valley. We've got a diversity of crops which I doubt can be matched anywhere. That makes it interesting. I like a little variety. But we've got some specialties, too. We're the number one county in the country—in the whole United States—in sweet-corn-seed production. And in alfalfa seed. And red-clover seed. And mixed grains. We're number five in sugar beets. We're way up in dairy production. And so on. We've never had a crop failure. There's been some reduced yields here, but never an out-and-out failure. And it all began from nothing. Sixty years ago, this county was a wasteland. It was nothing but sagebrush desert. We get only about eight inches of rain a year. It was irrigation that made the difference, of course. We have plenty of underground water here, but we don't irrigate with that. We don't mine our underground reserves, the way some states are doing. The water we use is mountain snow-melt, impounded in storage lakes."

The telephone rang. Samson turned and looked at it. But he answered it on the third ring. "Oh," he said. "How you doing? . . . Right. . . . Yes, so I understand. . . . That's right. . . . Well, you've sprayed enough acreage to know. . . . You bet." He laughed. "But just remember, Roy. Remember what Hugh Homan told you about malathion and the paint on automobiles. It acts like a solvent."

Samson hung up. "That's enough," he said. He stood up. "Let's get out of here. Let's go see how the season is going. I'll take you for a little drive."

Hugh Homan is the entomologist assigned to Canyon County. I met him the following morning—a thickset man of thirty-eight with a hard blue jaw and heavy black brows and sideburns. He invited me to join him on a round of professional calls. We drove out of town on a wide gravel road in a dirty white Volkswagen with a big can of Treflan weed killer bouncing around in back. The sky overhead was fresh and blue, but there were cloudy mountains on the horizon. Homan's right hand, on the wheel, was missing the thumb and forefinger. "This fellow I want to see first is a fruitgrower named Norman Vermeer," he said. "He's got a problem with sandburs in one of his orchards. I should have seen him yesterday, but I had to go over to Boise and testify in an accident case. A farmer was burning a crop residue, and the smoke blew across the road, and a driver came along and couldn't see, and stopped. Another car came up and didn't see him sitting there, and smashed into him. Killed him. So his family is suing the farmer for negligence. I testified on farming practices. Burning crop residue instead of tilling it back into the soil is bad farming. But I had to testify that they do it all the time. It's common practice. Farming is a hazardous occupation, and one big reason is carelessness. I grew up on a farm just north of here, in Payette County, and I learned my lesson early. I was just sixteen when I lost my fingers. I was running a balky old corn picker, and I tried to reach under the rollers to fix something without turning off the engine. The only lucky thing was, I happened to be left-handed."

We slowed to turn off onto a bumpy lane, and my window filled with a sudden sugary jasmine smell of wild currant. There was a fence-line thicket of blossoming bushes just across the road. A yellow-headed blackbird was perched on one of the flowering branches.

"Now, there's a pretty sight," Homan said.

"The blackbird?" I said.

"What?" he said. "Oh—heck, no. I mean that old rooster

pheasant marching across that field. I've got a date with him for next fall. This is real good country here. I mean for farming *and* living. We start off in September with a season on doves. Then sage grouse. Then quail: bobwhite and mountain and valley—all three. Then pheasant. Then, up in the hills, chukar and Hungarian partridge. That's good, hard hunting. Then ducks and geese down along the river. Then, later on, if you've got the ambition to pack into the mountains, there's elk. I reload my own shotgun shells, and last fall I used a hundred pounds of lead, in one-and-a-quarter-ounce shot. So you can see I did a little bit of shooting. But I don't have any trouble enjoying my weekends any time of the year. We've got trout fishing in the spring, and there's bass and perch in the lakes in summer. And there's good skiing up in the mountains. This isn't just the place where I was born and raised. This country here is my *home.*"

We pulled into a rutted driveway between a big storage barn and a little white house in a sombre grove of pines. Beyond the drive were the pink-canopied aisles of peach orchard. A tall, blond smiling young man came out through the pines to meet us. He was Vermeer.

"Hugh," he said. "This sandbur situation here is serious. Those little farmers are mean. They made trouble for me with my pickers last fall. You know those fishhook barbs—they'll dig right through your pants. My pickers couldn't stand it. And you know about good pickers."

"I know they're hard to get," Homan said. "But maybe I can help. Anyway, I brought you this can of Treflan. I want you to try it. One quart to the acre in forty gallons of water. Then we'll see. Where are they giving you trouble—in your peach orchard there?"

"They're in my plums. You want to take a look?"

"You bet. Your peaches look good, Norman. Did you light for that frost back there?"

"I probably should have. I took a chance. And for once I was lucky. I understand they're hurting bad on stone fruits up in Washington."

"So I hear."

Vermeer laughed. "Well, you know how we feel about that. We sit down every night and pray that Washington freezes out. Then we might have a chance to make some money."

"Hey," Homan said. "You really do have some sandburs here."

"They're healthy little farmers," Vermeer said. "And these plums are one of my best crops. They all go back to New York—they're all for the kosher market."

"That's a good contract market."

"It is—but, you know, I wonder about those people back there. They buy all the plums I can grow, but they've never tasted a real plum. I mean a ripe plum. To get them there in the condition the market wants, I've got to pick them three weeks early. But they're really good plums when they ripen on the tree. The pickers always leave a few on every tree for us."

"The consumer is the boss."

"That's the trouble. The consumer eats with her eyes. It's funny, isn't it? She won't buy an apple unless it looks like a picture. It has to be big and red and shiny. But you and I and every grower knows that a little green adds flavor, and the redder the skin the tougher it is. I doubt if I'd even grow a red Delicious if she didn't make me. I might grow Jonathans or Rome Beauties. This is the best Rome country in the world."

"She'll change her mind someday," Homan said. "The fashion will turn to something else. Remember the Baldwin and the McIntosh and the old Arkansas Black."

"I know she'll change," Vermeer said. "And then I'll have to pull out half of my orchard."

We followed a long flat, empty blacktop road. Flanking it were boundless potato fields. Then the land began to dip. We passed a hopyard, with its twenty-foot poles and overhead wires and clustering, climbing vines. We came around the slope of a crumbling, sunbaked butte. We passed a barn remodelled into a house, and then a leafy alfalfa field. We turned into a drive at a gray shingle house with a straggle of sheds and shacks in back. There was a sound of hammering from behind the sheds.

Homan shut off the engine and leaned on the wheel. "This is a highly successful alfalfa-seed operation," he said. "It's a partnership. A couple named Trueblood live in that barn over there, and an old batch named Wally Burrill lives here. Bud Trueblood grows the alfalfa, and Wally raises the bees. Alfalfa is pollinated by a species of leafcutter bee. Those sheds with the open fronts are mobile bee boxes. Domesticated leafcutter bees don't live in hives. They nest in the holes of perforated boards called bee boards. The average board will have around two thousand holes, and there are usually twelve cells—twelve bees—to the hole. The bees are kept in refrigerated hibernation until just before blossomtime. Then the boards are hung in the sheds and hauled out to the field. Alfalfa pollination requires a lot of bees—between seven and ten thousand to the acre. And only the females work. This kind of beekeeping is full of problems. But that isn't why I'm here. There isn't much that I can teach Wally and Bud about their business. They're exceptional. What usually happens, I learn from them. So I like to stop by whenever I'm around this part of the country. And Mary Trueblood is a real good cook."

The hammering stopped, and a gray-haired man with a bony face and rimless glasses appeared. "I heard you drive in," he said, "but I was up on the roof of a shed. I've finally built me some sheds I like."

"I was looking at that new one over there," Homan said. "How come you're using planks?"

"Oh, Jesus," Burrill said. "I got sick of that goddam plywood. It's so goddam phony. But that isn't the only difference. These new sheds have all got double roofs for good ventilation. I want to make those little bastards comfortable. And I'm hinging the bottom planks on all three walls for the same reason. They're just as sensitive to heat as they are to cold."

"A lot of growers don't seem to realize that," Homan said. "They have to learn the hard way."

"You're goddam right," Burrill said. "A bee don't come alive until the temperature gets to seventy plus, and he'll die at one hundred and five. You've got to watch the little bastards. I remember one morning a couple of years ago I was making a round of my sheds. The early sun was shining in the open fronts, and the temperature up at board level—about chest level—was seventy-one degrees, and the bees were dropping out of their holes. But the floor in the sheds was still cold, and they lay there turning numb. What I did was grab a broom and race around sweeping them out —sweeping them out into the sun. And son of a bitch—it only took a minute of sunshine. Then they sat up and flew off to start making me some money. I could have lost every goddam bee I had."

"A lot of people have," Homan said.

Homan and I had noon dinner with the Truebloods and Wally Burrill in Mary Trueblood's kitchen. The Truebloods are in their fifties. She is a pretty woman with soft gray hair, and he is tall and lanky and burned to leather. We sat in comfortable chairs at a long table with a centerpiece of red tulips. We began with roast lamb, baked potatoes, and fresh green asparagus, and finished with cherry pie and coffee. The asparagus had been cut (by Mrs. Trueblood) only that morning from a volunteer stand along a fencerow. In Canyon County, asparagus is a weed. The seeds are spread by birds, and the plants thrive wherever they can escape cultivation—in the shelter of fences and around the trunks of orchard trees.

"I remember when we took out our orchard up home," Homan said. "My job was to dig up the asparagus roots around the trees. Those roots were harder to get out than the stumps."

"I've broken a plow on asparagus roots," Trueblood said. "I detest it with a purple passion. Except when it's here on my plate."

The stove on which the asparagus, and everything else, was cooked was a coal stove—a big black cast-iron turn-of-the-century Majestic range.

"I spent years finding that stove," Mrs. Trueblood said. "I wouldn't cook on anything else. Coal heat is the perfect cooking heat. Of course, it's more trouble than gas or electricity, but that's true of so *many* things. So many good things take trouble. Like this homemade bread we're eating. And homemade pie. And home-grown vegetables. I love my Majestic stove. And one day when I was up in Bud's mother's attic I found another treasure. It's hanging there over the stove: 'The Majestic Cook Book.'"

"Hell's bells," Burrill said. "Everything worthwhile takes trouble."

"I had to learn that for myself," Trueblood said. "I had to go all the way to college to find out how to farm. My father sure never taught me. He farmed on the principle of let's hurry up and make as much as we can right now and never mind what happens to the soil. It never occurred to him to give nature half a chance. But the things I finally learned weren't new. A year or two ago, I picked up a copy of the Department of Agriculture *Yearbook* for 1902—and it's all in there. Crop rotation. Soil conservation. Cultivation. The Extension Service tried to teach it to my dad, but he couldn't be bothered. He couldn't even be bothered to irrigate right. It was easier to overwater, so he leached his soil away."

"There are still a lot of farmers like your dad," Homan said. "We've worked out a little table at the office. We figure that maybe two percent of the farmers are truly receptive to new ideas. They're men like you and Wally. We call them innovators. Then comes a group of fifteen percent that we call early adapters. Then comes a middle group of sixty percent. They're the regular majority. They come in when the ideas are pretty well established. Another fifteen percent are the late adapters. They're the ones that say, 'Hell, I'm doing all right, these new ideas are probably just a flash in the pan, so I guess I'll wait and see.' And then there's those that never adapt."

"We got one of those bastards for a neighbor," Burrill said. "He told me he wouldn't think of using fertilizer. He said it made the weeds grow too fast."

"A lot of farmers come to our meetings just to get away from their wives," Homan said. "Or maybe to see their friends. They don't even try to learn."

"Learning is hard work," Trueblood said. "But, good Lord, so is chukar hunting."

The Snake River swings up from the south a mile or two west of the Trueblood farm, and Homan and I crossed it there on the Homedale Bridge. The river was fast and muddy, with many brushy islands, and the banks were lined with drooping willows. On the other side of the river, beyond the one-street village of Homedale, the road began to rise. Our destination was a hilltop orchard owned by a man named Shults. "Garfield Shults," Homan said. "He called me out here a couple of weeks ago for advice on spraying his apple trees for scale. I want to see how good a job he did. Garfield sells all his fruit at retail. He's an old-fashioned door-to-door peddler, and he makes enough to live the way he wants to. His real interest is grafting—experimenting with different species and varieties. I met a man from Cornell at the annual meeting of the Entomological Society of America last year. 'So you're from Idaho,' he said. 'I wonder if you know a man named Garfield Shults. He just wrote and asked me for some New York McIntosh slips.' Garfield's known from coast to coast."

Shults's orchard was a jungle. Towering, tortured, unpruned apple trees. Bushy pears and peaches and plums. Reedlike saplings half buried in thigh-high grass. We found Shults down on his knees hacking at the roots of an apricot stump. He stood up to greet us—a small, ragged, beaming man in a khaki sun helmet. "Hugh," he said. "You know something? I think that spray did good."

"I think so, too," Homan said. "All the scale I've seen is dead." He rubbed his hand along an apple branch. "Nothing left but dust."

"And that tree there was just about lathered with them."

"That's right. But, my God, Garfield—when are you going to mow this grass? This is no way to grow fruit."

"Oh, I'm going to mow it. Don't worry about that. But right now I've got something to show you. Here's a row that's really dizzy. I've got prune plums growing on an apricot tree. The way I figure—if the prunes freeze out, I've still got a crop of apricots."

"Right."

"This whole section is dizzy. This dizzy-looking tree is my experimental laboratory. I've got it growing seven or eight different apples—Roanoke from Virginia, McIntosh from New York, Splendor from New Zealand, and Spies and Jonathans and Romes. And I've got a mystery apple here. I crossed a red and a golden Delicious. It's got those wide Delicious shoulders. But it's pink, Hugh—it's just as pink as a peach blossom. Oh, and here's a berserk Bartlett pear. Now, what the heck did I do here? I've forgotten, except that it keeps as good as a Bosc. And here's another berserk tree where I've forgotten exactly what I did. But I'll be watching it. I'll find out in a couple of months. That's half the fun. Is it going to be something delectable? Or merely edible? Or do you feed it to the horses? But I wanted to ask you, Hugh. What am I going to do about those bugs?"

"I keep telling you, Garfield. We can't get rid of bugs. We can't *eradicate* them. We don't even want to. They've got their place."

"OK. But what do I *do?*"

"You learn to live with them, Garfield."

Homan and I climbed back up through the overgrown aisles in a susurration of bees. We came out of the orchard dusk and into the hilltop afternoon. Garfield is like so many farmers, Homan said. "They're chemical activists. We're trying hard to change all that. We're trying to teach them that insecticides are the last resort. They mean you've failed at proper control—biological control. Our target orchard insect is the codling moth. It puts the worm in the apple. But when we first learned how to kill the codling moth chemically, we also killed the predators of the spider mite, and the spider mite became a very serious problem. Then we started using less toxic stuff on the codling moth and spared the predators. Now we're working to control the codling moth by confusing him at breeding time with a synthetic female scent. I think the farmers are beginning to listen to us. Not because they're fascinated by the idea of biological control. They listen because they're businessmen, and insecticides cost money. They cost a lot of money."

The senior home economist in the Canyon County office is a tall, fair, blue-eyed woman of thirty named Beverly Montgomery. Mrs. Montgomery and I had a cup of coffee together in her office. It is a windowless room with a desk, a filing cabinet, and a big 4-H poster: "I pledge my Head to clearer thinking, my Heart to greater loyalty, my Hands to larger service, and my Health to better living, for my Club, my Community, and my Country." "My work is mostly with our nutrition-education program," she said. "This is a rich county in many ways, but we have a lot of low-income families—welfare and food-stamp people. We have poor white people and poor Mexicans. Our Japanese families all seem to be self-suffi-cient. I would say that at least one-third of our population needs nutritional guidance. It's distressing how poorly informed they are, and how improvident. At the first of the month, when they have some money, they eat well. I mean, by their standards—ham-burger, hot dogs, potato chips, Cokes, and the snack foods they see advertised on television. Television is a problem. It's the only source of information that these people have. They don't read newspapers or magazines, and few of them have had much school-ing. Television commercials are their guides to living. Well, they tend to blow their budget in the first two weeks of the month. The third week is pretty tight. And by the fourth week they are often quite literally down to plain rice or macaroni. With no sauce, no butter—nothing. Then they get their checks or stamps, and they're so hungry for good food they'll blow it again on impulse—on strawberries at seventy-nine cents a pound, or half a dozen avo-cados at forty cents apiece. And this is where television comes into it again. They will spend their food money for something like Geri-tol. Our work is to help them stretch their food dollar—to help them get the most and the best for their money. It isn't easy work. We can't work directly with these people. We represent something they don't understand. They're suspicious and resentful. We have to reach them through their own kind of people. I have five white and three Mexican aides. These are superior women I have been able to attract and interest in our program—women I have trained. They are often neighbors of the people we wish to help. They can go into those homes and talk to the women there—the poor, un-happy teenage wives who send their kids to school without break-fast. They're down on life. Everything is too much for them. They've given up. But my aides are dedicated and patient. They go in and show them how to plan. They show them how to buy. They show them how hot cereal is cheaper and more nutritious than the cold cereals they hear about on television. They teach them how to cope."

We were driving out through a misty morning countryside—John Henry, who is the Canyon County livestock specialist, and I—in an old Mercury sedan with a mobile weighing chute clanking along behind, to weigh some calves at the farm of a breeder of purebred Red Angus cattle. Henry is forty-one years old—a big, bald, round-faced, slouching man—and he was dressed in the uni-form of the stockman: olive-green coveralls and pointed boots. "You know what they say about getting a farm these days," he said. "There's only two ways. Either you inherit it or you marry into it.

This old fellow we're going to see, this Layton Todd, he founded the operation, but he and his son are running it together now. What we're going to do this morning is weigh some calves for registry with the Red Angus Association. These calves are all around two hundred days old, and if they're up to standard they should weigh around five hundred pounds. I like working with cattle, but I guess I prefer it this way. My wife and I both like living in town—she plays the organ at the Latter-Day Saints. I grew up on a stock farm. My dad had one of the first Black Angus herds in Idaho. Red Angus is something new. I started milking at the age of six, and at eight I was out there shovelling manure, and when I was old enough for 4-H work I started feeding steers. I saw a lot. I saw my dad knocked down three times and almost killed one day by a dairy bull. Dairy bulls are always inclined to be mean. I got knocked around and cut up pretty good quite a few times myself. And I saw one of my kid friends out baling hay one day, and he slipped and went into the baler. It wired him up like a bale of hay, and the plunger cut him in two. I left the farm when I left home for college. Besides, my dad is still working our place. I got my B.S. in animal husbandry and M.S. in animal nutrition. This work is exactly right for me. I like to teach. I like to be of service, to make some impact. And everybody knows you. You're a leading citizen." He laughed. "I mean—Well, gosh, I get my picture in the paper at least once a month."

A sign appeared just ahead on the left: "Black Dust Angus Farms." Henry turned off the road, and we clanked down a lane past a block of cattle corrals tumultuous with bellowing cows and moaning calves. There was a heavy smell of manure and the sour and sickening stink of ensilage. We pulled up at a loading chute halfway down the block. Layton Todd, a red-faced man in coveralls and a big straw hat, was leaning against the chute. Inside the chute, tinkering with a gate, was a pink-cheeked younger man. That was his son, Ze Todd. ("People are always asking me about my name," he later told me. "They ought to ask my dad and mother. They saw this movie about Jesse James just before I was born, and Jesse's wife, her name was Zee. My dad and mother had pretty well decided that I was going to be a girl, and that name of Zee appealed to them. And when I turned out to be a boy, they dropped an 'e' and gave it to me anyway.") Henry got out and unhitched the weighing chute, and Layton Todd came over and gave him a hand. It was a narrow barred cage on wheels, with a drop gate at one end. Henry and Layton hauled it up alongside one of the corrals. Ze pushed his corral gate open and swung it back to form a pen between the corral and the chute.

"I got three calves here, John," Layton said. "The only trouble is, there's one that's a little too old and two a little too young. Can we adjust? I'd hate to have you turn right around and drive on back to town."

"No problem," Henry said. "A few days don't make all that much difference."

"They're big, too. I tell you, John—these Red Angus calves, they grow faster than the Black. They got that hybrid vigor. All right, Ze. Let's start with that little bull."

A howling, balking, slobbering calf came stumbling through the loading chute. Ze Todd trotted in behind it, swinging a ski pole cut off short for a goad. He prodded it across the makeshift pen and up to the weighing chute. The gate was up, and Henry stood ready to drop it closed. I leaned up over the fence to watch. The calf shied and lurched—and skittered into the fence. The impact bounced me off and sat me down hard on the ground. I heard Henry shout, and Layton call, "Turn him, Ze! He's got himself bass-ackwards." The calf gave a long, despairing cry. Layton now had a rope around its neck, and, with Ze prodding and Henry waving it on, it dodged, bawling and blubbering, over the threshold and into the chute. The gate dropped with a crash. The little bull stood heaving on the scales. The cows and calves in the corrals all raised their heads and bellowed.

The two other calves were heifers. One was about the size of the little bull and the other was somewhat larger, but they both went almost readily into the weighing chute. The bull was the youngest (one hundred and eighty-seven days) and the lightest (three hundred and forty-five pounds). The larger, and older, of the heifer calves weighed four hundred and ninety-four pounds. It was the last to be weighed. It lumbered back into the corral, back through the staring cows and calves, back to its bellowing mother—drooling, wide-eyed, whimpering.

We stood and watched it go.

"The fuss they make," Henry said. "They act like they think they're beef. If they only knew how lucky they are. They've got the easy life. Nothing to do but breed."

"They got it easier than the breeder," Layton said.

"Dad's right," Ze said. "Breeding cattle isn't like raising, say, chickens. A full-grown purebred bull is a lot of animal. He can service six or seven cows in a day, and it's easy enough to get him started. The trouble is, those cows all look alike to him. So the problem is to get him to service them all—to move him on from number one to number two and from her to number three. All you've got is that ring in his nose. It isn't only that bulls can be mean. They're big—they can weigh a ton. I mean, two *thousand* pounds. An animal that big can give you just a little nudge and you'll feel it for a couple of weeks."

"It's like getting nudged by a truck," Henry said.

Samson said, "Which field is it, George?"

George—George Shavers—turned and spat out a wad of tobacco, and lighted a cigarette. "It's both," he said. "But this eighteen acres here is probably the worst. I've only had it just three years, and I've done everything I could, but don't seem to do no good. I don't know, Merle. The guy that had it before me, he must have let it run down for twenty years."

"I'll bet he did," Samson said. "Well, let's go take a look. You want to take my truck or yours?"

"Mine," Shavers said. "Yours looks too nice and new for these old fields. You know, on top of everything else, I think I've got some gophers coming in. I found a couple of holes the other day. But I wonder what they're going to find to eat in that damn field."

Shavers climbed under the wheel of an old Ford pickup, and Samson and I squeezed in beside him. Samson sat with his tools in his lap—a foot-long tubular soil probe, like a giant apple corer, and a dozen paper soil-sample bags marked "University of Idaho Agricultural Extension Service Soil Testing Laboratory Take Soil Samples Carefully Take a Representative Sample Use Separate Bag for Each Sample." We moved off across the field, jolting against the grain of the furrows.

"There was a young guy down at the café," Shavers said. "He told me manure didn't do no good. I think it was just a theory he had. So I didn't pay no attention."

"I don't know who that young guy was," Samson said. "But he sure wasn't any farmer. The only possible drawback to manure is that it might bring you in some foreign weeds. But I don't call that much of a drawback."

"It ain't to me," Shavers said. "I've already got every damn weed there is."

"OK, George. Let's pull up here."

We got out in a following cloudburst of dust. It passed, and the air cleared, and I could see the sudden rise of the mountains, twenty miles away. Samson squatted down and worked his probe into the soil as far as it would go. He extracted a core of crumbly earth. He sifted it through his fingers and into a sample bag.

"Sandy loam," he said. "But you've got some clay down deep. I don't like that much. Suppose we move on down the line a couple of hundred yards and try again. Maybe this isn't typical. And, of course, the laboratory may have something else to say."

"I like a sandy loam," Shavers said.

"I do, too," Samson said. "If you water it enough. And often enough. And you need organic matter. I do think you're going to need a lot of manure for this field. Twenty tons to the acre, at least. But I like the tilth. I can see you've worked at cultivation. I don't see all those weeds you were talking about."

"It's cultivation, all right," Shavers said. "It ain't weed killer. I think weed killer is the lazy man's way."

"It's one of his ways," Samson said. "You know what they say. There's two kinds of farmers. There's the one that's got weeds and the one that's got money."

"There's the one that calls the county agent," Shavers said, "and the one that don't bother."

"Right," Samson said. "And there's the one that wants to sleep till seven o'clock in the morning and knock off work at three in the afternoon. He sells his farm to one of the big corporations."

There was the sound of children's voices from a back room at the Canyon County office. I walked down the hall and looked in. On a low platform at one end of the room was a demonstration kitchen, and sitting around a table at the other were ten little girls of eleven or twelve and a pretty young woman in white slacks and a sleeveless blue jersey. Most of the girls had pale-blond hair, most of them wore dresses, two wore glasses, one was fat, one was a foot taller than the others, and one had an arm in a sling. The woman was Lenora Fields, the other home economist, and this was a 4-H class.

" . . . and Charlie," Mrs. Fields was saying, "is Charlie who?"

"Calcium!"

"That's right. And Charlie Calcium helps make what?"

"Teeth and bones!"

"And where is a good place to get calcium for good teeth and bones?"

"Milk!"

"Right. Now, Patty is Patty who?"

"Patty *Protein!*"

"And what does Patty Protein give?"

"Energy!"

"That's *right.* And where is a good place to . . ."

Arthur Walz, the area potato-and-onion specialist, and I had an early breakfast at Pollard's Drive-In Cafe. He is a tall, thin man of fifty with sandy-red hair and pale-blue eyes and freckles. We ordered bacon and eggs, and they were served, as usual, with hashed-brown potatoes. Hashed-brown potatoes are the grits of Idaho and the West. We ate to Bill Anderson on the jukebox singing "It Was Time For Me to Move On Anyway," helped ourselves at the cashier's desk to toothpicks and an after-dinner mint, and headed south in a gust of wind and a spurt of rain. Walz opened the glove compartment and got out a pair of sunglasses, and the sky began to clear.

"We've got a name for that," he said. "We call it an Idaho rainstorm. Two or three drops of water and a lot of wind, and then the sun comes out. I think we're going to have another nice hot sunny day for our trip. It's a trip I don't make any oftener than I have to. Owyhee County—the county where we're going—is the biggest county in my area, and it has the fewest people. As a matter of fact, it's one of the biggest counties in the United States. It's almost as big as the state of Massachusetts. But it's very rough country—mostly mountains and high desert. The only real crop is potatoes. There happen to be some very big producers, though, so I have to make a tour every couple of months or so. Those mountains up ahead are the Owyhee Mountains. 'Owyhee' is a phonetic spelling of 'Hawaii.' We had a gold rush here in the early days, back in the eighteen-sixties, and it seems that a lot of the prospectors were Hawaiians. One big bunch of them had the misfortune to get massacred by the Indians. So the other prospectors started calling the place where it happened Owyhee."

We crossed the Snake River at the village of Marsing. Marsing was the beginning of Owyhee County. We stopped there for gas and to pick up the Owyhee County agent—a calm, square-built, gray-haired man named Glenn Bodily—and then continued south. It was a different countryside on this side of the river. The fertile Canyon County flats gave way to stony sagebrush hills and salt-grass hollows and occasional towering purple buttes. The river wound among the hills, and there were river meadows here and there, sometimes with a cow or two grazing in them. The air was hot and dry, and the sky was a hazy blue. A grove of trees appeared, like a mirage, ahead.

"That's Given's Hot Springs," Bodily said. "It used to be a famous resort."

"It was nice," Walz said. "People used to drive all the way

down from Caldwell for a picnic in the shade of those old locust trees. Now all they want to do is stay at home with the air-conditioning on and watch the television."

The wilderness returned. Walz touched his lips with a protective salve, and pointed to a big falling-down frame building on the river-bank a mile or two away. "And there's a short history of Owyhee County," he said. "That started out as an Indian fort. Then they turned it into a ferry house. Then it was somebody's barn. Now it's nothing."

The road swung away from the river. We began to climb through an even wilder, even emptier countryside. And then, on a hilltop far ahead, a cluster of buildings came into view. A filling-station café. A one-story yellow brick building with a flagpole in front. Half a dozen houses. We passed a sign: "Murphy, Ida. Home of All-Girl Rodeo." We pulled off the road and into the filling station. A plump blond girl in jeans and boots watched us from a bench at the door of the café.

"Murphy is our Owyhee County seat," Bodily said. "And that is all it is. They put the seat here in the early days because this is more or less the middle of the county. It's about halfway between the two settled areas. That brick building there is the courthouse. There's nothing else but that and this and a post office. Well, let's go have us a cup of coffee." He opened the door. "Hello, Teddy."

"Hi, there," the girl said.

"Teddy," Walz said. "What's the population here now? About thirty?"

"Oh, no," she said. "I think it's up around seventy. But if you really want to know I'll find out. I'll count it."

We drank our scalding, watery coffee at the counter. The only other customers were two old men with stubbly sunken cheeks, wearing faded overalls and big hats and silently drinking beer. Be-hind the counter was a fat woman with a pile of bright-red hair. Teddy was waiting for us when we came out.

"I was wrong," she said. "It isn't seventy—it's only fifty-five. I guess a couple of families must have moved away."

After Murphy, the road began to worsen. There were potholes in the asphalt, and patches of cobblestone gravel. The mountains were edging closer. They rose higher and higher, with many thrusting peaks, but the slopes were green and gently rolling. "I've been chukar hunting all through here," Walz said. "Appearances are de-ceiving. It looks easy from here. But when you get up close—when you really get up in there—it's rough. You climb and climb and climb, and then you happen to stop and look back. You know you've been working, but when you look back down at all those shelves and rockslides, it scares you. It's a shock to see what you've been climbing through. And way, way down there is a tiny little speck, and you realize: My God, it's my car."

"This is all rough country in here," Bodily said. "It's pretty close to desolation. Some of Owyhee County is like Canyon County—all it needs is water. But this is different. Sagebrush is a good indicator of topsoil. Its size and abundance tell you something. But you don't see any sage along here. There's nothing but shad scale and rabbit brush. That white dust you see out there is bentonite clay. That's your soil, and it's almost impervious to water."

"They used to use bentonite to seal their irrigation ditches," Walz said. "It's almost as tight as cement. Bentonite is real bad news to farmers."

"You bet it is," Bodily said. "And a lot of farmers have had to find that out the hard way. I've seen them trying to plow it. But you know something, Art? That fork back there—I'm not too sure we're on the right road. You can get lost in this damn country."

"Not really," Walz said. "Somebody's bound to come along and find you in a day or two."

The road ran on through the featureless flats. There was nothing to see but the mountains and an occasional sculptured butte. The road turned and dipped and twisted down a hill. We crossed a little bridge with a trickle of creek below. Beyond the bridge were three or four houses. Then a ramshackle Pepsi-Cola store. Then a big stone Catholic church in a grove of poplar trees. Bodily gave a grunt and sat back.

"OK, Art," he said. "We're in Oreana. But I haven't been down through here in quite some while."

"Oreana is one of our Basque colonies," Walz said. "They used to run sheep in here, but now it's mostly cattle. I don't know how they're making out."

"They do all right," Bodily said. "There's pretty good grazing on this side of the creek. They're interesting people. I remember a fellow just south of here who had a little stock operation. I came down with a specialist, and we looked over his range and his water and all the rest, and we worked out a nice expansion program for him. We were there for most of a day. And then he shook his head. 'I don't know,' he said. 'I think I'm happier the way I am.'"

Walz had two afternoon appointments. Both were with big potato growers whose holdings were on the high sagebrush plains beyond Oreana. We stopped on the way for a sandwich at the Black

Sands Cafe, in a tourist camp on the shore of a storage lake at the confluence of the Snake and one of its tributary rivers. The lake was a strange sight. Its waters were blue and sparkling in the sun, but the shores were arid desert. There were no trees, no greenery of shrub or grass. The gray, dusty desert brush ran down to the beach banks, down to the edge of the water. The only sign of life was six or seven coots floating at the mouth of a marshy cove.

After the lake, the potato fields—high and hot and windswept—had a look that was almost lush. The first of the farms was a corporate enterprise with some five thousand acres under cultivation. "We're running a little planting experiment here," Walz said. "Potato plants are usually grown about nine inches apart. We're trying them here at six inches. This is a big operation, with a big production, but they want to make it even bigger. That's why they're big." He and Bodily and a section lessee spent half an hour together—strolling along an endless field, stopping and talking, pointing and moving slowly on, nodding and frowning and tracing boot-toe patterns in the dust. I joined them for a while, and then went back to the shade of the car. The other farm was a two-thousand-acre fraction of a family operation. Walz was there to meet a group of salesmen and test two types of humidifier for use in a new potato-storage barn. I watched the tests with one of the family, a polite young man named Blaine Mecham. He had on the usual battered boots and imitation-leopardskin cap. "No," he said. "I went to Utah State. My people are Latter-Day Saints. And I didn't go to ag school. After all, I was raised on a farm. I thought I'd do better to learn something I didn't already know. I majored in sociology, and my minor was ag economics. Then I worked for a year for the Bank of America in Fresno. Then I was ready to come back home and go to work. I hardly ever do any physical work myself. But I'm always here. I drive around and keep the men going. The market doesn't matter too much to us. We don't grow baking potatoes in this area. That's all done in the eastern part of the state, where it's high and cool. Our potatoes here grow too big for baking. We sell our crop by contract to the processor. If you've ever eaten any frozen French fries, you've probably eaten some of our potatoes. No, we don't live up here. We live in town—in Mountain Home."

We drove back to Marsing through the last heavy heat of the desert afternoon. I like to see a good operation," Walz said. "And we've seen a couple today. They aren't as common as some people like to think. The day of the hick is long gone. Farming is a real profession now. It demands a lot of a man. I've never seen a good farmer who wasn't above average in intelligence. He has to know how to handle men, he has to be able to plan, and he has to be able to manage land—he has to understand the land. I've known potato growers to get a yield of three hundred and fifty hundredweight to the acre and still go belly up. They were thinking yield when they should have been thinking quality. Quality is work. You don't get quality by sitting around the café drinking coffee at ten o'clock in the morning. You have to live with the crop. That's one thing that hasn't changed. The best fertilizer is still the grower's shadow. We try to teach them that."

It was almost six o'clock when we dropped Bodily off at his office. The sun was low, and the air was beginning to cool. We crossed the river and climbed up through darkening orchards to the flats. The burgeoning fields began—mint and onions and alfalfa and beets and corn and beans—and there was a smell of blossomy sweetness. It was strange to think that this had once been a desert as forbidding as much of Owyhee County. I had a curious feeling that I had spent the day in the past. Owyhee County was a survival of the original Idaho. I had been given a glimpse of what Washington Irving saw for days on end when he passed this way in 1810. "It is a land," he wrote in *Astoria*, his account of that journey, "where no man permanently resides; a vast uninhabited solitude, with precipitous cliffs and yawning ravines, looking like the ruins of a world; vast desert tracts that must ever defy cultivation and interpose dreary and thirsty wilds between the habitations of man."

Walz said, "Are you in a big hurry to get back to town?"

"Not particularly," I said. "Why?"

"I want to make a little detour for a minute."

He turned off the highway and down a dim gravel road. We drove slowly along for about a mile and pulled up at a twilit potato field. Walz opened his door and got out.

"I'll be right back," he said. "There's something I . . ."

He hopped across an irrigation ditch and climbed the bank and walked out to the edge of the field. I watched him standing there in the gathering dusk with his hands on his hips, looking down the long, sprouting rows. He came back and got under the wheel and started the engine.

"Something wrong?" I said.

"Wrong?" he said. "Oh, no. I just wanted to see— This field

belongs to a fellow I've been working with. He had a little problem, and I've been a little worried. So I thought I'd just stop by and see. But it looks real nice, doesn't it? I think we're going to do all right."

[1973]

5. A Window on the Oligocene: Teller County, Colorado

There are few more beautiful natural parks than the mountain valley that encloses the village of Florissant (pop. 102), in Teller County, Colorado, about a hundred miles southwest of Denver, on the western slope of the Front Range of the Rockies. This valley has been variously known as South Park and Castello's Ranch, but it now takes its name from the village. It is ten miles long and a mile or two wide, and it follows a gently winding course, with many sudden, serpentine arms. The valley floor is a rolling meadow. It flows, deep in grass, around an occasional thrust of rust-red granite outcrop, and it is framed on the east and west by low hills crowned with open groves of ponderosa pine. Florissant is high country—almost nine thousand feet—but above its highest hills, encircling the infinite distance, are the peaks of higher mountains. There are antelope in the Florissant valley, and deer and elk and bear and badgers and coyotes and porcupines, and in July the meadows are a garden of wild flowers—bluebells, yellow clover, purple loco-weed, pink trumpet phlox, alpine daisies, brown-eyed Susans, flaming Indian paintbrush. The beauty of Florissant, however, is not its only natural glory. It has another, a rarer and a richer one. Beneath the flowering Florissant meadows lies a treasury of paleontological history. Florissant is one of the richest repositories of plant and insect fossils in the world.

A fossil is an impression of a prehistoric organism which has been preserved in the crust of the earth. Fossils are formed in many ways. These include freezing, drying, petrifaction (or the replacement of organic by mineral matter), and encasement under pressure in asphalt, amber, sandstone, shale, or volcanic ash. The Florissant fossil beds were formed by a series of volcanic eruptions that began some thirty-eight million years ago. This places the beds, by geologic time, in the Oligocene epoch of the Cenozoic era. Florissant was then, as now, a valley, but it was a highland rather than a mountain valley, and it had a mild, humid, probably subtropical climate. A wandering stream flowed south through the valley, and the banks of the stream and the slopes above it were covered with willow and oak and pine and beech and giant sequoia. The first, progenitive volcanic eruption changed that distant scene. Its convulsions deposited a levee of volcanic mud at the mouth of the valley, blocking the outward flow of the stream, and the stream thus dammed became a pond, and the pond became a lake. Fish flourished there, and insects swarmed, and trees and shrubs grew dense along the shore. The volcano presently came to life again, and for perhaps three million years there were frequent wild eruptions. With every eruption, a cloud of fine volcanic ash blew into Florissant. The ash fell thickly on the lake, and as it settled it carried with it to the bottom a multitude of leaves and insects and tiny fish and stored them there in a thin, impressionable casing. Millennia passed, and the layered deposits of silt and ashy shale accumulated. The lake slowly shrank from a depth of forty feet to only a foot or two, and finally drained dry. It was then, around thirty-four million years ago, that a final and cataclysmic eruption occurred, and the whole of the lake was buried in a flood of boiling lava. That perfectly sealed the formed and forming fossils, and preserved them for man's eventual discovery.

The Florissant fossil beds were discovered almost a hundred years ago. A field geologist named A. C. Peale is generally accepted as their discoverer. Peale made his find in the course of a study for the United States Geological and Geographical Survey in the summer of 1873. A few years earlier, in 1870, the community that came to be called Florissant (from *floraison*, meaning "season of flowers") had been established as a trading post by a wanderer known to local history as Judge James Castello, but if Castello had then seen and recognized the fossil beds that lay in his domain, he left no record of the fact. Peale did. He included an account of his find in his formal survey report. "About five miles from the mouth [of Beaver Creek]," he noted, "around the settlement of Florissant, is an irregular basin filled with modern lake deposits. The entire basin is not more than five miles in diameter. The deposits extend up the branches of the creek, which all unite near Florissant. Between the branches are granite islands appearing above the beds, which themselves rest on granite. Just below Florissant, on the north side of the road, are bluffs not over 50 feet in height, in which are good exposures of the various beds. The following section gives them from the top downward: 1. Coarse conglomeritic sandstone. 2. Fine-grained, soft, yellowish-white sandstone, with bands that are more or less argillaceous, and containing fragments and stems of leaves. 3. Coarse gray and yellow sandstone. 4. Chocolate-colored clay shales with fossil leaves. At the upper part, these shales are black, and below pass into— 5. Whitish clay shales. These last form the base of the hill. The beds are all horizontal. Scattered around are fragments of a trachyte [a volcanic rock], which probably caps the beds. . . . I had thought it possible that the beds were of Pliocene age. The specimens obtained from bed [i. e., stratum] No. 4, of the section above, were submitted to Professor Lesquereux, who informs me that they are . . . 'Upper Miocene.' . . . The shales were so soft and friable that it was rather difficult to obtain any specimens. About one mile south of Florissant, at the base of a small hill of sandstone, capped with conglomerate, are 20 or 30 stumps of silicified wood."

The authoritative Professor Lesquereux to whom Peale submitted his specimens for dating was the celebrated Swiss-born American paleobotanist Leo Lesquereux, and it was he, together with two equally eminent associates, who made the first scientific evaluations of the Florissant fossiliferous shales. His associates were the paleozoologist Edward Drinker Cope and the founder of American insect paleontology Samuel Hubbard Scudder. Scudder was the first scientist to follow Peale to Florissant. He made the first of many visits there in the summer of 1877, and spent five strenuous days examining the visible beds and collecting fossils for later laboratory study. His account of that first visit, which appeared as part of a comprehensive report ("The Tertiary Lake Basin at Florissant, Colo., between South and Hayden Parks") in the *Bulletin of the United States Geological and Geographical Survey* in 1882, was ecstatic. "The very shales of the lake itself," he noted, "in which the myriad plants and insects are entombed, are wholly composed of volcanic sand and ash; fifteen meters or more thick they lie, in alternating layers of coarser and finer material. . . . The upper half has been eroded and carried away, leaving, however, the fragmentary remains of this great ash deposit clinging to the borders of the basin and surrounding the islands; a more convenient arrangement for the present explorer could not have been devised. . . . The insects preserved in the Florissant basin are wonderfully numerous, this single locality having yielded in a single summer more than double the number of specimens which the famous localities at Oeningen, in Bavaria, furnished Heer in thirty years. Having visited both places I can testify to the greater prolificness of the Florissant beds . . . and the quarries are fifty times as extensive and far more easily worked."

Scudder also inspected the "silicified wood" to which Peale had alluded. "Our examination of the deposits of this lacustrine basin," he noted, "was principally made in a small hill, from which perhaps the largest number of fossils have been taken, lying just south of the house of Mr. Adam Hill, and upon his ranch. Like the other ancient islets of this upland lake, it now forms a mesa or flat-topped hill about ten or a dozen meters high. . . . Around its eastern base are the famous petrified trees, huge, upright trunks, standing as they grew, which are reported to have been five or six meters high at the advent of the present residents of the region. Piecemeal they have been destroyed by vandal tourists, until now not one of them rises more than a meter above the surface of the ground, and many of them are entirely leveled; but their huge size is attested by the relics, the largest of which can be seen to have been three or four meters in diameter. These gigantic trees appear to be sequoias." Scudder ended his report with a new estimate, concurred in by both Lesquereux and Cope, of the age of the Florissant beds. They were neither Pliocene (two to ten million years ago) nor Miocene (ten to twenty-seven million years ago) in origin. They were Oligocene.

The first Florissant fossils to be properly studied were those collected by Scudder in 1877. That visit, though brief, was prophetically productive. In the mere five days that Scudder spent in the beds, he and three companions (two fellow-scientists and the local rancher Hill) gathered a total of around five thousand specimens. The quality of the material also was prophetically high. "The shales of Florissant," Lesquereux enthusiastically noted, "have preserved the most delicate organisms—feathers, insects, small flies, petals, even anthers and stamens of flowers." Lesquereux, being a botanist, reviewed the plant specimens. He was able to distinguish some ninety different species. All of them were species long extinct, but most were recognizable as prototypes of modern plants. Fossil vertebrates were reviewed by Cope. He found few satisfactory specimens, and fewer species. His report listed eight species of fish and two of birds—one a kind of plover and the other a finch. Scudder himself reviewed the insect and arachnid fossils, and it was chiefly his report that brought the Florissant beds to international scientific attention. He tentatively identified literally hundreds of species. They included thirty species of wasps, fifty species of ants, eight species of flies, fourteen species of spiders, five species of grasshoppers, sixty-five species of the order that embraces aphids, cicadas, and leafhoppers, and—to his particular delight—a wealth of butterflies. "Having examined more than ten years ago all the butterflies that were known in the European Tertiaries," he wrote in a separate survey report, "the American forms that have been exhumed at Florissant, in Colorado, in presumably Oligocene beds, have especially interested me. There are, altogether, seven species, more than have been found at any other locality in the world, and only two less than all that are known in the imago state of European deposits."

The paleontological importance of Florissant that Scudder first proclaimed has been ardently confirmed by many other paleontologists. At least a dozen major scientific expeditions have worked the Florissant beds and assembled large and comprehensive collections. Scudder added to his original collection by almost annual visits until his retirement in 1892. The first academic expedition to Florissant was sponsored by Princeton University. Its members worked there through the summer of 1880. That study was followed, in 1902, by a second Princeton expedition, this one jointly led by Henry Fairfield Osborn, of the American Museum of Natural History, and W. B. Scott, of the British Museum. Other expeditions have come to Florissant from the American Museum itself, the Denver Museum of Natural History, the University of Colorado, the University of Iowa, Washington State University, Humboldt (California) State College (led by the distinguished paleontologist H. D. MacGinitie), and the University of California, and Florissant fossils are prominent in the collections of most notable natural-history museums. There has always been plenty for all. The Florissant deposits are extraordinarily rich. According to a recent computation by Frank M. Carpenter, Fisher Professor of Natural History at Harvard, they have yielded up some eighty thousand explicit specimens of insects alone, and fossil plants are even more abundant. This multitude of specimens represents well over a thousand different species of life—around eleven hundred insects and arachnids, a hundred and forty-four plants, and sixteen vertebrates. The insect specimens include a total of nine species of butterflies and four species of tsetse flies, the now uniquely African vector of trypanosomiasis, or sleeping sickness. Moreover, despite a century of scientific scrutiny, the variety of the Florissant beds has almost certainly not yet been exhausted. Every expedition turns up new material. As recently as 1965, on a casual, one-day visit, a United States Geological Survey paleontologist named Estella B. Leopold discovered a fossil palm leaf, the first such specimen ever un-

earthed at Florissant, and a totally unexpected find. It was also—
like most of the Florissant fossils—an excellent specimen.

The diverse and overflowing excellence of the Florissant fossil
beds is not their only distinction. They are equally distinguished in
the eyes of science by their age. Most other beds laid down in the
expanses of the Tertiary period of the Cenozoic era (from two to
seventy million years ago) are either younger or older than those at
Florissant. Florissant stands midway in time between the Miocene
epoch, which began twenty-seven million years ago, and the Eo-
cene epoch, which began fifty-five million years ago, and its fossiliferous shales are thus a clear and precious view of life through
several million otherwise inscrutable years. There is only one other
Rocky Mountain source of Oligocene fossil plants. That is a bed at
Ruby Valley, in Montana, but specimens there are so few and far
between that collectors work it not by hand with a geologic hammer
but with a bulldozer. The Florissant record has scope as well as
clarity. Its documentation of a particular place at a particular time is
almost incomparably complete. The freak of nature that created
Florissant preserved in each of its several stratifications a comprehensive flora and fauna—a total ecosystem. "If a single layer of
paper shale in the Florissant beds could be uncovered simultane-
ously over its entire surface," Dr. Leopold has said, "we would
have a detailed picture—a photograph in rock—of Florissant as it
was some thirty-eight million years ago. As a volcanic tomb, Florissant is a kind of Pompeii of the Oligocene. It's a kind of Dead Sea
Scroll of evolution. There is simply nothing like it."

Florissant was for centuries an occasional Indian hunting
ground. The Utes camped and hunted there on their summer raids
against the Pueblo towns in what are now New Mexico and Ari-
zona, and so, at times, did the nomadic Arapahos. The white dis-
coverers of Florissant were the mountain men of the second
generation. They trapped and explored and roughly mapped that
part of the Rockies in the eighteen-forties and fifties. A tall tale of
the period, told by a trapper on his return to Taos from a mountain
journey (and recorded in a government guide to the area), was
probably inspired by the petrified stumps at Florissant: "Pa'dners, I
need a pewtrified forest of pewtrified trees with their pewtrified
limbs chockful of pewtrified birds a-singing of pewtrified songs."
With the arrival, in the eighteen-seventies, of the trader James Castello and the rancher Adam Hill and others of their kind, the settlement of Florissant began, and the valley is now—hills and
meadows and fossil beds—in well-documented private ownership.
The owners of the Florissant valley are cattlemen; the growing sea-

son there is too short for any crop but grass. One of the dozen present owners of its twelve thousand acres operates a small tourist concession on the side. Two of them own lands embracing the remains of the petrified stumps. One of these also owns the bed from which Scudder extracted his first collection of fossils. This bed is open, for a fee, to the public, and visiting scientists have always been freely and warmly welcome there. They have also always been hospitably received by the owners of the other celebrated fossil beds—the bed worked by the first Princeton expedition, the University of California bed, a bed exposed by a cutting dug in 1887 for the now abandoned Colorado & Midland Railroad. The respect of the owners of Florissant for science has undoubtedly been a factor in the preservation of its fossil beds for continued scientific study. It has not, however, been an important one. Florissant has been largely preserved by the accident of nature that made it cattle country.

It has long been felt that the fossil riches of Florissant are too fragile to be so lightly guarded. The desirability of some defense against the human compulsion to rearrange nature which would be stronger than a long winter and a short summer was briefly considered as early as 1921. In that year, a group of interested scientists and others suggested that Florissant be brought into the protective embrace of the National Park Service. The suggestion received a politely sympathetic hearing, but no action was taken, and the interest of even its sponsors faded away and finally vanished under the impact of the Depression and the Second World War. It was revived, in 1953, by Edmund B. Rogers, then (he has since retired) the superintendent of Yellowstone National Park, with a testimonial based on firsthand exploration and entitled "Florissant Fossil Shale Beds, Colorado." Rogers's recommendation excited sufficient influential interest to set in motion the standard salvational procedure. This involved a pilot study, a preliminary report, and a formal proposal, and it proceeded at the standard pace. A formal proposal to preserve six thousand of the twelve thousand acres at Florissant as a Florissant Fossil Beds National Monument was approved by the director of the National Park Service in 1962. The following year, an enabling bill was introduced in the House of Representatives. It died, ignored. A similar bill was introduced in 1965, and it was similarly received. Two years later, in 1967, the House was offered a third Florissant bill. An amendment to it reduced the size of the proposed Monument from six thousand to one thousand acres. This truncated preserve attracted a wave of penny-pinching support, and the bill was approved with little opposition and sent

along to the Senate. There it once more died. Another year went by
and another Florissant bill was conceived. The new proposal dif-
fered from its predecessor in that it restored the cut in acreage and
originated in the Senate. It was introduced on February 4, 1969. A
few days later, an identical bill was introduced in the House. The
winter passed, and also the spring. Then, on June 20, the Senate
approved its Florissant bill. The House bill remained in committee.
Summer came on.

I went out to Colorado toward the end of July and paid a visit to
Florissant. I saw it in the company of one of its many champions,
Theodore R. Thompson, then the superintendent of Rocky Mountain National Park, at Estes Park, Colorado. He picked me up in
Denver in a green Park Service station wagon at around eight
o'clock on a hot, dry, cloudless morning. We drove south on the
throughway to Colorado Springs, and then west through Manitou
Springs and under the loom of Pikes Peak and over the crest of the
Front Range at Divide and down the long western slope between
browning grasslands and scattered groves and climbing woods of
aspen and ponderosa pine. We passed a lonely filling station with a
sign over the door: "We're from Illinois. Where are you from?"
There were mountains, some of them still furrowed with snow, all
around the horizon. A highway sign appeared ahead: "Florissant 8
Mi." Beyond it was a piercing orange Day-Glo billboard: "West-
wood Lake Estates." The highway began to climb. Another billboard came into view: "Trout Haven Estates 2½ Mi." A gravel road
led off to the left. Another mile, and another billboard appeared:
"Colorado Mountain Estates. ½ Acre Lots." Then another: "Wagon
Tongue Home Sites—Florissant."

"This country is changing fast," Thompson said. "That's why
we're fighting hard for the Monument. We think it's now or never.
It used to be just tourists here. They'd stop and then drive on. Now
it's subdivisions—vacation houses. Everybody wants an A-frame
in the mountains."

"Why an A-frame?" I said.

Thompson shrugged. "They're practical," he said. "Especially
in snow country. And they're easy to maintain. But I think it's more
than that. The A-frame is a kind of status symbol out here now."

We went down and around a bend. There was a rutted road on
the left and a big welcoming billboard: "Lots. $15 Down. $15
Month." The roadbed climbed steeply up to a cluster of new
houses. One of them was an A-frame.

"This is the edge of the Monument," Thompson said. "The proposed area all lies south of the highway and beyond that ridge over there. That's the village straight ahead. That's Florissant."

Florissant was a highway hamlet. Most of it was strung out along the right-hand side of the highway—a liquor store, a shingle-sided post office, a filling station, a real-estate office. On the other side were a log-cabin motel and café. A man in overalls was sitting on a bench in front of the post office. There was a billboard sign near the real-estate office: "4 Seasons Fun. Wilderness Estates." We turned left at the motel onto a gravel road that led south through a break in the ridge. The road wound up through open groves of pine and rolling wild-flower meadows. Black Angus cattle were grazing knee-deep in flowers in the meadows. A sky-blue bluebird —a mountain bluebird—flew across the road and into a clump of trees. This was the Florissant valley. This was the Florissant I had heard and read about. On a rise a mile or so away stood a long, low clapboard building with a covered gallery all around it.

"That's the Singer place," Thompson said. "It used to be the Florissant railroad depot, back in the old Colorado & Midland days. Bob Singer bought it and had it moved up there in 1924. The Singers have a little over eight hundred acres in the area, and their land includes some petrified stumps and a very good fossil bed. As a matter of fact, it's old Scudder's bed, and you'll want to see it. Their main business is cattle, but they also run a museum and tourist operation in the summer. If the Monument ever goes through, their house will probably be the administration building. Temporarily, anyway."

"How do the Singers feel about the Monument?" I said.

"Oh, they're for it," he said. "They see the need. They want to protect the beds. Most of the longtime owners here want the Monument. Except that some of them are getting a little impatient. You saw that development back there on the highway. That could have been part of the Monument. So could some of the lakebed west of Florissant. It was included in all the Monument plans until the owner finally got tired of waiting for Congress to act, and sold it. Now it's what they call Colorado Mountain Estates. And there's another, even bigger piece of the Monument that has just been sold to land-development companies."

We parked in a parking lot at one end of the Singer house. I got out to stretch my legs while Thompson went off to look for Bob Singer. The Singer house was unmistakably a vintage railroad station. It had a bow-window bulge in front that must have been the stationmaster's office, and the encircling covered gallery was the remains of the old passenger platform. I looked off across the valley. It was easy to visualize the railroad station as it had once been. I could easily picture the group of turn-of-the-century paleontologists climbing down from the red plush Pullman cars. I could see their heavy, high-buttoned suits and their high-crowned derby hats and their stern mustached faces. They were as sharp and true as a period photograph. But I couldn't picture anything of the past that lay under the meadows. All I could see were the rolling meadows flowering in the sun, and they looked like any pretty mountain meadows.

Thompson came back around the corner of the house. With him was a tall, tanned boy of seventeen or eighteen. He was a serious-looking boy. Thompson introduced us.

"This is Tim Singer," he said. He reached into the car and brought out a roll of plastic specimen bags and two geologic hammers. He handed me one of the hammers and stuck the bags in his pocket. "Tim grew up in this country, and he knows his fossils. He's going to show us around the old Scudder bed."

"I could show you something else, too," Tim said. "I'll show you our biggest petrified sequoia, if you want to see it. It's more or less on the way."

"I'd like to see it," I said.

"It's a fine specimen," Thompson said.

We followed a path up a slope behind the house. Halfway up the slope, the path levelled out and broadened into a sunken shelf. A big, furrowed, marble-like column was rooted in the middle of the shelf, like a fountain in a formal garden. That was the sequoia. Tim cleared his throat and changed his voice.

"This is the largest petrified tree in the world," he said. "It's fourteen feet tall and seventy-four feet in circumference. It weighs forty tons. It used to be much taller. In 1892, around forty feet were cut off the top to show at the Chicago world's fair, and souvenir hunters have been chipping at it for a hundred years. They estimate that the living tree was three hundred and fifty feet tall."

We stood and looked at the stony stump. It was curious, but that was all.

"OK," Tim said. "Let's go on to the fossil bed."

Scudder's famous fossil bed was even less impressive than the stump. It was not much more than a ditch. It was a wash, a gully, a shallow gulch about fifty feet long worn into the flank of a grass-grown ridge, and we were walking up its dusty floor before I knew what it was. The floor of the bed was rubble, and the walls were crumbling strata of gravel, shale, and rocklike volcanic tuff. The tuff formed the uppermost stratum. There was a crust of it just under the carpet of meadow sod. Then came a foot or two of shale. The rest of the bed was gravel.

Thompson stopped and kicked at a pile of rubble. He picked up a slab of shale about the size of my hand. It was laminated like a piece of plywood in layers of gray, tan, and rusty red. He turned it on edge on a chunk of tuff and tapped a gray layer with the adzelike blade of his hammer. The slab split cleanly apart. He held out two smooth gray faces of shale.

"Nothing," Tim said. "Here's a better-looking piece. Try this."

It was a better piece. Thompson split it apart, and on one of the gray faces was a buckshot scattering of tiny brown specks. They looked like tiny burns.

"What do you think?" he said. "Charcoal?"

"Probably," Tim said. "It might be a bunch of little mosquitoes." He pulled out a magnifying lens and took a closer look. "I guess it's just charcoal, though."

There was another gray grain on the piece of shale. Thompson tapped it in two. He gave a startled grunt, and showed us one of the halves. On it was the imprint of a little leaf.

"Hey," Tim said. "Look at that one."

"Not bad, huh?" Thompson said. "How would you identify it, Tim? It looks a little like birch."

"Or elm," I said.

"It does," Tim said. "But I don't think it's either of those. I don't think it has any modern equivalent. I think it's a shrub they call *Fagopsis longifolia*. It's fairly common in these beds."

"Whatever it is," Thompson said, "it's a real nice specimen."

It was a beautiful specimen. I sat down on a hump of landslidden gravel and examined it with the magnifying glass. It looked like an actual leaf—a dry, brown, fallen autumn leaf. Every detail was perfectly preserved. The leaf stalk was there, and the midrib, and the delicate opposite veins. Only the very tip was missing. It was an almost flawless fossil image. But to me it was more than that. The petrified stump was merely a monstrous relic. This was a recognition. I remembered a phrase from my reading. It was one of Estella Leopold's apothegms: "Florissant is a window on the Oligocene." The window had opened in my hand, and I was looking in.

We spent an hour and a half in the fossil bed. We found a dozen fossils or fossil fragments—twigs and charcoal, bits of leaves and a fully formed willow leaf, a faint impression of a fly. None of them compared in quality with the little *Fagopsis* leaf, but that was only a disappointment. It didn't really matter. The *Fagopsis* leaf was revelation enough. It was almost two o'clock when we climbed out of the bed and walked back to the house, and long past time for lunch. Thompson and I left Tim at the house. We got a couple of cans of Fresca from a vending machine on the gallery and a bag of diner sandwiches from the car and sat down to lunch in the grass at the edge of the parking lot. We looked out at the sunny sweep of the wild-flower meadows as we ate. They were still wonderfully pretty meadows, but it seemed to me that I saw them differently now. I could see them now for what they really were.

A little distance up the gravel road from the Singer ranch, we came to a gate with a sign: "Pike Petrified Forest." This was the other sequoia-stump concession. We didn't stop. The gate was fastened with a padlock, and we didn't have time to see if anyone was at home. The road ran on through the rolling meadows for another mile or two. Then the land began to rise on the left, and a winding row of hillside houses thrust suddenly into view. A graded road led up from the gravel road through a wide rustic gateway with an arching log-cabin roof. Across the arch stretched a thirty-foot sign: "Colorado Mountain Estates." On the right of the gateway, there was a billboard sign in the shape of a house: "Colorado Mountain Estates. ½ Acre Lots." Beyond the gateway was a street sign: "Arrowhead Lane." We turned up Arrowhead Lane.

"There are two more places that I want you to see," Thompson said. "This development is one of them. There are around a thousand acres here, and they should have been part of the Monument. They're a natural part of the Florissant valley. I can't really blame the original owner of this land for selling. The Monument has been hanging fire too long. But it's a pity. The present boundary line of the Monument is that fence right over there."

"That's pretty close," I said.

"It's a little too close for comfort," he said. "It gives the residents of Colorado Mountain Estates a beautiful view, but it could mean a lot of population pressure, a lot of wear and tear on the Monument. Let's hope we don't lose any more land this way."

"Are there fossil beds in here?" I said.

"I don't know," he said. "But Florissant is all the same geology, so I suppose there are. Or were."

We turned off Arrowhead Lane and drove through Amherst Circle. The houses we passed were cabins or A-frames. They were new but already aging, and they looked cramped and crowded together. Half an acre isn't much land in the mountains. We turned into Badger Circle. The unsold lots between the houses were unspoiled stands of pine. There was a distant view of the farther valley from the top of Badger Circle. A woman with a mop in her hand and a cigarette in her mouth came out of one of the houses. She stood on the porch and shook out her mop and watched us go by. We circled back to Arrowhead Lane by way of Pinewood Road.

We drove back down the valley for about a mile. The road forked there, and the fork on the right was a shortcut back to the highway. We took that fork. It led across the valley, and the land began to rise toward the flanking eastern hills. Just ahead, on each side of the road, were ditchlike excavations. The excavations looked familiar. They looked like well-worked fossil beds.

"That's right," Thompson said. "They're famous too. The one on the right was opened back in 1880 by the first Princeton expedition, and the other is the University of California bed. But that isn't what I particularly wanted you to see. I came out this way to show you something that has us all in quite a sweat."

The road cut through a stand of aspen and emerged again into meadowland. Thompson slowed the car, swung off on the shoulder, and stopped. There was a ditch at the edge of the shoulder and a barbed-wire fence at the top of the ditch. In the grass near the fence lay a big, shiny twenty-foot length of galvanized sheet-metal piping—a brand-new culvert liner. Just beyond the culvert liner was a parked bulldozer.

"This meadow forms the eastern end of the Monument," Thompson said. "It's part of a tract of around seventeen hundred acres. It used to belong to one of the old Florissant families. A few months ago, they sold it to land developers in Colorado Springs. It was the same old story. It was Colorado Mountain Estates all over again. Except that this time the people behind the Monument—scientists and conservationists and others—went to court. They went before the Circuit Court of Appeals in Denver and came out with a restraining order that temporarily enjoined the owners from building roads or doing any other excavation work. That was only the other day—on July 10. And the order expires on July 29. What happens then is hard to say. But that culvert shows you what the syndicate expects."

I left Colorado the following day. Two weeks went by. I watched the New York papers, but there was no mention of the Florissant affair. Then, around the middle of August, I got a letter from a friend in Denver. The letter enclosed a clipping from the Washington bureau of the *Rocky Mountain News*. It read, "The House Monday approved on a voice vote a bill creating the 6,000-acre Florissant Fossil Beds National Monument 35 miles west of Colorado Springs. The bill now goes to the Senate, where approval of technical amendments is expected. The Senate earlier passed a measure identical in substance to the House version. Following anticipated Senate passage, the measure will go to President Nixon for his signature. . . ." The story had no dateline, but the date of issue was printed at the top of the clipping. It was August 5. That had left a week for the unleashing of the bulldozer. Too bad, but not irreparable. On August 20, President Nixon signed the bill bringing Florissant under the protection of the National Park Service. A few days later, the bulldozer had vanished and the culvert liner had been hauled away.

[1971]

6. Wheat Country: *Pratt, Kansas*

I came to Pratt (pop. 6,885), the seat of Pratt County, in the windy high plains of south-central Kansas, on an afternoon in early spring. I came down from the north on U.S. Highway 281, through an enormous verdant countryside of sprouting winter wheat. The high plains were originally almost treeless, and the only trees that I could see now were the work of man—an occasional windbreak wall of cottonwoods and Russian olive and bushy Eastern red cedar standing along a faraway horizon. Highway 281 is a narrow blacktop road, not much wider than a driveway, and the wheat, still only a couple of inches high, had the look of grass, of lustrous lawn. I had the feeling, mile after unchanging mile, of drifting up the endless approach of some great estate.

A darker green appeared up ahead. It broadened and lifted into a canopy of treetops. But it wasn't another windbreak. It was Pratt. An organpipe cluster of grain elevators, the skyscrapers of the plains, thrust up through the trees, and just beyond them rose two silvery, spider-legged water towers. The wheat-field lawns gave way to rough pasture. There was a low white building on the right: "Central Well & Pump." And on the left: "Pratt Implement Co." A vacant lot with a barbed-wire fence plastered with tumbleweed, and then: "Mid-Kansas Iron & Metal." There was a railroad crossing, a siding with a string of Southern Pacific freight cars, and a yellow brick depot off to the right. The highway widened. Its two lanes became four. Its blacktop became brick—old, polished, rosy-red paving brick. There were sidewalks shaded by big honey locusts, and houses—most of them two-story houses and many of them built of brick—set in tidy little lawns. I passed beneath the two big water towers, and glanced back and up. One of them was twice the size of the other. Lettered in black on its shining flank was "COLD." The other was labelled "HOT." ("Ah, yes—the water towers,"

Ned Kelley, the production manager at KWLS, the Pratt radio station, said when we met a day or two later. "That's one of the things I like best about Pratt. It has a sense of humor. I came here from Kansas City by way of Denver and a few points in between, and it's my experience that most towns take themselves too seriously. Pratt doesn't—not even in the sacred realm of high-school athletics. Around the region here, we've got the Cunningham Wildcats, the Medicine Lodge Indians, the St. John Tigers, and the Skyline Thunderbirds. But the Pratt team is the Greenbacks, whose mascot is the Fighting Frog.") The wide brick street was Main Street. The trees, the lawns, the comfortable houses continued for five or six blocks to a traffic light—to First Street. First Street was two-thirds the width of Main Street, and it was conventionally paved with asphalt and concrete. Beyond the intersection was South Main Street, the business district—four long blocks of stores and offices, of wide sidewalks graced with more shading locust trees, with flowering plants in decorative planters, with wooden benches, weathered but unvandalized. The curbs were solid with angle-parked cars, there was stop-and-go traffic on the wide red street, and pedestrians were waiting dutifully at the crossings. Just across the intersection, in front of Skaggs Ace Hardware, a policeman with a chalk stick was strolling along the curb, marking the tires of the cars parked there.

There are no Pratts residing in Pratt, and there have never been any. The town of Pratt takes its name from the county, and the county was named for a young native of Massachusetts, Caleb S. Pratt, who came to Kansas in 1854, soon after its establishment as a territory. He was in his early twenties and one of the early beneficiaries (or recruits) of the Massachusetts Emigrant Aid Company. The company was an abolitionist organization dedicated to quickly populating the prospective state ("Bleeding Kansas" in the company's emotional literature) with like-minded activists in order to stem the threatened spread of slavery westward from the neighboring states of Missouri and Arkansas. Pratt settled in Lawrence, on the eastern edge of the territory, and rapidly made a name for himself in territorial politics. When the Civil War broke out, he enlisted in the First Kansas Infantry, was elected second lieutenant, marched off to Missouri, and was one of the Union casualties in the costly Confederate victory at Wilson's Creek. In death, he became something of a local hero, and in 1867 the newly constituted Kansas state legislature named a newly constituted county—hundreds and hundreds of square miles of billowing buffalo grass, which few white men had ever even seen—in his honor.

The name by which the town of Pratt was originally known was Pratt Center, and for good reason. It was situated, by the artful design of its founders, in the exact center of the county. (That center was, and is, the intersection of Main and First Streets.) This was done in the hope of achieving its designation as the Pratt County seat. The hope was realized, of course, but not without a struggle. In 1884, when the town was incorporated, Pratt County contained some thirty distinct and belligerently ambitious communities, according to the local historian J. Rufus Gray (who died, toward the end of my visit, at the age of ninety-five). Pratt is now, for all practical purposes, the only town in the county. The others are all dead and gone, or dying—a dozen little houses here, a boarded-up red brick school there, a boarded-up red brick bank (with a cornerstone marked "A.D. 1907"), a boarded-up filling station (with a rusty manual pump and a dial still reading "27½ cents per gal."), a fly-specked grocery store with a post office in a corner, a clapboard Methodist church. But, more than that, Pratt is the only town of any size for six or eight counties around, and it is in conspicuously robust health. Its South Main Street business district is intact and flourishing, and includes a minareted Moorish movie theatre that shows first-run Hollywood films seven nights a week. It has an eighty-four-bed hospital—the Pratt Regional Medical Center, which is served by a staff of fourteen physicians, augmented by a rotation of preceptors, internes, and residents from the University of Kansas School of Medicine—that was recently thoroughly modernized at a cost of seven million dollars. Most of its business and professional leaders are relatively young: the average age of the members of the Rotary Club is forty. Pratt has a daily newspaper—most unusual these days in a town so small—called the *Tribune*, whose news editor, Doug Weller, is twenty-five. There are few houses for rent in Pratt, and almost no apartments. There are very few houses for sale for less than fifty thousand dollars, and those few are older houses on the older streets. There are, however, many houses newly built or being built (for a hundred thousand dollars or more) on the treeless outskirts of town. The older residential streets in Pratt are named for trees (Elm, Maple, Cherry, Walnut) or states (Iowa, Illinois, Ohio) or Presidents (Washington, Garfield, Cleveland, Grant). The newer streets reflect a more contemporary imagination: Park View Drive, Sunrise Avenue, Sunny Lane, Meadow Lark Lane. (I actually saw a meadow lark one day at the end of Meadow Lark Lane.) Pratt is only too contemporary in still another respect: its one hotel—the Parrish Hotel, an eight-story structure built in 1931—stands derelict just off South Main

Street, the victim of inadequate off-street parking and the American traveller's preference for the easy come-and-go of a motel.

Pratt has six motels. All of them are on First Street (which becomes U.S. Highway 54 beyond the city limits). Five are on the town's eastern outskirts; the other is a mile or two to the west. I stayed at the Hillcrest Motel, on a just perceptible knoll on East First Street, in a more than comfortable room—big bed, television and radio, three Andrew Wyeth reproductions on the walls, a refrigerator under the bathroom sink. "Well," one of the women in the Hillcrest office told me when I expressed some surprise at the last, "a lot of our guests are in oil, you know. They're roustabouts and rough-necks. And they like to come back and put up their feet and have a nice, cold Coors." The view from my room was of the parking lot and the street (which became a drag strip in the later evening hours), and of a fire station (with a flag endlessly stretching and snapping in the hilltop wind), Steen's IGA Food Liner (in whose parking lot the racers often parked to talk), and the Pratt Monument Company, with a little graveyard of shiny new red or gray tombstones out front. The Hillcrest has no restaurant, or even a coffee shop, but that was a tolerable inconvenience. Pratt has some twenty eating places, no more than half of them devoted to regional specialties (Taco Grande, Pizza Hut, Kentucky Fried Chicken) or fast food. Most towns the size of Pratt have, at best, one more or less satisfactory place to eat. Pratt has either four or six, depending on one's way of reckoning. Three of the four—the Kitchen, the Uptown Café, and the Main Place—are on South Main Street; the fourth (Mayhew's) is out west of town, on Highway 54. But Kansas is one of those states in which liquor may be bought only by the bottle, not by the single drink. That is to say, a drink may not be bought in a bar or a restaurant. It may be bought only in a "club." Pratt has its American Legion Club, its Elks Club, its Park Hills Country Club, and two others, of more general membership—the Brass Ring and the Club D'Est. I was made welcome during my stay at both of these last. I usually breakfasted at the Kitchen, where the waitresses were uniformed in red jackets and white trousers and shoes (and, had they not been women of mature years, might have been mistaken for cheerleaders), and where the pancakes, bacon, and eggs were so good that I saw them on diners' plates at breakfast, lunch, and even dinner. I lunched at the Main Place (where the luncheon specialty was a bowl of navy beans and ham plus a slab of excellent corn bread, and where one of the waitresses habitually wore high heels and knickerbockers) or at the

Uptown Café (where I overheard a little boy complain to his mother, "I don't *like* water—it's too *sour*," and watched a little girl eat a plate of potato chips by dipping them one by one in a glass of Coca-Cola) or (because its specialty was deep-fried channel catfish) at Mayhew's. The Brass Ring occupies the basement of the Main Place restaurant and is owned and operated by the owner of the Main Place, and the Club D'Est is situated next door to the Uptown Café and is owned and operated by the owner of the Uptown Café. I patronized both of my clubs, but I ate most of my dinners at the Club D'Est. It offered a very good filet-mignon shish kebab (with Texas toast) and a standard salad bar that included (on alternate nights) fresh strawberries and cubes of watermelon. The bartender was a woman called M.F., who often told me as she served me my "Jack" (her code for Jack Daniel's) that she had never had a drink in her life. Both clubs were generally crowded, even on Monday night. The Pratt chapter of Alcoholics Anonymous meets at 614 West Fifth Street.

Pratt also has its municipal amenities, and to a considerable degree they are peculiarly its own. They include a local-history museum, housed in a large and attractive building and administered by the Pratt County Historical Society; a municipal park system (a swimming pool, tennis courts, trails) consisting of nineteen parks, ranging in size from one acre to ninety-two acres, and totalling a hundred and eighty-six acres; and the Pratt Public Library, open six days (and four evenings) a week, with a total of almost fifty-eight thousand books. All these came into being almost entirely through the gifts of individuals, and except for the parks they are largely so supported. "Pratt is not a poor community," Oneita Johnson, librarian of the Pratt Public Library, told me. "We have many fortunate people here—millionaires and such—and they are very generous with their good fortune. Our library is known around the state as the rich library. We have a budget of around eighty thousand dollars, and our income is always in excess of that. We quite literally have more money than we know what to do with. One single benefactor provides us with an annual income of nine thousand dollars simply for books. We opened in 1910, with a few shelves of contributed books and subscriptions to the *Literary Digest*, the *Ladies' Home Journal*, and the *National Geographic*, and as far as I know we've never had a moment of financial worry. We now spend nearly two thousand dollars a year for periodicals alone. We have an income of thirty-one thousand dollars from one bequest. That's the Millar Fund, which built this beautiful building. Mrs. Millar

was the widow of William C. Millar, who owned a large piece of
the old Frank Rockefeller ranch, next door in Kiowa County. Frank
was old John D.'s charming but worthless brother. He gambled and
drank and everything else, and John D. bought the ranch as a place
for Frank to go and straighten out. Frank died back East, in Cleveland, in 1917. When Mrs. Millar died, in 1957, she left us almost
four thousand acres. We lease it out, mostly for grass, but it also
has a very nice oil well on it. Mrs. Millar loved reading, especially
poetry and the Bible, but you know she never borrowed a single
one of our books? She always bought her own. Our lawyer has told
us we're in another will that's even bigger than the Millar Fund.
Oh, yes—we have a lawyer to help us acquire our endowments.
People sometimes need a little persuasion. We have so many wonderful patrons. I'm going to Wichita tomorrow with Cuma Zeltner,
one of our staff, to buy a computer. We've been wanting a little
personal computer for a long time, and, lo and behold, we've just
received an anonymous gift that will make it more than possible.
Cuma will be our programmer. She took some courses at the college here last winter."

"Oh, you bet," Les Jacobs told me. "These people here have
money. They have a net worth. They own their own homes, they
own their own farms, they own their businesses." Jacobs, tall, pre-
maturely gray, carefully dressed, and brilliantly manicured, owns
and operates Les Jacobs: Chevrolet–Olds–Cadillac, on East First
Street. "The car business has never been so bad," he said. "But
even so, we made a profit in 1981. The Midwest is still the new
frontier. There's real growth here. We've got water, we've got jobs
—the unemployment rate in Pratt County is about two percent.
And we're centrally located. We're only about a hundred and fifty
miles from the exact geographic center of the country. We're all-
American here, and the Olds is king. The Eighty-eight. These people aren't interested in small cars, foreign or domestic. They want a
full-size car—full comfort, room, luxury. And they can afford it.
But a car is not a status symbol to them. They'd be embarrassed to
drive a Rolls-Royce. I say the Olds is king, but this is also Cadillac
country. Our business is off, but not the Cadillac end. We count on
selling at least two big Caddies every month. We've never sold less
than twenty-four a year. I personally know of a hundred and seventy-five Cadillac owners in Pratt County. The Cadillac is the only
car they know, these big farmers. They've been driving one for
twenty-five or thirty years. Financing? Interest rates? They couldn't
care less. They just sit down and write me out a check. The mon-

eyed people here have always been in wheat—with some cattle on the side. But now, a lot of them, they've also got oil."

"Oil—I'll tell you about oil," a man at the Brass Ring bar told me one evening. He was about forty, and dark—dark hair, darkly tanned, and wearing a dark-blue Lacoste jersey. He was drinking Chivas Regal with a splash of 7UP. "When people think of oil, they think of Mobil or some guy with an oil well on his place. Like 'Dallas,' right? Well, I say oil is jobs. It's a whole bunch of jobs. It's a dozen different jobs before the oil even comes out of the ground. Somebody has to go out and write the lease for the land, and arrange the right-of-way. Then the surveyor comes on. Then the dirt contractor. He gets the site ready for the rig. Then the drilling company. Then the casing goes in. Then the valves, the tanks, the pipeline. Then there's transportation. Then pumpers. And then, way down there at the end of the road, there's the refinery. All those guys working, that really makes a community boom." He took a gulp of his drink. "And the money they make! My God, a roustabout—even a roustabout—he makes eight or ten dollars an hour. . . ."

"Well, *I* sure hope this oil thing lasts," Kim Page, one of the waitresses at the Club D'Est, told me. "I think it's great. I'm twenty-eight years old, and now that I'm divorced I'm just about the only girl my age in Pratt that isn't married. But there's a whole lot of unattached guys around. I mean all those roustabouts, those roughnecks, those oil-field guys. Which is neat."

On my first morning in Pratt, I drove down to the Kitchen for the first of many breakfasts there (the first of what must in time have totalled an appalling two or three dozen eggs, two or three pounds of bacon, and a foot-high stack of pancakes) and then set out on a stroll around the center of town. The first person I met smiled and nodded and said, "Good morning." So ("Hi, there") did the second. And the third ("How you doing?"), and the fourth, and so on. ("I sometimes think that that is the biggest difference," Iris Worthington, the manager of the Pratt Area Chamber of Commerce, told me. "I've lived in the city. I lived in Wichita before I came here. Small towns are friendly. They give you a chance to prove yourself. You're innocent until proved guilty. In the city, it's just the opposite. You have to prove your innocence.") The center of Pratt is compactly centralized. I walked a block north on Main toward First Street, and, standing on the corner of Main and Third, standing in front of the Peoples Bank, I could practically see it all—not only the stores and offices facing each other along South Main but also the public buildings. There, half a block to the west, was the Municipal Building, with the Pratt Public Library (as I later found) just behind it. There, a block to the east, was the post office (with the Pratt County Historical Society Museum behind it); the Pratt County Courthouse, in its park of lawns and walks and shaggy old ash trees (with the police department and the sheriff's office on the street beyond); and the cottagelike building that houses the Pratt *Tribune*. I stood there—gazing around, responding to greetings, enjoying the feel of the morning sun—and became aware of music. It was "The Poor People of Paris," muted but inescapable, and it came from overhead, from a speaker high on a light post. The center of Pratt is also unified by Muzak.

I went around to the *Tribune* and introduced myself. Doug Weller, the news editor, received me in a comfortably grubby office with a Teletype machine tapping away in a corner. He is a gentle young man with soft brown eyes and a bushy black mustache. "Everybody seems to like our Main Street," he told me. "It isn't our only brick street, though. We have almost seven miles of brick pavement. I think most of us wish that all our streets were brick. You've probably seen the potholes on our so-called modern streets. Main Street was the first paved street in Pratt. That would have been around 1918, and it was quite a project. Main Street, as you probably know, runs from the Southern Pacific tracks on the north all the way to the Santa Fe tracks on the south." He smiled a sudden smile. "Rufus Gray, our local historian, says that nobody lives on the wrong side of the tracks in Pratt. We all live in between. We almost had an uprising here a few years ago. The State Highway Commission wanted to overlay Main Street with blacktop. They said brick was too much trouble to maintain. Everybody protested—the Main Street residents, the Chamber of Commerce, everybody. And we prevailed. The city lifted the bricks, renewed the sand and concrete base, and relaid the bricks. Main Street is good for another fifty years."

Doug Cook, the Pratt zoning administrator, gave me a delighted look. His eyes were bright with conviction. "I know," he said. "A lot of people think that alleys are a thing of the past. Maybe most people do. But we think differently here in Pratt. We think they're part of the future. Pratt has always had alleys, and I think we always will. They belong in every practical urban plan. Nearly every east-and-west street in Pratt is connected through the middle of every block by a north-and-south alley. That goes for most of our streets—the new as well as the old. Our developers accept the rule. I'll agree that alleys are old-fashioned. Just like our brick streets! Listen! Alleys keep the trash off the street. They preserve streets from heavy equipment—garbage trucks, delivery trucks, trucks making gas or electric repairs. They separate neighbors, they provide a nice back-boundary line. They give our joggers a safe place to run. I could go on and on."

"Well, yes, I think that's true," Jim Harris, who is the manager of Dillon's, the largest of Pratt's three supermarkets, told me. "I'd say that Pratt is a pretty clean town. It's cleaner than most, anyway. But the reason isn't that the people here are any different from anybody else. The reason is that here in Kansas, like a lot of other places, we're turning the clock back. We're getting rid of the no deposit, no return on beverage bottles and cans. It's actually a community service that we and Safeway and the others perform. With, of course, the cooperation of Coca-Cola and Pepsi and all the rest. We don't get a thing out of it ourselves except the satisfaction. But that can be very satisfying. There's a deposit here of ten cents on a regular-size glass soft-drink bottle and twenty cents for the quart size. A lot of people, of course, don't bother with the return. They don't care—they're in the littering habit. But the kids know better. You see them out there working the streets and parks. They bring the stuff in here by the bag. We pay them the regular deposit for the bottles and twenty cents a pound for aluminum beer or pop cans. And they never walk out of here with less than two or three dollars."

Paul Epp, the proprietor of Epp Coins & Supply, at 112 South Main Street, gave me a thoughtful look. "OK," he said. "If you're interested, the 'Coins' part means I'm in the numismatics business. I buy and sell coins. The 'Supply' part means I also sell apparatus for finding coins. Like over there, that vacuum-cleaner-looking machine —that's a Garrett metal detector, one of the smaller models. I sell them to people who prospect for coins. People have been losing coins in this country—in parts of this country, anyway—for over three hundred years. The prospectors work the streets, old abandoned house sites, old fairgrounds—all kinds of places. When they tore up the old wooden sidewalks here in Pratt some years ago, the prospectors found a real bonanza. It's interesting what happens when you drop a coin. Most people think it sinks into the ground. Not at all. It lays there, and gradually the dust and dirt overlays it. It's like archeology. The depth dates a coin. There's a chart that spells it out. If you find a coin at a depth of, say, half an inch, that coin is circa 1979. If you find it at, say, one foot, that coin is circa 1787. Oh, a detector can detect at quite a depth—six to eight feet, some of them. Prospecting can be profitable. Nobody would pay up to six hundred dollars for a detector if it wasn't. Some of my customers have done pretty well. I know one guy here has made around eighteen thousand dollars. One guy bought one of my detectors and came back from an abandoned house up around Great Bend with three twenty-dollar gold pieces, three ten-dollar gold pieces, eight five-dollar gold pieces, and a couple of smaller ones. I offered him thirty-five hundred dollars for the lot, but he wouldn't take it. When I go on vacation, I always drive, so I usually take a detector along. I usually pick up something."

I parked my car in my slot in front of my room at the Hillcrest Motel, and got out and looked up at the sky. There was a great cloud rising in the west—a great black cloud—and it was moving fast. It was only a little past five, but the afternoon had dimmed almost to dusk. I heard a rumble of thunder. I walked the few steps to my room and unlocked the door, and the sky overhead was all black cloud. The thunder rolled again. I closed the door—shoved it, heaved it closed against a surge of wind. I stood in the dark and listened to the wind. There was a sudden rage of rain on the windows, on the roof. I went over to the windows and looked out. The parking lot, the rooms across the court were barely visible. But the downpour wasn't rain. It was hail. It was a blizzard of hail—of hail the size and exactly the look of mothballs, pelting down, blowing in waves in all directions, gathering in drifts. It was a wildness I have never seen before. The light began to change. The cloud was moving, thinning. The hail slackened, became rain, became a spring drizzle. Then the cloud was gone. The afternoon came blazing back. I opened the door and stepped out. The air had a vivid freshness, and a smell—a strange, almost unearthly smell, a smell that was almost a flavor. It was strange but also familiar. And then it came to me. It was the smell of watercress.

I saw Doug Weller at the *Tribune* the next morning, and we talked about the storm. "That was a little unusual," he told me. "Even for Kansas. I mean the hail. We've got a story coming up in the paper this afternoon about a guy here who was doing some laundry, had his washer and dryer going, when the hail began. He says he rushed over and turned the things off—he thought he'd left a pocketful of change in his jeans. The wind wasn't anything really special. We *do* get a lot of wind here. But people have the wrong idea about Kansas. They seem to think that Kansas is the home of the tornado. That's its reputation, but we don't deserve it. Kansas is only number three in the nation. The leading tornado states are Texas and Oklahoma. But we know who's to blame. We blame our reputation on *The Wizard of Oz*."

"You've noticed that, have you?" Lois Fischer, one of the beauticians at Beauty Boutique, said to me. "Well, it's true. Our women don't go in for high-fashion hairdos. They simply can't. Not with the wind we have here. Imagine Dolly Parton or somebody crossing Main Street— what all that hair would look like when she got to the other side! There is just no way you can back-comb hair in Pratt and have it last. We do mainly asymmetric cuts—what they used to call windblown—and curlies, long or short. Curlies are really practical. You don't have to mess with them, and the wind doesn't mess with them, either."

Howard K. Loomis, the president of the Peoples Bank, is a tall, solid, immaculate man of fifty-five (gray suit, white shirt with button-down collar, striped necktie) with a wide, warm, squint-eyed smile. He was smiling now. "No," he told me. "You don't hear much complaining here about the wind in the summertime. A twenty-mile wind feels pretty good when the temperature is hanging around a hundred and ten degrees. Or higher. They used to say that if it wasn't for the wind, when a farmer went out to open his mailbox on a summer afternoon he'd have to use a pot holder. The wind makes life bearable here in July and August. For one thing, we don't have to cool our swimming pools, the way some places do. And the wind can be a blessing in wheat country. Kansas is the leading wheat state, and Pratt is one of the leading wheat counties. We've got about two hundred thousand acres in wheat. Our annual production is about six million bushels. So wheat is what matters most. The wind minimizes the disease problem. It helps keep the rust down. But if you want to talk about wheat I suggest you talk to Richard Konold. Dick has a nice place out southeast of town. I'll give him a call."

I got up to go, and Loomis followed me to the door. He stopped there. "Dick is a very nice guy," he said. "This place is full of very nice people. I was born and raised in Omaha, and I worked for several years in Kansas City. My wife was a Kansas Citian. But we were both delighted when I got a chance to come to Pratt. There's something about a small town. There's a quality. I'll tell you what I mean. When our oldest boy was seventeen, he was out one night and he was going through Lemon Park pretty fast. One of the town cops saw him and stopped him and got out and came over to the car. He stood there for a moment. Then he shook his head, and said, 'Why, Art Loomis! I'm ashamed of you!' And Art came home hanging his head.''

Konold—Richard Konold, a tall, lean, leathery man of fifty-odd, in boots and a ventilated implement-company cap—stopped the pickup we were riding in and rolled down the window. We were on a farm road hardly wider than the truck, in a treeless, fenceless, totally featureless landscape of billowing green that stretched off to every horizon. He propped an elbow on the windowsill, and stared. "Look at that!" he told me. "Just *look* at it! This is *wheat* country! You're looking at nothing but wheat for fifteen miles in every direction. You're looking at an *ocean* of wheat. Now, I call that pretty. This country was made for wheat. The first settlers, back in the eighteen-seventies—they knew that the minute they saw it. They only made one mistake, the first folks here. They saw there was two kinds of country here—shortgrass country and tallgrass country. They thought the taller the grass, the better the soil, so that was what they grabbed. Then came a bunch of Negroes, followed by a bunch of German Baptists. They took what was left, the shortgrass, and, of course, that turned out to be the best. There are still some German Baptists here. You've probably seen them around town in their big black hats and bonnets. I don't know what happened to those Negro settlers. This land here was all shortgrass country. Wheat is a real good crop to grow. It's the easiest crop to raise I know. It just does everything right. It's a dryweather crop, and Pratt County is fairly dry. We average maybe twenty-four inches of rain a year. Rain is crucial at planting time, in the fall, but after that too much rain will hurt it. I call it a miracle crop. You can think it's down and out and all burned out, and then comes a shower of rain, and it jumps right back. It's a double crop. Planting time is late September to early October, and the wheat sprouts pretty fast. When it gets up to three or four inches, you can turn your calves in to graze for a few weeks. Most wheat farmers run a few cattle. Almost everybody's farm has some rough acreage that is only good for pasture. Well, you move your calves out before they graze your wheat too short. Then the cold winter comes, and the wheat hibernates, just like an old bear. That's when the *good* farmer goes back to school. They have classes at the college here on tractor mechanics, refrigeration, irrigation, a whole bunch of subjects that it pays a farmer to know—day classes and night. The wheat begins to green up around February, and you can turn your cattle back in for another few weeks of grazing. Or, if you don't have any cattle, you can rent the grazing out. We harvest in June, and after that you start tilling—getting the land ready for fall planting. I've learned two things about farming. An old stockman told me when I was just starting out with some cattle that there is usually a time every year when you can sell a calf and make money. Whenever you can make a profit, sell. Never hold out for a better price. That's the way to go broke. The same thing goes for wheat. I've got some storage tanks. I don't have to sell my wheat the minute it's cut. Equipment is the farmer's biggest problem, his biggest expense. I've got about the minimum. Two tractors, one of them a spare. Wheat drill. Tandem disk plow. Chisel plow. Spring-tooth cultivator. I don't own a combine. A combine goes from eighty thousand dollars up, and you only use it for two short weeks at harvest time. I pay a custom cutter to come in and cut my wheat. I consider that one of the freedoms of farming. Like being your own boss, like taking a day off when you feel like it, like looking out the window and saying, 'That's my land.' Like living out in the open air."

The highway was bordered on the left by the jungle beauty of a mile-long windbreak of impenetrable cedar and Osage orange and on the right by wheat—by mile after mile of rippling, skittering, shimmering green—but Paul Hartman, the Pratt County extension agent, drove with his eyes fixed only on the road. From time to time, we passed another car, and the index finger of his right hand lifted off the wheel in salute. Hartman is twenty-eight years old, big and serious, with a ruddy round face and soft brown bangs. "Here we are," he told me, turning off the highway and onto an unpaved county road. "That's the Preisser place up ahead—that new little house and those big equipment sheds. Larry is what they call a custom cutter. A custom cutter harvests other folks' wheat for a contract fee. He supplies the combines and the semis and everything else. Larry and his wife and their two little boys and a couple of hired hands start out down in Texas and work the harvest north. Larry grows a little wheat himself, but it wasn't him who called me out here. It was his wife, Karen. Look at their place. Two little pine trees, and the rest of it open to every kind of wind and weather. She wants some planting—some wind protection and, I guess, a little beauty, too."

We pulled up between the house and the nearest towering equipment shed, and Hartman opened his door. A Doberman pinscher came loping up from behind the house. Hartman closed his door. He touched the horn. The front door opened, and Mrs. Preisser—blue-eyed and blond, booted and jeaned—came out. She spoke to the dog, and he sat. He sat and rolled over and grovelled. Mrs. Preisser shook her head and laughed.

"Come on in," she said. "You don't have to worry about a big baby like Duke. We'll go in the office. I've drawn up a little plan of what we need. Larry's out in the shed working on a wrecked combine. A dumb kid up north last summer turned it over—said he could handle it, and he couldn't. My little boy Jeff could have done better. I'm serious. He respects an eighty-thousand-dollar piece of machinery, he understands it. He's been driving a truck since he was four. Well, there's my plan. I want protection from the wind, and I also want some shade. I think maybe I'd like to have some Chinese elms for shade. Not cottonwood. Cottonwood drops those little white things off."

Hartman and Mrs. Preisser sat down at a desk in a corner of the office. I walked around the room. The windows gave on a bare front yard, the two lone pines, the dirt road, a field of wheat, a dusty, distant horizon. There was a big framed photograph on one of the walls: four combines moving abreast across a field. The combines looked as big as houses and as menacing as Abrams tanks. There was a framed sentiment on another wall: "God could not be everywhere so Hecreated mothers." There was a bookcase full of what I took to be the Preissers' winter reading: *The Exorcist, Business Law, Tom Sawyer, Up the Down Staircase*, a French-English/English-French dictionary, *Adolescent Development*, Bertrand Russell's *Marriage and Morals*.

Hartman was saying, "OK, then. We'll go with buffalo grass for the lawn."

MRS. PREISSER: "We can't do a garden. Or any fruit trees. We're away too much all summer."

HARTMAN: "Right. Now let's talk about wind protection. One thing to remember is that your wind protection extends ten times the height of the tree. A row of ten-foot trees will give you shelter for a hundred feet in. I'd like to go with two rows of trees twelve feet apart, with a twenty-foot space down the middle of the belt to allow for cultivation and cleanup. You don't want your windbreak to grow up in thirsty weeds. I say go with Eastern red cedar. And I always say use small plants. The trauma of transplanting sets a bigger tree back. Start with foot-tall trees or less, and in five years they'll be up a good five feet."

MRS. PREISSER: "I'd like some color. I mean, all these green fields."

HARTMAN: "OK, for a color accent let's think about a redbud. And maybe a goldenrain tree."

MRS. PREISSER: "I like yellow."

HARTMAN: "And some ornamental shrubs. I like pyracantha. I like spirea. You and Larry talk it over. So now we come to shade. You'll want a little more than those two Austrian pines. Especially in back, where the boys play. You could think about hackberry. Or moraine locust. You mentioned Chinese elm. I'd say maybe eight main shade trees. You can add your accents later."

MRS. PREISSER: "I guess so. But about how much—"

HARTMAN: A lot of this stock comes out of the state forestry program. It's part of our job. A planned planting like we've been talking about can increase the value of your place by twenty percent. I think we can do this for under four hundred dollars."

MRS. PREISSER: "Oh? Oh, really!"

We turned off the dirt road and back onto the highway. Hartman was looking a little sombre. He shook his head. "You know," he said, "you've got to admire those people. They're young, but they're already the last of a breed. They've got the old-fashioned frontier kind of guts. Can you imagine the investment Larry Preisser has back there? In equipment alone? You know what those combines cost—and he owns three. No, not owns. He's buying them from the finance company. When Karen tells him what that planting program will cost, he'll probably laugh. Four hundred dollars! That's small change in his ledger. Karen and him, I'll bet they know some sleepless nights."

One of the almost daily features of the Pratt *Tribune* is a front-page box (lower left-hand corner) called "Vital Stats." Part of "Vital Stats" is an abbreviated deaths column. I found myself glancing at it every afternoon when I picked up my *Tribune* at the Hillcrest Motel office, but it was several days before I understood my interest. What had interested me, I then realized, was the advanced age of the local people listed there. On that afternoon, I made a note of the day's "Vital Stats." The list read "Eva Davis, 89, Pratt. Carl Devers, 82, Norwich. Nellie Stansill, 86, Pratt." A few days later, the list read "Clyde Sayre, 80, Mullinville. Ethel Williamson, 100, Macksville. Alpha Robinson, 81, Newton. Dorothy Gatz, 83, Pratt."

I mentioned this enviable longevity to Deborah Toombs (30) the next morning. Mrs. Toombs is a public-health nurse and the administrator of the Pratt County Health Department. "I don't know," she said. "But I'll tell you what I *think*. I go to Wichita for two days every month. And when I come back from all that rubbing elbows

I'm just like this—nervous, shaky, practically hypertensive. I think the reason people here live so long is simply country life, small-town life. We don't have all that stress."

I drove out east of Pratt one balmy afternoon with a retired head roustabout named Max Mathis for a look at the apiaries from which he annually extracts five hundred gallons of honey and a comfort-able supplementary income. "My dad—I don't know why—he was afraid of bees," Mathis told me. "I learned beekeeping from my grandfather, McKinley Monroe Mathis, down in Fairview, Okla-homa. He taught me all he knew, and he knew plenty, but it turned out there wasn't any hurry. He lived to be a hundred and two years old. At the time of his death, he was the oldest Mason in the world. I've always kept bees. I like those little fellows. Of course, I realize a fellow can die of a bee sting if he's that sensitive to it. But I've been stung I don't know how many times—I reckon a couple of times every day in the season. It hurts, but it don't really bother me. I'd rather be bit by a bee than a chigger. The only thing I hate about being bit is it kills the bee. He loses his stinger, and that's the end of him. I keep around nine thousand bees. That's about the most one man can handle. I've got about twenty-five hives in each of my four apiaries. There are four main breeds of honeybees that I know of. There's the Caucasian breed. There's the Midnite breed and the Starline. And there's the Three-Banded Eyetalians. Mine are almost all Eyetalians. I'm really sweet on those Eyetalians. Now I'm going to turn off here. This rut-track runs down to one of my apiaries. And on a nice day like this my bees will be stirring, so I think you'd better roll up your window. That tweed jacket you've got on—bees don't like wool. It's got an animal smell."

We parked a dozen feet or so short of the first row of white box hives. The hives faced south, and each had a little veranda in front, and the verandas were crowded with bees sunning themselves and coming and going. There was a scraggly windbreak behind the hives, with a red squirrel hopping and gawking from branch to branch. "They're just beginning to feed themselves," Mathis said. "They're getting tree pollen mostly. They love that wild plum. After the trees comes alfalfa. I have an arrangement with the farmer who owns this land. My bees pollinate his alfalfa, and I get the honey. After alfalfa comes red clover. The honey season runs from May 15 to September 30. The last honey flow comes from golden-rod. A lot of folks buy my late honey because they think it's good for their hay fever. Bees are real interesting. I buy a new queen every year for each of my hives. Each queen comes to me in a little screen-topped wooden box. There's the queen in there, and there's six worker bees, and there's a lump of sugar candy for food. The queen, you know, can't or won't feed herself. That's why the workers. The first thing I do when the boxes arrive is take out the workers with my tweezers and turn them loose—my workers won't accept strangers. But my bees are interested in the queen, and they start feeding her from the candy. Pretty soon, they're ready to take her for their queen. A queen bee—you've never known such a specialized machine. All she does is lay those eggs. She won't feed herself, she won't clean herself, she can't sting, and she's a pretty poor flier. But she's smart. She knows just how many eggs to lay and when. If the feed gets short, she cuts back on laying. The mystery to me is the drone. It's the drone that mates with the queen, but only one drone wins out and mates with her. Except for mating flights, the drones just lay around the hive and eat what the workers bring in. They're really drones. The workers are really workers. They just plain work themselves to death. They get the nectar and make the honey and feed the queen and keep her clean and tidy. They also take care of the hive. When a bee dies, the workers gather around and carry him outside and dump him. They keep the hive spick-and-span. They also police it. I mean, they can deal with intruders. Twice in my life I've been checking out a hive and I've found a mouse in there. A dead mouse. I don't know how or why he got in, but the bees had stung him to death and wrapped him up and sealed him off with bee gum."

Bill Hampton, Jr.—a big, round man of forty-three with a big, round face and a big mustache—is a partner in the law firm of Hampton, Hampton & Schmisseur, and the judge of the Pratt Municipal Court. "There's money here in Pratt County," he told me. "There always has been. This is wheat country. But the people here respect success. They don't resent it. Equal opportunity is a reality here. So we're kind of blessed with the kind of people who try not to intentionally break the law. I think you could walk up and down South Main Street wearing the biggest diamond ring in the world and ten pounds of gold chain around your neck, and nobody would do more than just admire it. I park my car in the lot out back, and I could leave the keys in the ignition if I wanted to. The only reason I don't is I don't want to tempt some poor, weak-minded soul beyond his strength. I'm not talking about murder, of course. We've known murder here. I'm talking about crime."

* * *

"Oh God," Marsha Cook Ioerger said to me. "Do I remember! How could I ever forget? It was the first big story I ever covered." Mrs. Ioerger is twenty-eight years old, a slim, spirited strawberry blonde, and a reporter (*the* general-assignments reporter) on the Pratt *Tribune*. "OK, it was on a Monday morning—Monday morning, October 22, 1979. I came into the office and started to take off my coat, and Doug Weller came over with this strange look on his face. He said, 'Keep your coat on.' He said, 'You're going out to the feedlot.' He said, 'They've found the body of a woman out there. There's been a murder.' I looked at Doug and kind of laughed. But he wasn't kidding. I said, 'What am I supposed to do?' He just said get going. So I did. The Pratt Feedlot is about five miles out north and west of town, off Highway 281. I kept thinking, Oh, my God! When I got out close to the feedlot, I came to a bunch of parked cars, and the sheriff's car was blocking the road. Ray McGuire, the sheriff, told me they were waiting for an agent of the Kansas Bureau of Investigation and they didn't want anybody near the body till then. So I sat there in my car. They'd found the body around eight o'clock, and it was around nine o'clock by now. I sat there till almost eleven. All they could tell me was that the body was in some brush near the road. I sat there thinking eerie thoughts. I had my camera along, but I was afraid of what the body might look like. I thought I ought to be feeling real bad about that poor lady, but I was really just intrigued. That made me feel gross.

"Well, the K.B.I. guy finally arrived. He was a guy I knew named Gary Pettijohn, and I finally began to get some information. They had found a knife, a big butcher knife, in the grass across the road from the body, and some footprints. Also a lot of her clothes —her coat, purse, and shoes. All she had on was jeans and a blouse. They hadn't identified her yet. But there was a kind of coincidence going on. There was a woman named Lila Wright who worked the late-night shift at the E-Z Stop convenience store, on East First Street. A little before five o'clock that morning, a truck driver—a regular customer—stopped at the E-Z Stop for some coffee, and the place was open but there wasn't anybody there. Mrs. Wright was gone, and so was her pickup. The trucker called the store manager at his home, and the manager came right down and checked things over and found almost three hundred dollars missing. So he called the police. At about six o'clock, Gene Tritt, one of the Pratt cops, found the missing pickup just off Highway 281, about three miles from the body. The chief of police, Paul

Garst, found some footprints there, too, and got pictures of them. Well, by the time they let me go up where they'd found the body, the body had been taken away. All I could do was sort of look around and hurry back to the office. I was in a tizzy. I was involved in a real professional-type thing. I mean, I was entirely shook. But Doug was holding everything, and I sat down at my typewriter and decided to just write the facts. Which I did, and Doug ran the story on page one with the headline 'BODY FOUND, POSSIBLE LINK TO KIDNAPPING.'

"That afternoon, after we had gone to press, the police announced the identification. It was Mrs. Wright. She was thirty-four years old, separated from her husband, and she had a daughter by an earlier marriage named Tammy Berschauer. Tammy was eighteen and had just left Pratt High, and she identified her mother. That was about all the news I had for my follow-up story the next day. The headline Doug put on it was 'NO HARD EVIDENCE IN MURDER CASE,' and he gave me my first byline on the story. I had another investigation-continuing story the next day—Wednesday, October 24. The police were waiting for the results of an autopsy. But things were happening behind the scenes. I got it all later from Gary Pettijohn, the K.B.I. agent. What was happening was this: Tammy Berschauer had also been working at the E-Z Stop, and after a few days—after the funeral and all that—she went back to work there, on the afternoon-to-midnight shift. But her boyfrien was worried about her being there all alone, so he started coming to work with her. And there was this neighborhood guy. His name was Mikel E. Trumbly. He was eighteen years old but looked younger, and he was big and strong. My little sister remembered him from Pratt High. She said he had a wandering eye, but he was real quiet and hung out with younger guys. Well, this guy, this Mikel, came to the E-Z Stop almost every evening, and he always bought a 7UP and maybe a couple of magazines. The footprints that the police had studied were the prints of tennis shoes, and they were the same at the scene of the murder and at where the pickup was found. The police took the pictures they had made down to Midwest Athletic, and the people there identified them as made by Adidas shoes. One night after Mikel had been in the E-Z Stop and gone, Tammy's boyfriend said to Tammy, 'Did you notice that that guy was wearing Adidas tennis shoes?' They talked about that, and pretty soon they got an idea. I guess you could say they decided to play detective. So when Mikel came in the next time, Tammy smiled at him and said, 'Hey, I like your shoes. I want to get a pair like them for my brother.' I guess Mikel thought he was getting a compliment.

Then Tammy said, 'Look, I want to get your size—I think my brother wears the same.' So she asked him to come outside and step in a muddy place and then step on a paper sack. He did, and she got a nice print, and she turned it over to the police. And it matched the other prints.

"That was on Monday, November 5th. Gary Pettijohn called Mikel and asked him to come down to the police station, which he did, and they had a long visit. Anyway, Mikel confessed. It seems that he had been kind of flirting with Lila Wright at the E-Z Stop, and I guess she must have acted in a way that made him think she was serious. We'll never know exactly what happened that night, but he came in the place with that knife. He took whatever money there was in the register, and forced her out to the pickup and made her drive out toward the feedlot. He told her he was going to rape her. But he said if she didn't try to fight or anything, he would only just rape her. He wouldn't kill her. I guess she agreed. And afterwards, when she tried to get away, he got scared and chased her and caught her and stabbed her in the abdomen. Then he took off in her pickup.

"The rest of the story is that Mikel pleaded guilty to charges of first-degree murder and kidnapping, and his pleas were accepted, and the judge sentenced him to life in prison. Oh, I forgot to tell you. The E-Z Stop had offered a reward for Lila's killer. Five thousand dollars! And Tammy got it."

Mrs. Ioerger sat for a moment, looking down at the scattered notes and clippings on her desk. Then she shrugged, and gathered them up and stuck them away in a drawer. She lighted a cigarette. "But, you know," she told me, "the strangest thing—the really weird thing—was the way the people here reacted to it all. They kind of tried to close their eyes. You could hardly find a soul in town who would say that they had ever known Mikel Trumbly. They just pretended that what had happened could never have happened here."

[1983]

7. Countryside: *Crawford County, Missouri*

I went down to Missouri—down to Crawford County, in the foot-hills of the Ozarks, some ninety miles southwest of St. Louis—to see something of the Meramec River and a white-water tributary called Courtois Creek while they both were still there to be seen. The Meramec, like so many other rivers in America, has had the misfortune to catch the eye of the Army Corps of Engineers, and the Corps (with the usual approval of the construction industry and a handful of well-placed land speculators) plans to build a dam across it. The dam would cost (at the latest estimate) around a hundred million dollars. Its purpose would be to create a thirteen-thousand-acre lake (suitable for motorboating, water-skiing, flat-water fishing, and surrounding with vacation homes) that would also serve as an emergency reservoir for St. Louis should the Mississippi River happen to run dry.

I had arranged to float the Courtois for ten or twelve miles, from a point just below its source to its junction with the Meramec, and then on down the Meramec for two miles to a point called Onondaga Crossing. Most of Courtois Creek would be swamped in the backwaters of the dam, and that stretch of the Meramec, though many miles above the proposed dam site, would be buried under fifty feet or more of dead, muddy water. There were eight of us in our elegiac party. My companion, and the stern man in my canoe, was a young boating guide and naturalist—green-eyed, dark-haired, fiercely mustached—named John Igleheart. There was an engineer named Duane Woltjen and his wife, Judy, a registered nurse, both founders of the Ozark chapter of the Sierra Club. There was a geologist named Don Rimbach—a big, bald man with a big red beard—whose special interest is caves and springs. (Crawford County is rocky country, and its rocky bluffs and outcrops are riddled with caves. The Meramec Dam would flood at least a hundred considerable caves, including the celebrated Onondaga Cave.) The others in the group were Dennis Drabelle, counsel to the Assistant Secretary for Fish and Wildlife and Parks of the United States Department of the Interior, and Todd Vogel and Robert Howard, both wildlife biologists assigned to the Kansas City-area office of the Fish and Wildlife Service. Vogel and Howard are by way of being specialists in the mammalian order Chiroptera, or bats. Several of the threatened caves are known to be the winter habitat of *Myotis sodalis,* the so-called Indiana bat, a species protected by the Endangered Species Act.

I had my first sight of the Courtois from a low-water crossing, or surfaced ford, called Blount's Bridge. That was where we had agreed to meet and put in. Igleheart and I were the first to arrive. We were delivered there after a big country breakfast by a friend in a road-worn Volkswagen with a bumper sticker that read "STOP Meramec Dam—A Crime Against Mother Nature." We watched the car turn and grind back up a long, wooded, rut-tracked hill, and then walked down to the ford. Our canoes were beached on the downstream side on a hump of gravel bar. The Courtois was full and fast and a gleaming, glittering, almost Caribbean green. It looked more like a river than a creek. The far shore, fifty or sixty feet away, was a craggy limestone cliff screened with willow brush and big, towering, overhanging sycamores. The water along the foot of the cliff was still and deep. We stood and listened to the silence—to the voices of birds, to the stir of a breeze in the trees, to the riffle of moving water. We stood there in the joy of the pearly morning and waited for the others. There was no hurry. It was hardly nine o'clock, and we had the whole long day ahead of us.

We moved off in a flotilla of four canoes. The Woltjens took the lead. Igleheart and I were in second position, and the others ranged away two or three lengths behind us. I sat in the bow and looked down through four feet of water as clear as the morning air at the coppery cobblestone bottom sliding quickly up and then past and away. We were moving nicely, faster than a fast walk. I had forgotten the feel of speed one gets on an Ozark float—the illusory power of natural movement that makes a galloping horse between one's knees seem faster than a racing car.

I looked back at Igleheart. He nodded and smiled. "I don't know why, either," he said. "It's true, though—there's nothing truer. But we really are moving, you know. We've got a current here of maybe four miles an hour. This is a fast river. Duane tells me it has an average gradient of eight feet to the mile. They've got a numerical scale for classifying streams like this for flow and difficulty. It starts at one and rises to six. Six is practically a waterfall. The Cotaway is rated at two."

"The what?" I said.

Igleheart laughed. "You said you used to live in St. Louis," he said. "Then you've got to know how Missouri pronounces its French place-names. They write the name of this river the way it's spelled on the map, but 'the Cotaway' is what they call it."

The Woltjens sat idle and drifting up ahead in the slack water of a slough. They waved and beckoned us over. We pulled out of the current and floated down through the sudden dark and damp of willow shade under the bank.

Judy Woltjen was beaming. "Isn't it great!" she said. "Isn't it just gorgeous!"

"It's beautiful," I said. "I've never seen a prettier river."

"Yes," Woltjen said. "That's why we waited for you. I thought you might be interested to know where you are. This is roughly the point where what I call the scene of the crime begins. If they build the dam, this will be the mouth of the Cotaway. From here on down will be nothing but lake."

"At normal pool," Judy Woltjen said.

"That's what I mean," Woltjen said. "And normal pool is the level of water they try to maintain. It's the minimum. At flood pool, or high water, the lake will probably reach up pretty close to where we put in."

"That would be the end of the smallmouth bass," Igleheart said. "They like it cold and clear. They can't take that warm lake water, or any kind of pollution. And this is the best bass stream I've ever fished." I cocked my head and listened. It was the rush and rumble of faster water. There was another rapids coming up. It sounded like a good one.

"No problem," Igleheart said. "I was through here only a week ago. But I think maybe I'd better handle it alone."

I shipped my paddle and hunched down in my seat. I listened to the rising surge of the chute. We came around an arm of gravel bar and into a chop of foot-high whitecaps. The cliff, with its trailing brush and clinging trees, closed in on the right. The canoe gave a sudden slide, like a slip on ice. The chute loomed—a sunken log, a bony snag, a tumble of rocks, a skin of seething water. We scraped,

crunched, lurched, and were through. We skittered almost broadside into a pool. Igleheart brought us around. The pool narrowed
and deepened. The channel cut hard to the right, under the jut of
cliff, under a lowering colonnade of sycamores. A hanging branch
the size of my thigh reached down and across. I ducked, and leaned
away.

I kept on leaning. I couldn't stop leaning. And the canoe went
over. I went in and down and slid on my side along the pebbly
bottom and turned over and came up gasping. I grabbed for my
paddle and, with my boots and jeans dragging like lead, splashed
through four feet, three feet, two feet of surging cold water, and up
the slipping slope of the gravel bar.

I got my breath, and looked back. Igleheart was still in the
water, stumbling backward, hanging on to his paddle, holding the
swamped canoe. I got rid of my paddle and gave him a hand with
the line. We hauled the canoe up onto the bar and tipped it over. A
soggy jacket slopped out from a thwart—mine. And a soggy flannel shirt—Igleheart's. And the remains of a package of cigarettes
—Igleheart's. I took off my shirt and wrung it out. I thought I
might be able to flap it dry. There was nothing I could do about my
pants and boots. But the sun was well up now and the air was
almost hot. They would dry well enough on the body.

The first of the other canoes came down through the chute and
under the hanging branch. It was the two biologists, Vogel and
Howard. They saw us standing stripped to the waist and dripping
on the gravel bar. They stared, and pulled up, and landed.

Vogel said, "Wow—what happened to you?"

"I leaned the wrong way," I said.

"It's worse than that," Igleheart said. "So did I."

A little spring-fed brook came spreading in from behind a gravel
bar, and the Courtois widened for a stretch below it. We paddled
peacefully together, two abreast, down a winding avenue of
sunny open water. The cliff had shifted across to the other shore,
and its ledges were aflame with cascading columbine. There was
a woodpecker (a pileated woodpecker, somebody guessed from
the sound of it) knocking somewhere in the woods above. A
little green heron the color of slate watched us from a sycamore
stump on the bank.

"That's a new sign of the times," Woltjen said. "The sycamore
stump over there. You'll see a lot of stumps like that from here on
down. The sycamore is going the way of the cypress and the black

walnut—it's getting to be an endangered species. It's a bottomland tree, and it's running out of environment. But the reason it's being cut along here is the dam. Sycamore brings good money. They use it for butcher blocks and barrels and things like that. The people are trying to get as much out of their land as they can before the dam goes in. Uncle Sam drives a pretty hard bargain, you know. With ordinary people, anyway."

"I don't really blame these people," Judy Woltjen said. "I can understand how they feel. But what if we manage to stop the dam?"

"Which we will," Rimbach said.

Woltjen shrugged.

Rimbach was in the stern of the canoe just ahead. He suddenly sat up and braked with his paddle.

He said, "Hey! Hey, look! Look at him go!"

I looked. It was a frog—the head of a frog—in a slough. It was the big, spotted, pop-eyed head of a bullfrog swimming across the mouth of a slough toward a cluster of blossoming lily pads. I kept looking. The frog climbed up on one of the lily pads and squatted there in the shade of a yellow blossom. I watched it sitting there, and I knew I had seen it all before. But where? And then it came to me. A picture emerged, rose vividly up from the depths of my childhood—a picture of a smiling green frog sitting cross-legged on a lily pad in the tiny, shiny pages of *The Tale of Mr. Jeremy Fisher,* by Beatrix Potter.

Igleheart said, "What time have you got?"

That startled me. I felt a touch of alarm. I had forgotten about my watch. It was not, as far as I knew, waterproof. I took a cautious look. And relaxed. "Ten to one," I said.

"Good," he said. "Then we're not too far from on time. That gravel bar down there on the left—that's Bob Bass's landing, where I told you we'd be taking out for lunch. Bob won't be there. I understand he's up in St. Louis on business. But that doesn't matter too much. It's Mrs. Bass who's giving us lunch, and she's French. She and Bob met in Paris. So I guess you know what to expect."

I had heard a lot about Bass. I knew that he was a big landowner in Crawford County, and a man with many and varied business interests in Steelville, the county seat. He was also, I gathered, a leader in the movement opposing the dam. There didn't seem to be much doubt about that. His interests included a canoe-rental business. Several of his canoes were pulled up on the gravel, and we passed them on the way to the house. There was a printed placard exhortation fixed on the bow thwart of each of the canoes. It was headed "DON'T DAM THIS RIVER," and continued, "Meramec Park Reservoir, a dam now partially funded for construction by the Corps of Engineers, will make a reservoir of the Courtois, Huzzah, and upper Meramec Rivers. The beauty and value for recreation of these natural streams is too great to sacrifice for a man-made reservoir at this location. Do not be cheated out of your natural heritage. Stop the dam. Join us. Citizens Committee to Save the Meramec, Inc. Box 88, Leasburg, Missouri."

Our lunch could hardly have been more *déjeuner:* Quiche Lorraine. Filet of sole and fresh white asparagus. A chilled Muscadet. Mrs. Bass, an attractive young woman in jeans and a blue denim shirt, sat at the head of the table and nibbled and sipped and smoked. "It is every kind of a crime," she said. "It is fantastic. Our land here on the river has been in my husband's family since the Civil War. We have six hundred and forty acres —what you call a section—and they wish to flood it to make recreation. The thought of turning food-producing land into a lake at a time like this is imbecilic. To say nothing of the price they offer! We know enough to say no. And so do some others. But there are many people here—old people, simple country people—who don't understand. They think if the Engineers wish to buy your land you must do as they say and sell. They think they have no rights."

"It's really neat," Rimbach said. "When a man is accused of a crime, the police sit down and read him his rights as a citizen. But when the government wants to buy his land, nobody tells him anything."

We dropped, thumping and skittering, through another tight, splashing, headlong chute—and there was our kingfisher again. It was perched on a skeleton cedar branch overlooking a pool. It turned its big, awkward, tufted head, and gave us a look of exasperation. It stepped off the branch and once more flapped heavily away downstream.

Igleheart said, "That's how many times—three?"

"Four," I said.

"Then I doubt if we'll see him again. He'll be running out of territory. You can push him only so far, and then he turns back. He's more afraid of trespassing on the next kingfisher than he is of us."

We crossed the pool. We moved through a cloudburst of swarming mayflies. We followed the channel around a double horseshoe bend and down a chute so shallow that we had to get out and wade. We slopped back aboard and glided into the pool below. There was a buzzard hanging like a puff of black smoke in the sky high overhead. There was a pair of brown flycatchers courting or fighting in a dogwood tree. There was a turtle asleep on a log. There was a beer can shining in a couple of feet of water near the bank. But Igleheart was right. The kingfisher was gone—doubled back to its own domain.

Igleheart said, "Hold it!"

He was staring at the beer can. He looked shocked. He poked down and touched it with his paddle. It lurched slowly over, and his face cleared. He stepped overboard and reached down and picked up the can. It wasn't a discarded can. It was a can of beer—Old Milwaukee beer—unopened and intact.

"It looks like somebody else took a spill," he said. "We don't get many slobs on this river." He climbed back in and opened the can and dropped the tab in the bottom of the canoe. He took a swallow. "Too bad it isn't Bud," he said, and held out the can to me. "But at least it's good and cold."

We beached our canoes on the bank of a slough, and Vogel and Rimbach led the way along the bar and up a steep and slippery path to the twenty-foot mouth of a cave. Above the cave, above its overhanging upper lip, the cliff rose fifty or sixty feet to a crown of brush and scrub. We stepped into the chamber and into another season—into a dank, autumnal chill. The floor was rough with rubble and the charred remains of campfires, and the walls were pitted with cracks and niches. Overhead, the ceiling soared. Beyond, at the end of the chamber, were the openings of two dim and disappearing passages.

"They call this Bat Cave," Vogel said. "I don't know who named it, but he had the right idea. It's been an Indiana-bat habitat for maybe hundreds of years. And a good one. Look at all those holes. This rotten old limestone is just right for roosting. It gives them a perfect toehold. That's the way they hibernate, of course—hanging by their toenails."

"What did they estimate the size of the colony at, Todd?" Howard said. "Around three hundred? That sounds reasonable. This is a fair-sized cave. Those passages go back a hundred feet or more."

"I don't think anybody's been all the way back," Rimbach said.

"Bats are interesting," Vogel said. "Especially colonial bats. I mean the way they hibernate. They kind of feel their way into it. Early in the fall—in early October, say—they start drifting into their cave. They begin to group up a little—sort of getting the feel of each other. They're not colonial in the summer, you know. They separate into pairs to breed. And when the fall comes on, they have to get used to grouping again. Nobody knows just why they group together in clusters. It's probably a combination of physical and psychological factors. They're warmer—the temperature is stabilized—when they're packed together. And they are probably more comfortable psychologically. There's comfort and security in numbers."

"What happened to the Indiana bat?" I said. "What makes it an endangered species?"

"It's like every other problem in nature," Vogel said. "The trouble is man. We keep destroying their habitat. The Indiana bat is a particularly demanding animal. Its summer habitat is a sycamore tree, and the only place where it will hibernate is a limestone cave like this. These caves are a little cooler and more humid than most. And there aren't many such caves—they're in Indiana, in Kentucky, a few in Illinois, and here. Another thing, of course, is that people just don't like bats. They come into a cave and build a fire, like you see here, and that disturbs the bats if they're hibernating. The smoke and noise, and more. People think nothing of shooting bats or stoning them or whatever comes to mind. I'm not really crazy about bats myself. But that isn't the point. The point is they fill a niche, they have their place in nature, they're part of the biological chain, they're terrific eaters of nocturnal insects—they help keep things in balance. It's possible that people can be taught a little basic biology, can be made to understand. But that won't do much good if the habitat is already destroyed—the way this cave will be if the Engineers build that dam."

"There isn't any doubt about the destruction," Woltjen said. "We estimate that the lake would be about thirty feet deep at this point, completely filling the cave."

We were travelling together two abreast again. The Courtois had joined the Huzzah just below Bat Cave, and a mile or so farther on the Courtois-Huzzah had joined the Meramec. The Meramec was really a river. It was fifty yards wide bank to bank—from the craggy gray cliff on the left to the gravel bar on the right—and deep: ten or twelve feet deep in the channel. The sun blazed steaming down. Rimbach's face was as red as his beard, and he had a wet handkerchief draped on his big bald head. I thought of the cool of Bat Cave.

A figure came into view. It was a fisherman, a white-haired man in bib overalls, standing at the end of a long tongue of gravel, with a pail at his feet and a fly rod in his hand. He watched us coming, and nodded a greeting.

"How's the fishing?" Rimbach called.

"Oh, the fishing's fine," the man said. "But the catching—that ain't so good."

Rimbach laughed. "I know what you mean," he said.

"I figure the water's too close to the shore," the man said.

"It'll be a lot closer if they build the dam," Rimbach said.

"Screw the dam," the man said.

There was a throbbing murmur from somewhere down beyond the bend ahead. The murmur rose to a mutter, and then to a snarling roar. It was the first noise I had heard all day—the first unnatural sound. We were only a bend or two from our taking-out place at Onondaga Crossing, and I thought for a moment that it might be one of the cars coming down to the landing to meet us. But it wasn't that. It exploded into sight—a man and a woman raging up the pool in a skiff with an outboard motor. They blasted past in a stink of gasoline fumes. We lurched and teetered, and emerged from their wake. But the gasoline stink was still there. It hung in the air like a foretaste of the future.

Onondaga Cave lies deep under the cliffs that overlook a river crossing. The road that led us to the cave was flanked by woods on the river side and, on the other, by pastures and occasional fields of young corn. White-faced cattle, knee-deep in grass, watched us from the pastures. It was the morning after our float. Vogel was driving. Drabelle, next to him, said, "Hey—look!" A sign was coming up on the shoulder. It read "STUPENDOUS!" Beyond it, in the classic Burma Shave manner, was another: "AMAZING!" Then "IT'S EVEN GOOD!" And, finally, "ONONDAGA CAVE." But that series was only the beginning. There was another set half a mile farther on: "IF YOU WANT / YOUR EYES TO GO GAGA / COME AND SEE / "ONONDAGA." And, just after that, another: "THE DISTANCE TOO FAR? / TOO HOT IN THE CAR? / RELAX AT THE CAVE / YOUR NERVES YOU'LL SAVE."

Onondaga Cave is a commercial cave, and its exterior is conventionally commercial—a big welcoming sign, a paved parking
lot, and a long low, L-shaped white clapboard building with a kind
of vestibule in the form of a wigwam. We walked through a gift-
and-souvenir shop and down a hallway past a café. Information
along the way defined "Onondaga" as an Osage Indian word meaning "Spirit of the Mountain," and noted that the cave was discovered by Daniel Boone in 1798. It was opened commercially in
1904, as an adjunct of the St. Louis world's fair. We passed through
a room with piles of speleological literature on tables. The entrance
to the cave was at the far end of the room—the mouth of a grotto
with a ramp sloping gently down. The passage was clearly but
indirectly lighted. The footing was concrete scored for safe walking. The walls and ceiling were raw, jagged, sweating limestone the
color of taffy. There was a faraway sound of rushing water—an
underground stream. There was a steady drip of water seeping
down through the rock from the woods and fields in the upper
world. Rimbach took the lead. "I know this cave like I know the
way home," he said. "I've surveyed every known foot of it, and the
official map is mine. I even discovered a fair-sized grotto that nobody knew was there. We call it a cave, but it's really a series of
caves. All told, with all its arms, it covers about a mile. A good
part of it has never been thoroughly explored. A scientist digging
around in here one day last year excavated an old bone that turned
out to be the leg of a kind of peccary extinct since the last Ice Age.
Where we are now, if they build the dam we'll all be up to our
knees in water."

The passage opened into a chamber eerie with glittering, dripping stalactites and stalagmites. They rose in stumps. They fell
from the ceiling in spears and swords and bayonets. They curtained
the walls with draperies. A shadowy opening led to the chamber
beyond. We moved toward it through a strange, shining, yellow,
taffy-colored glow. The ceiling seemed lower. It was like walking
through a late-October drizzle. There was a break in the wall, and
the rising sound of water. I caught a glimpse of a stream across a
slippery slope of rock. "Nobody knows where that stream comes
from," Rimbach said. "It disappears and reappears. They call it
Lost River. At this point, if they build the dam we'll all be over our
heads in water. That's at normal pool. The Corps, of course, keeps
saying different, but I know what I'm talking about. I've measured
it."

Rimbach touched a switch fixed in the cavern wall, and the

lights went out behind us. He touched another, and the darkness ahead dissolved into beckoning light. We were moving into a kind of canyon. An abyss appeared on the left. We followed a walkway cut into the rock on the right. We edged around a bend. The light seemed to brighten. We stepped into an immensity of glittering space—a block-long chamber with a soaring ceiling hung with hundreds of stalactite chandeliers. In the distance, halfway down the chamber, the floor lifted into a hummocky island, and on the commanding summit of the island stood two monstrous conical stalagmites. "They call this the Big Room," Rimbach said. "I understand it's second in size only to the Big Room at Carlsbad Caverns, in New Mexico. It's eight hundred feet long by two hundred feet wide by eighty feet high. Those big stalagmites are called the Twins. The darker one is Bob and the other is Mary. I don't know how old they are. They've always been here. But think of the millions and billions and trillions of drops of water it took to build them. Let's get a little closer. Do you see that band of red tape around the middle of Mary? That marks the approximate level of the lake at normal pool."

We were deep in the cave now—deep in the heart of its darkness, moving through a watery light, with dark behind us and dark ahead. There was an almost oppressive sense of layers and tiers and pressing thicknesses of rock piled overhead. I was thankful for Rimbach, for the chain of lights, for the ramps and steps and walkways that could be followed back and up and out. A seep of water from the dark above touched my nose and ran icily down my cheek.

The walkway turned and followed a tongue of rusty orange rock out and across the cavern. There was water deep down in the gallery on the left—a dark, still, well-like pool, spangled with reflected light. Rimbach stopped at the tip of the tongue and looked back. "Now, this is something really neat," he said. "They call this the King's Canopy. I guess it is a canopy—all those folds and all. I call it a bridge. I mean, it bridges the room. But whatever you want to call it, it's the biggest of its kind in the world. They estimate it weighs around sixteen hundred tons. And it's onyx. It's made of *solid* onyx."

We stood and looked down at sixteen hundred tons of semiprecious stone.

We came out into daylight, out into the sun, out into the dry and warming air. I gave a shiver of real relief. The cave had been an extraordinary experience, but I was glad to have it behind me. Vogel lighted a cigar. Rimbach unwrapped a candy bar. Drabelle had a faraway look on his face. "You know," he said. "I think they need a new Burma Shave jingle here. A different kind of message. And I've invented one. It goes:

> *To the Engineering Corps:*
> *Stop and Think Again Before*
> *Onondaga Cave You Slaughter*
> *With a Flood of Muddy Water."*

"Hey," Rimbach said. "That's good, Denny. I like that. I really do. But—" He took a bite of his candy bar. He chewed and swallowed. "I'll tell you something, though. I don't think we're going to lose this fantastic cave. I don't think the Corps will build this dam. For two reasons. One is the growing local opposition. The other is the site. They'd be inviting an engineering disaster. Or a financial disaster—an astronomical cost over-run. Or both. They couldn't have picked a worse site for a dam. Where they want to build it is the most cavernous section of the whole two-hundred-mile length of the Meramec. You've seen Onondaga—how susceptible dolomite limestone is to erosion. This country is all little Onondagas. There are at least nine miles of known cave passages within a three-mile radius of the site, and there are plenty more that haven't been found and mapped. It's like building a dam on a sponge. It'll fill and fill and fill, and then it'll start to let go. The Corps will sooner or later learn the truth. They're going to have to make a thorough geological examination of the site. And when they do, I think they'll do like Denny says. They'll stop and think again."

I stepped out on the ledge that formed the brink of the cliff, and looked down, straight down, two hundred feet or more, at the Meramec. This was a good six miles below the landing at Onondaga Crossing, and the river, winding in from behind a point of woods on the right, was wide and slow and a shining bottle green. Across the river, beyond a brushy island and the brushy farther shore, stretched a rolling pasture with a scatter of grazing cattle, and beyond the pasture was a long hedgerow, and beyond the hedgerow were a tiny house and a barn and sheds, and then another pasture rising in the dimming distance to the lift of a wooded ridge. I stood on the ledge and looked out across the wide green river and the

wider, greener fields. It was the loveliest countryside I had ever
seen in America—the loveliest and the most serenely peaceful and
fulfilling. I wondered if I would ever see it again. I wondered, in
spite of Rimbach, how long it would be here for anyone to see. I
knew, because Rimbach himself had told me, that when or if they
built the dam this would all be lake—the whole of this fruitful
valley, from halfway down the cliff almost to the beginning of the
ridge on the far horizon.

AUTHOR'S NOTE:

One of Jimmy Carter's first acts after his inauguration as President
in 1977 was to review the projected operations of the Army Corps
of Engineers. Many of these projects, he decided after consulta-
tionwith representatives of the states involved, were either unneces-
sary or undesirable, and he ordered them terminated. The proposed
Meramec Dam was one of these.

[1975]

8. Solo: Jal, New Mexico

The Jal General Hospital stands on a little rise on gravelly ground just west of the town of Jal, in the rich Permian Basin oil fields of southeastern New Mexico. It was built as a unit of the Lea County hospital system in 1961; it has fifteen double rooms, an emergency room, and two operating rooms; and it serves a community of almost forty-five hundred people. The hospital staff consists of one full-time registered nurse, two part-time registered nurses, seven full-time licensed vocational nurses, three part-time licensed vocational nurses, two nurse's aides, an office manager, two secretaries, a dietary supervisor and four kitchen workers, a janitor, a housekeeper, a laboratory and X-ray technician, and a physician. The physician, whom I recently got to know, is a general practitioner of forty named Elwood L. Schmidt, and he is the only doctor in town.

I came to Jal from Texas—West Texas. I drove from the airport at Midland through Odessa and Notrees and Kermit in a rented car with the radio shouting Pentecostal hymns: "I will never let the Devil win/I will never compromise with sin." Kermit is fifty miles from Odessa, and Jal is eighteen miles (and just across the Texas—New Mexico line) from Kermit, and it was desert all the way. It was flat red sand and gray gravel, mesquite and bunchgrass and tumbleweed, and there were oil wells everywhere. Most of the wells were pumping, and often in the distance there was a silver skyline cluster of bulk-storage tanks and fractionating towers. Along the road were red warning signs: "Caution: Low Pressure Gas Line," "Caution: High Pressure Oil Pipe Line," "Caution: Telephone Cable Underground." There was always a circling hawk in the high blue sky overhead, and the driver of every car I passed raised a finger from the wheel in greeting. I spent the night at the Circle A Motel, on the eastern outskirts of Jal (where I learned from a Chamber of Commerce brochure that the town took its curious name from the cattle brand of an early settler named J. A. Lynch), and ate an early breakfast with a crowd of hardhat roustabouts at a highway café called Theresa's, and then drove out to the hospital to meet Dr. Schmidt in time for his morning rounds.

The hospital is a long, low building, built of cement blocks painted the color of adobe, with a dusty planting of yuccas out front. I left my car in the parking lot and went into the waiting room. There was a row of chairs along one wall, and across from them were a bench and a little table piled with tattered magazines. On the bench lay a gray-haired man in work clothes and stocking feet. He was asleep and snoring, and he smelled of beer. Through a doorway at the end of the room was a long corridor lined with closed doors: "Emergency Room," "Men," "Janitor," "No Smoking." The "No Smoking" door opened, and Dr. Schmidt emerged—a big man with short, light hair, a long, flat nose, and a wide, smiling mouth. His trousers were green, his jacket was a green-and-brown check, his shirt was yellow, and he wore a yellow-and-brown-striped tie. Behind him came a young nurse in a white uniform.

"This is Edna Jean Featherston," he said. "Edna Jean is one of our L.V. N.s, and she is also my rounds nurse this morning." He looked down at the man on the bench. "This poor fellow lost his wife a couple of years back. She died here at the hospital. Sometimes, when he has a few too many, he comes up here to sleep it off. Memories, I suppose. Well, I've got some patients to see. Let's get going."

The rounds cart was waiting down the corridor, in front of the nursing station. It was a metal teacart spread with medical supplies and equipment. Eight patients' charts in metal binders hung on a rack at one end. Dr. Schmidt took a swallow of coffee from a mug on the cart and hung a stethoscope around his neck. Mrs. Featherston got behind the cart, and we followed him down the hall—past a painting of an oil well with cacti and mountains in the background, past "Nursery," past "Laboratory"—to an unmarked door on the left. He took a chart from the rack (*Bruce Marts, 45. Turbine operator, El Paso Natural Gas Co. Duodenal ulcer*) and opened the door.

"How do you feel, Bruce?"

"I feel good. I feel like a fiddle."

"Have you stopped smoking?"

"Well . . ."

"All right. If I send you home with some tablets, can you function?"

"You mean can I work? I think so. I'm ready to try."

"All right. Now hear this. Cigarette smoking is *not* good for your ulcer. This is accepted by medicine as a *fact*. So *don't*. Whatever the temptation. Or provocation. Whatever happens on the job. Whatever somebody says to you. Or whatever they don't say. I know what I'm asking—I haven't had a cigarette in my mouth for sixteen months three weeks and four days, but I still remember the pleasure. I remember, but I don't smoke. And I don't have an ulcer. So."

"Well—I'll keep trying."

"I'll see you at my office in, let's say, two months."

"All right. But, you know, I've been laying here thinking. I mean, all that terrible pain, and you say this ulcer wasn't no bigger than the end of a matchstick."

Robert Snider, 27. Machine operator, Trans-West Pipeline Mainte-nance Co. Upper respiratory infection.

"I didn't hear you hacking as I came down the hall. You must be getting better."

"I been coughing."

"Let's take a look at your ears. Well, that looks better. Now let's see your throat. Uh-huh. And your chest sounds pretty nice. How about your belly?"

"Well, it don't really ache. It just feels sour down there."

"You've got a good X ray. No ulcer. And the signs are good. But I think we'll check your stomach acids. It's no problem unless you gag easily. It's just a matter of putting a tube down your throat."

"Whatever you say. But I sure don't feel like going home. I still feel sour."

Jack McKeown, 68. Cotton farmer. Observation.

"Well, Jack, you're looking a lot better than you did when they dragged you in last night."

"I feel a lot better."

"Let me hear your heart. Bang, bang, bang—real good. Real strong. Now give me your arm. I want to check your blood pressure. Mmm. OK. No problem there. And the electrocardiogram we took last night was fine. I think we'll take another—just to be sure. But now I want to know a little more about what happened. You weren't doing a whole lot of talking last night. All I know is you were sitting in the pool hall and all of a sudden—what? You passed out?"

"I don't rightly know. I was setting there watching some fellows playing dominoes, and I come on gradually sick. I felt dizzy, like I was drunk. But I hadn't had a drink of anything all day. Not even a Coke. I hadn't even eaten anything since breakfast. I drove up to

Lubbock, where I got a farm, and I started to work breaking land and I guess I just forgot about dinner. Then I come back home and stopped at the pool hall, and that was when it happened. The next thing I knew was some fellows were shaking me and I was wet with sweat and I must have been asleep."

"Jack, I think you're crazy. I think you're a plain damn fool. You drove—how far is it to your place?"

"It's a hundred and ten miles, about."

"You drove a hundred and ten miles up and a hundred and ten miles back, and plowed I don't know how many acres of land, and didn't eat any dinner or even drink a Coke, and you're sixty-eight years old. There may be something serious here, and I'm sure going to find out, but I doubt it. My guess is you just plain wore yourself out."

"Well, I'm resting now."

Johnny Mack Owen II, 9. Father, office clerk, El Paso Natural Gas Co. Possible duodenal ulcer.

"Good morning, Johnny Mack. What's that you're reading?"

"It isn't reading. It's a crossword puzzle."

"How's your belly?"

"It feels OK."

"Let's see what it sounds like. Mmm. It's growling pretty good."

"Did you get the X rays done?"

"I did. And they don't show an ulcer. They don't show what we call a crater. That's like a little hole. But I don't think that means you haven't got an ulcer. It's like when you're out hunting and you find some deer tracks in the snow. Then you see some deer droppings. Then you come to a tree where a deer has rubbed his horns. Well, you haven't seen an actual deer, but you know there's one around. You presume he's there. It's the same with you. We don't see an ulcer, but we can presume from various signs that it's probably there."

"Oh. I'd like to go deer hunting in the mountains sometime."

"I'm sure you will."

"What's a 'mimic'?"

"What? Oh, you mean for your puzzle. It means to make like. To imitate."

"Like a monkey?"

"Right. I'll see you tonight."

* * *

Laura Lee Whipple, 31. Husband, welder, Jal Welding & Machine Works. Vomiting.

"I don't know. I guess I'm some better."

"No more nausea?"

"Not really. And I did eat some breakfast."

"Good. And you didn't have any nausea yesterday. Well, why don't I let you go home? I guess I will. Now—what to do at home. Frequent small meals. I won't try to tell you that this is the end of it. That would be a story. But the end will come—it's bound to come when the baby is born. You know that from the last time."

"I don't know why I feel this way, Doctor. I didn't feel like this when I was carrying my first baby. I felt real happy. And the second one, too. It seemed to begin with the third. And now—you know, I think this is the worst of all."

"Yes. Well. And now—when you see your friends, what are you going to say? Do you have to say, 'I've been in the hospital for three days because I'm pregnant again and I can't keep a thing on my stomach'? No, you don't. Tell them this: 'I had a touch of hyperemesis gravidarum.'"

"What in the world does that mean?"

"It means 'I'm pregnant and I can't keep a thing on my stomach.'"

Joe Don Evans, 31. Radio operator, El Paso Natural Gas Co. Bronchitis.

"Joe Don here is one of my showpieces. Am I right, Edna Jean? He's one of the very few patients I've ever done a tonsillectomy on. I don't believe in routine tonsillectomies. I think it's a pernicious operation. Most doctors feel the same. It's the public that believes in tonsillectomies. They want to have the children's tonsils out because it's a tradition. It's American. But Joe Don was a different case. His tonsils were a mess. They had to come out. How are you this morning?"

"I'm not as miserable as I was."

"Your chest sounds good. Is it hurting any?"

"I don't hurt anywhere."

"Maybe we can get you out of here by Sunday. The only thing your tests still show is a little white-blood-cell elevation."

"Let's make it Saturday."

"Saturday? You got a big night planned?"

"You know about Saturday—it's Hal Baker's barbecue. Aren't you and Fay going?"

"What's he barbecuing?"

"Goat, man. You tell him, Edna Jean. San Angelo goat. Hal and them were out getting mesquite for the fire last week."

"Well, then. I guess you might be there. I'll think about it, anyway."

Lavinia Tredway, 52. Husband, housepainter & roustabout. Acute bronchitis & anxiety state.

"They tell me you're still coughing."

"Not too much."

"And you're still on those damn cigarettes."

"I've been trying not to."

"Well, keep trying. It's your only hope. Now breathe for me. I want to listen to your chest. You sound better—and you look a little bit better. What does your husband say?"

"He come in here last night thinking to be nice by visiting me. He'd changed his clothes and everything. I guess it was for me. But I don't know. It wasn't too good. We got a little nervous."

"Was he—"

"I don't believe he'd had a single drink. You know, Doctor, I just don't understand this drinking. I don't mean him. I mean me. I don't ever really want a drink. I mean, why do I take that first drink? That sure isn't my idea of a good time. People say there's nothing to do around here but drink. But I know people that don't drink. Maybe I ought to play cards. Or go to the cockfights. I wish they had a movie. I like to cook a good dinner. But something always seems to happen. You know that burn on my elbow— where I leaned on a cigarette? I didn't even feel it. "

"How much were you smoking then? How many packs a day?"

"Three, I guess. No, I'll be honest—it was more like four."

"Well, you've made some progress. And you're pretty well dried out."

"I don't even like the taste of *beer*."

William Harris, 28. Electrician, El Paso Natural Gas Co. Back pain.

"Good news, Bill. The X rays of your back are all right. Nothing showed. How do you feel?"

"I feel better. I feel real good."

"Those are sweet words to a doctor. You mean, no pain at all?"

"Not really. You know, I wish I knew how this happened. That motor I was lifting, it didn't weigh much more than a hundred and fifty pounds, and I can lift that easy. Heck, I'm a weight lifter, you know that. I guess what I did was pick it up a little twisted."

"I'll bet you dropped it real fast."

"Oh, I didn't drop it. It hurt like heck, but I carried it on over to the pump. Shoot, you can't just drop a valuable electric motor like that."

"Swing your feet over the side of the bed and let's look at your reflexes. Good—that's good. I think you are a whole lot better. Now let's see you stand up. Now walk over to the door and back. That's right—keep walking. Yesh, offisher, I can walk that there line as straight as anybody. Very good. Now, I'm going to give you some exercises. You know them. You learned them in the service. They'll give you something to do when you're tired of reading— what's that magazine there? . . . Oh? Well, now. I didn't know you were a drag racer, Bill."

"Oh, sure."

"Bill, I will say you're much farther along than I expected. But I have to say this. There's always a chance that you'll cough and *bang*—a setback. I'm telling you so you won't worry if it happens. It's not at all uncommon with a back like yours."

"What do you call a back like mine?"

"I don't know. There isn't a name for everything. It don't have to have a name to hurt, and it don't have to have a name to be treated. I know folks like to have things named. But I can't always oblige."

"Well, I'll try not to cough."

Harris was the end of morning rounds. I looked at my watch: it was nine-twenty. We went back up the long hall. Johnny Mack Owen's door was open. He was sitting up in bed with the television on, a model airplane in his lap, and a book in his hand: *The Mystery of the Mountain Cave*. We left Mrs. Featherston and the cart at the nursing station, and the duty nurse handed Dr. Schmidt a handful of memoranda. He stuffed them in his pocket. The sleeper was gone from the waiting room. Outside, there was a pale-blue Mercury sedan parked at a "Doctors Only" sign.

"Have you got a car?" Dr. Schmidt said. "Well, leave it here and ride back to my office with me. You can pick it up later. We'll be coming back here again. And, probably, again. Well, that was nice and quiet, wasn't it? No crises. Although I must say I've been a little bit worried about Bruce Marts and that ulcer of his. I mean, this isn't his first one."

"You seem to see a lot of ulcers."

"Right. There *are* a lot of ulcers. Johnny Mack's dad has one, and so does his mother. I don't know why. I wish I did. Except that most of the plants here work their people on rotating shifts—tours, they call them. That can play hell with the human body. I never take any chances with an ulcer. They frighten me. I have an old fellow in the hospital at Kermit who has me scared to death. I was conditioned on ulcers by a teacher at medical school. I'm from South Texas, and I studied at the University of Texas Medical Branch, at Galveston. I graduated in 1956. That's where I met my wife. Ila Fay is a Texan, too, from Amarillo, and she's also an R.N. She worked until the children began to come along. Well, that teacher taught me that an untreated ulcer was a cocked pistol. When something suggests an ulcer to me, I want that man in the hospital. Of course, hospitalization isn't the problem here that it is in so many places. We usually have a bed, and the expense doesn't matter too much. Our big industry in Jal is El Paso Natural Gas. They've got four big plants and their Permian Division offices here. I understand there are pipelines under practically every inch of Lea County. Anyway, El Paso has a very liberal health-insurance program. They take good care of their people. El Paso built my office in order to get a doctor here. Not me—my predecessor, Dr. O'Loughlin. And they charge me a very nominal rent. Dr. O'Loughlin left soon after I arrived, in 1961. He's practicing in Abilene now. I wish he had stayed here. I wish I had *some* help. You know, it's almost funny. I came here because Dr. O'Loughlin needed help. I was practicing in Slaton, Texas, up near Lubbock, and Slaton was over-doctored. It was full of doctors, and I had so little to do I was bored to death, and when the Jal Chamber of Commerce advertised for another doctor I jumped at the chance. And now look at me! I haven't had a day off in four months. Solo practice has its satisfactions, but this is just a little too solo. My God, when my wife and I want to be alone for a little while at night I've got to take the telephone off the hook." We turned off the highway and drove down a long, bare block of little brick houses set in little bare yards. We passed a new brick post office on a lawn with a flagpole. We turned into Main Street, a wide business street with a concrete mall down the middle and two blocks of one-story buildings—Wacker's Variety Store, City Barber Shop, Jal Recreation Center, Aunt Dorothy's Cafe, Roy & Rena's Bar, Midget Cafe, Bob's Superette, Cactus Bar, New Mexico Bank & Trust Co., Bert's Place, Lewis Drugs, Jal Cleaners, McKeown's Dry Goods. We turned off Main Street and pulled up at a one-story cement-block building painted pale blue. It was planted with evergreens, and there was an inscription above the door: "Jal Medical Center."

"We'll go in the back way," Dr. Schmidt said. "The waiting room is just a waiting room, and it's probably full of folks. I see patients from when I get here in the morning until they let me leave for lunch, and from when I get back until they stop coming. Everything opens off this hall. That door on the left is our X-ray room, and this one here is the laboratory. My girls do simple X rays and routine laboratory tests. I like to have a white blood count when somebody's got a cough or such. These four numbered doors are consultation rooms. The girls bring the patients in and get their histories and get them ready, and I see them in turn. My private office is here on the right, and this is the general office. I want you to meet Mary Butler. Mary is my receptionist and bookkeeper. And these lovely girls are the nurses. They work for me, and their husbands all work for El Paso. Cecilia Davis. Joan Roberts. Nadine Brookings. All right, girls. Quick—while I've got a chance—some coffee. And what are you all grinning about?"

"Here's a present for you, Doctor," Mrs. Davis said.

"Oh? Hey—chocolate-chip cookies. And homemade. Where did they come from?"

"Dana Riggs brought them in on her way to school."

"Well, now. Wasn't that nice!"

"What I want to know is this," Mrs. Butler said. "Why are you getting presents from a pretty girl like Dana?"

"I let her correct my grammar when she was in here yesterday," Dr. Schmidt said. "I let her think she knew the difference between 'shall' and 'will.'"

We drank our coffee (sweetened with saccharin and stirred with a wooden tongue depressor) in Dr. Schmidt's office. The office was hung with framed diplomas and certificates—from the University of Texas at Galveston; from White Cross Hospital, in Columbus, Ohio (where he interned); from the American Academy of General Practice—and his desk was piled with books and papers and periodicals, and decorated with two standing photographs. One was a studio triptych of his children (three small boys), and the other was a grinning chimpanzee in a doctor's white coat, with the caption "Whatever it was you had, you've got it again." Dr. Schmidt sipped his coffee and looked at his mail and ate a chocolate-chip cookie. The telephone rang, and he answered it ("Oh? No—that's not too good. . . . Yes, I do. . . . I'll turn you back to Nadine. She'll give you an appointment") and wrote something on a memorandum pad and ate another cookie. There was a knock at the door, and Mrs. Roberts looked in. Dr. Schmidt nodded, and drank the last of his coffee and stood up. We went out and across the hall to a numbered door with a folder clipped to the panel. He took down the folder and gave it a glance *(Mrs. Burma Cusenbary, 33. Husband, electrician, El Paso Natural Gas Co. Pain)* and opened the door.

"You, too? That husband of yours was in here just the other day about cutting his finger half off. What's *your* trouble?"

"You're going to laugh at me. But my jaw hurts. It hurts when I chew. It's like there's something wrong with my wisdom teeth. Only I don't have any wisdom teeth anymore."

"Very good. Your description is excellent. There's a six-hundred-page book devoted to the joint where the jaw hooks onto the skull, and it doesn't say it any better than you did. They call it the temporomandibular joint. Has it ever locked on you?"

"Oh, yes. That's what is so embarrassing. Sometimes when I'm laughing I can't close it—I have to take my hands and *push* it shut."

"Well, you can get arthritis there like anywhere else. The question is, what do we do?"

"I suppose you could amputate my jaw."

"That may not be necessary. Let's try aspirin first. Let's say eight or ten tablets every day, and take them at mealtime. I think that may be all you need. If not, we'll start thinking about a dentist. How's Phil doing?"

"He's fine. But he was lucky, wasn't he?"

"He could have lost the end of his finger, you mean? Yes, he was lucky."

Cavin Horne, 5. Father, rig operator, El Paso Natural Gas Co. Cough.

"Good morning, Mrs. Horne. Good morning, Cavin. So your mother is making you play hooky from kindergarten."

"I didn't want to take any chances, Doctor. He was coughing again, and he had a fever of 101.2 last night."

"Mmm. I don't hear any wheezing. I don't find any evidence of pneumonia. I think he's just back on his old bronchitis. You're a pretty experienced patient, aren't you, Cavin? We've got a real big history on you for a boy of five—including a duodenal ulcer. But we'll lick 'em yet."

"I wonder, Doctor. His sister, you know, she went through a period like this, with a regular cough and a runny nose, but she finally outgrew it. Do you think maybe Cavin will do the same?"

"Could be, I guess. But you're right about kindergarten. I'm afraid Cavin will be playing hooky all the rest of the week."

"Did I tell you we're moving? I think where we're going there may be less dust. I hope so—for all our allergies. What do you think?"

"I think it's dusty everywhere."

Benjamin May, 21. Production dispatcher, El Paso Natural Gas Co. Knee.

"That's an ugly-looking knee. What did you do to it?"

"It's a floor burn. I got it playing basketball out at the plant. Then it like got infected."

"So I see. Now I'll tell you what you're going to do. One: get some soap and work up a thick lather on your knee. Two: rub this ointment on it. Three: here are some penicillin tablets. That's for the infection, in case it's strep. I could do a ten-dollar laboratory analysis and wait five days for the results to come back, but I'm going to save you time and money and assume it's strep."

"OK."

"Now, wait a minute. That isn't all. I'm going to give you a free lecture. The subject is that red stuff you painted on your knee— whatever it is. That's what caused all this trouble. I know this goes against your lifelong American sports tradition, but never, *never,* NEVER put that red stuff on a wound. It burns it. It irritates it. It's *no good* on broken skin. And try to keep from falling down for the next five days."

Cynthia Wood, 8. Father, head of W. E. Gray Roustabout Service. Rash.

"Doctor, I want you to look at this child. I don't know what you're going to say, but I got to thinking and worrying. Her first bumps come out about a week ago. Now those on her back look like they're getting well. The ones on her stomach there, they're the newest ones. Now, what comes to my mind was the chicken pox."

"Oh?"

"That's right. That's exactly what I got to thinking."

"Well, let's take a look. I'm looking at your stomach, Cynthia. And now I'm pinching something between my fingers. What do you think it's called?"

"Fat?"

"Right. And what do you think you ought to do about it?"

"Diet?"

"Right. You don't want to be a big fat girl that can't play and have any fun. Now, about this rash. I don't think it's chicken pox. I don't think it's an allergy, like hives. I think these are some kind of bug bites. Do you-all have a dog?"

"A dog? We got a hound."

"Good. I suggest you go on home and look him over for fleas. Meanwhile, I'll give Cynthia some oral antihistamine for the itching. And let me know about the dog."

Jack Leisure, 46. Jal Water Dept. Ulcer.

"This is just a checkup, isn't it, Jack?"

"That's right. I'm doing real good. I think that ulcer is all healed up."

"I think so, too. I think it started healing the minute you sold your filling station and went back to work for the city."

"I know it did. I shouldn't never have tried it on my own. It don't make me happy to be the boss. I'd rather somebody else had the worries."

"You had a sad experience. But I guess it was instructive."

"I learned a lot. I learned that when you give your friends credit and they don't pay, you lose your money and you lose your friends, both."

Mrs. Sandra Phillips, 22. Husband, welder. Pregnant.

"I don't know what I'm going to do with you."

"I'm too heavy, ain't I?"

"You're much too heavy. Do you know what you weigh? Two hundred and three pounds. Now, listen to me. Excessive weight gain in the first pregnancy is associated with a lot of troubles. It's courting disaster. I mean, it's dangerous. Your blood pressure is borderline high. Good nutrition is important for you and the baby, but too much is too much."

"My husband, he don't help me."

"What do you mean?"

"I try to cut down on eating and he gets mad. He goes on like crazy. He says I'm starving the baby."

"Well, I say you aren't. You tell him to stop practicing medicine. I don't tell him how to weld."

Mrs. Barbara Stirman, 57. Husband, pipe fitter. Gallstones.

"You're looking pretty good, Mrs. Stirman. I hope you feel that way."

"I guess I do—at times. But that diet you gave me. It's a problem. Everything is so difficult here. I guess I'm spoiled. My husband had three solid years of work in one place before we came here. We even had a house. I don't know, I get so sick of travelling from job to job. You know, we've been in Alaska and up in Montana and in Wyoming and over to Oklahoma. It was nice having a house. But now we're back in a trailer, and it's crowded and it's cold and the windows are drafty. And the stores here. You can't buy anything bigger than a match except you go down to Kermit or Odessa. You can't get skim milk. You can't get dry cottage cheese. That's what I meant about your diet. And then last night I ate something that made me sick. I guess it was the spaghetti."

"Well, that wasn't real sensible, was it?"

"I guess not. But I get so blue. Living in a trailer and all."

"How are you sleeping?"

"Oh, I sleep all right. I never complain about sleeping. But did you ever hear of somebody having triple vision?"

"I've heard of everything. Do you have it?"

"Yes."

"When did it begin?"

"I was going down the hall of the trailer, and it hit me just like that. It was like that vent you've got up there on the wall—I see three of it. It's a crazy feeling."

"I'm sure it is. But I don't think we'll change anything. I think we'll stay with the prescriptions you have for another two weeks. Then call me."

"I don't even have a telephone in that trailer."

Jennifer Hicks, 8 months. Father, pastor, Church of Christ Church. Cough.

"Well, Mrs. Hicks, how are you liking Jal by now?"

"I like it fine—we both do."

"I forget where you come from."

"From Roby. I come from Roby, Texas. That's up near Abilene. But I didn't live right in town. I lived, oh my goodness, ten miles out of town. That's how I come to mislike towns. Jal is just about right for me—for us. I'm not so much on this fast pace of living."

"Well, I know what you mean. But what's the trouble with Jennifer?"

"I thought she sounded croupy. She sounded awful croupy yesterday. And this morning she woke up crying."

"Her white blood count is normal. But I'm just a little bit worried. I'm wondering if this is asthma. But I have to say no to that. You don't see asthma in a baby under two. Does that mean she's likely to develop asthma later on? Yes, it does. It's very possible. Is there anything to do? Probably not. But we're going to try diet—a milk-free diet. And a dust-free environment. And I'm going to prescribe an antihistamine. Then we'll see."

"You think she's going to get asthma?"

"It's possible. But we can take comfort in the old saying: All that wheezes is not asthma. Suppose you bring her back in about ten days."

Mrs. Billie Beaird, 33. Husband, head of Jal Gas Co. Ear.

"Tell me about your ear."

"Well, it started out just itching. Then it got kind of sore. Then it started roaring. It's this left one. And it bothers me."

"OK. Now—open your mouth."

"You want to look in my mouth?"

"I thought I might."

"Then wait a sec. I got to get rid of my gum."

"I'll wait. All right? OK. Now turn your head so I can look at your ears. Mmmm. And you can go back to your gum if you like."

"I swallowed it."

"Well, that's getting rid of it. About your ear. I think what you've got is a nervous rash. I'm going to give you some eardrops. *My God!* I'm prescribing eardrops. Well, there are times when they are indicated, and this is one of those times."

Fernando Acosta, 28. Jal Water Dept. Burn.

"How in the name of God did you do it?"

"I spilled some sulfuric acid. I splashed some on my pants and —oh, Jesus, it burned right through to my leg. So quick. Then it began to hurt. I washed it off with soap and water, and somebody gave me this salve. Is it any good?"

"Only for the manufacturer. Give it to me. See that wastebasket over there? Now watch. Gone. I'll give you something that *will* help—an antibiotic ointment. But that damn stuff you had—it makes me mad. It makes me furious. Some damn fool congressman will stand up and raise Cain about the Pill. That gets his name in the paper. Why don't they speak out about these damn benzocaine preparations? They're promoted for topical anesthesia for burns and abrasions, and they help very little or none. They can actually be harmful. There are local reactions and systemic reactions and severe allergic reactions— all possible and all well reported. But I guess there's more goddam political mileage in yelling about the Pill."

* * *

Mrs. Eloise Dobbs, 38. Husband, feed store. Chest pain.

"This whole side of my chest hurts, Elwood. It really hurts."

"What about your heart—any irregular beat?"

"I haven't noticed any. Elwood, I just want to feel good again."

"That's a reasonable request. And I think it's very possible you will."

"But what do you think? Is it my heart? Is it my lungs?"

"Now, you won't believe this—but I don't know. I do not know. But I wonder. Are you lifting any sacks down at the store?"

"I lift some. But only fifty pounds or so. And only for the woman customers."

"I think you'd better let your lady customers lift their own sacks. If I know those ladies, they can do it just as well as you can. Maybe better."

Lester Sharp, 62. Operator. Pain.

"Well, Lester—what is it today?"

"I got trouble. That goddam pain."

"You mean your ulcer? Or your arthritis?"

"I mean my leg. That damn pain goes right down my leg. I called you the other day, but you were out."

"The girls said you called, but you didn't make an appointment."

"No, I didn't. I was in pain. I went to see a doctor in Kermit. But he didn't give me no satisfaction. None at all. Then I tried a chiropractor and—"

"All right, Lester. Don't tell me about your chiropractor, you hear? Or I'll get mad, real mad."

"I tell you this pain hasn't let me be in two whole weeks. Oh, damn, I need help."

"Then drop your pants and get up on the table. Is this the spot?"

"That and all around there."

"All right. I'm going to give you two injections. The first is a local anesthetic. Roll over on your belly and hold still. I said hold still. And this one is cortisone. I think—God damn it, Lester, hold still! You've got a three-inch needle sticking in your butt. How's your ulcer?"

"It's all right. It don't bother me much."

"Is that a fact? Well, I'm surprised. One of the girls saw you at the store the other day. She said you were buying a carton of cigarettes and a case of Coke."

"Ohhh. By God, I feel better already. I think you saved my life."

Dr. Schmidt and I had our lunch (or noon dinner) in Kermit. He had two Medicare patients in Memorial Hospital there whom he wished to see. Memorial, where Dr. Schmidt has staff privileges, is a large hospital with an intensive-care unit and other sophisticated facilities not available at Jal General. We stopped at the hospital first. One of the patients was an elderly woman in intensive care. The other was the man of whom he had spoken—an elderly man with a duodenal ulcer. ("Frank's been bleeding on and off all week," Dr. Schmidt said as we left the hospital. "I don't know how many pints of blood we've had to give him. He also has congestive heart failure and emphysema. But you noticed when we came into the room—there he was with a cigarette in his mouth.") Kermit is the seat of Winkler County, and we lunched (or dined) at a café on the courthouse square called Dolly's Family Style Meals. We shared a table for eight with five other men. Dr. Schmidt knew them all. The food was on the table, and we helped each other and ourselves. There was a platter of sliced pot roast and a bowl of chicken fricassee. There were yellow grits and mashed potatoes and giblet dressing and sweet potatoes with marshmallows. There were black-eyed peas and red beans and green beans and collard greens and carrots and broccoli and creamed corn and a gravy boat of pepper sauce. There was Waldorf salad and fruit salad and combination salad. There was corn bread and rolls and hot biscuits. There was a pound of butter on a plate and a bowl of grape jelly. There was iced tea and hot coffee. Dessert was peach cobbler. There was no tipping. We paid the cashier. There was a dish of after-dinner mints on the counter and a cup of toothpicks. Our lunches (or dinners) were a dollar and a half apiece.

"I don't eat like that every day," Dr. Schmidt said. "I usually go home for lunch. Although I will say Aunt Dorothy's Cafe in Jal has a real good meat loaf. When the weather is nice, I like to walk to lunch. It's about a mile from my office to home, and I need the exercise. Of course, it isn't easy. I can hardly walk a block without somebody driving by and stopping with something they want to ask me about. This is good country for walking. We don't have any hills, and it almost never rains. Our New Mexico weather is really pretty nice. They tell about a couple of old girls living up on the New Mexico–Colorado line in a strip of country that both states claimed. For a while, it was called New Mexico. Then Colorado took it over. Finally, the states agreed to submit the matter to arbitration, and the day the commission announced its decision one old girl came running home with the news: Their land was in New Mexico. The other old girl gave a sigh. 'Well, thank heavens,' she said. 'I tell you, Mary Flo, I just don't think I could have stood another of those Colorado winters.' I like that story. So true. And I like this kind of day. Not too cool. Very little wind. I suppose there are people somewhere out playing golf today. Dreams of bliss. Playing golf in the middle of the week. I've done it once or twice. I remember the last time. I was playing with a doctor friend in Kermit, and he mentioned a patient of his who was having a sleep problem. He was waking up very early and he couldn't get back to sleep. He lay there thinking. There were a couple of other things my doctor friend told me, and I said it sounded to me like a case of depression—endogenous depression. I said if the man were my patient I'd hospitalize him for some close observation. People like that have a high suicide potential. Just getting them into the hospital environment is sometimes a very big help. The home can be the enemy, you know. In that and a lot of other conditions. Anyway, I was eating supper that night when the phone rang, and it was my Kermit friend. He thought I would be interested to know that the fellow we were talking about that afternoon had just put a shotgun in his mouth and blown his head off."

It was almost two o'clock when we got back to the Medical Center in Jal. I counted five cars nosed in at the curb in front. One of them had a bumper sticker: "Why Not? Jal, N.M." The doors of all the consultation rooms were closed, and there were folders already clipped to the panels. Dr. Schmidt took off his checked jacket and sat down at his desk and looked at a long memorandum. The telephone rang.

"Yes," he said. "I was just looking at it. I'll see him on evening rounds. Thank you, Nadine. . . . What? . . . All right—put her on." He looked at me and made a long face. "Hello? . . . Yes? . . . Oh, no. . . . Oh, dear. . . . Oh, hell. . . . That's bad news. I guess we were a little too optimistic. Oh, yes—by all means. I'll have one of the girls make the arrangements. And don't you worry about anything. I'll see you tonight at the hospital." He hung up. "That was the pregnant lady we saw at the hospital this morning. Poor girl. As soon as she got home, she started vomiting again. I wish all my cases were as easy to understand as that. It's all very sad and simple. The only trouble is, I can't do a whole lot for her." He pushed back his chair. "Well, let's see what's on the program for this afternoon."

* * *

Steven Brooks, 16. Father, operator. Ear.

"Hello, Steve. My God—what did you do to your hair?"

"I guess I kind of let it grow."

"I guess you did—all the way. Well, what's this about your ear?"

"It's my right ear. It's just been, you know, ringing."

"Nobody fetched you like a clout on that ear?"

"Oh, no. But it seems like—You remember I had mononucleosis a while back. It seems like I've been noticing this ringing since about then."

"I guess there could be some connection. But that's pretty farfetched. Tell me more."

"Well, I wash my hair a lot. And then, of course, I've got this little rock band. I play drums."

"Go on. You have my full attention."

"Well, I spend a lot of time, you know, practicing? I mean, I set my drums between the speakers and turn them up pretty high. You think that could be it?"

"I think I'll see how well you hear this tuning fork. Now, tell me when you stop hearing the sound. . . . Yes? . . . OK? . . . Now? . . . Still hearing it? . . . Mmm. Well, your ears are balanced, and there's no hearing loss as far as I can tell from this. But amplified music—any kind of amplified music—can result in definite hearing loss. There have been a lot of studies on that subject lately. It's like working in a boiler factory. I suggest you lay off practicing for a few days. And before you play your next gig, get yourself a pair of earplugs. They won't keep you from functioning, but they will cut down the noise. That's all I can suggest right now—give your ears a rest. If the ringing continues or gets worse, we'll think about a specialist."

"OK. Hey—I just thought of something, Doctor. I get some noise at school, too. I take welding in shop."

"Get those earplugs."

James Day, 4 weeks old, and Donald Day, 2. Father, pipe fitter, El Paso Natural Gas Co. Cough.

"What's this—an epidemic?"

"It's really just Jamie, Doctor. Little old Jamie, he can't hardly breathe. The minute he lays flat, he starts snorting. Don here, he's just got himself a cough. Jamie started in coughing the night before last. He eats fine. It's just that he has a rough time breathing."

"Well, let's take a look. Mmmm. Uh-huh. Well. What are you feeding him?"

"I just now started him on a little rice cereal."

"You did, eh? Very good. You did right. I give you an A in my record book. I like to see all my four-week-old babies started on rice cereal. OK. Now, I'm going to give you some nose drops for Jamie. I think we can forget about Don. He's all right. But about the nose drops—let's don't overdo it. I don't like those things—you can get hooked on them. Have you got a vaporizer?"

"Have I got a vaporizer? In Jal, New Mexico? Is there anybody here who hasn't got one?"

"Probably not. But get yours out. And keep in touch. I sure want to know if Jamie starts running any kind of fever."

Richard Muncrief, 12. Father, operator, El Paso Natural Gas Co. Backache.

"Hello, Mrs. Muncrief. Hi, Rick. Now, who's got the nagging backache?"

"Well, for once it isn't me, Doctor. It's Rick."

"Where does it hurt, Rick?"

"Up here—up along the spine. It hurts worst when I first get up."

"How about when you urinate?"

"A little bit."

"OK. Let's see if I can find anything. Lean to the right. Now to the left. Now back. Now toward your toes—way down. All right. How about joint pain?"

"No."

"Hip pain?"

"No."

"Here—kick my hand. Now the other foot."

"Rick isn't a complainer, Doctor. He really isn't. But he says it hurts awful, and when he says awful he means *awful.*"

"I don't doubt it. But I hear from my son Paul that you're still making early-morning basketball practice at school. "

"Well, yes."

"I'll tell you what I think. This could be either a minor or a chronic muscle pain. Early-morning backache—is it early arthritis of the spine? I can't say. The only way to find out is to test. I think it's significant enough to warrant coming in to the hospital some weekend soon for some tests and X rays. If they're positive for arthritis, then we'll know what to do. Why don't you-all figure out a good time and let me know. How's your little sister, Rick?"

"She's OK, I guess."

"Actually, Doctor, she's been running a little sugar. Maybe I'd better bring her in."

"Maybe you'd better."

Mrs. Lillie May Dunn, 72. Widow. Heart.

"I've got some questions for you, Lillie May. It's been over a year since you've been in here—why? And when your sister made this appointment, she told me you'd stopped taking your blood-pressure pills—why?"

"I don't know. I never liked those pills, I guess."

"Well, how do you feel?"

"The same—terrible."

"In what way?"

"Like I got up early and worked hard all day long."

"Well, I guess you know what that feels like."

"I sure do."

"I'm going to check your blood pressure. You don't have to hold your breath. Mmm. OK. Have you been sleeping all right?"

"I sleep all the time. I slept through the television yesterday afternoon. My favorite show, too."

"Are you short of breath?"

"Some."

"I'll tell you your trouble, Lillie May. You've been neglecting yourself. You've gone into heart failure. When I listen to your chest, I can hear a lot of what we call moist rales—a lot of mucus."

"Is that serious?"

"Of course it's serious. I'm going to send you to the hospital. You need some looking after."

"All right. But when?"

"In about an hour."

"From now?"

"That's right."

"How about tomorrow?"

"Tomorrow? You got something planned for this afternoon?"

"No. Uh, no—it isn't that. It just seemed so sudden."

Mitchell Brininstool, 16. Father, head of X-L Transportation Co. Stomachache.

"Elwood, I thought you'd better have a look at this boy."

"Right. What's your trouble, Mitchell?"

"He's got stomach cramps, Elwood, and he's nauseated and he's got diarrhea."

"What have you been eating, man?"

"Sometimes he eats what we eat and sometimes he eats junk. Teenage junk. I was worried about appendicitis."

"You want me to take his appendix out, JoAnn? Let's wait a minute. I ought to examine him first. Can you describe the pain, Mitchell? Where does it hurt?"

"It like comes and goes."

"That sounds like colic. Did you burp him, JoAnn?"

"It doesn't bother me at night, I sleep OK."

"Well, seriously, I don't think it's appendicitis. The pain in appendicitis is right around—you don't mind if I draw a diagram on your belly? That kind of pain is around here. And yours is over here. Also, this is a colicky pain. It's a spasm—literally a nervous gut. It's probably emotional in origin. I'm going to give you a prescription for a gut sedative. That will quiet you down, and I think you'll stop hurting. You play basketball, don't you, Mitchell?"

"Yes, sir."

"As a matter of fact, you're one of the leaders?"

"Well, I'm the captain."

"Right. And you're a blood player, aren't you? You want to win?"

"Yes, sir. I guess so."

"And the Jal Panthers haven't had too good a season this year, have they?"

"No, sir. It's been real bad. We lost again on Monday."

"OK, Mitchell. JoAnn, I guess I'll see you at Hal Baker's barbecue on Saturday. I hear he's barbecuing a goat."

"Yes. But, Elwood—my Lord! You mean Mitchell's trouble is nerves? You mean at sixteen years old he's got nerves? Just like all the rest of us?"

Cynthia Hurta, 15. Father, grocery store. Sore eye.

"It says here you've got a sore eye, Cynthia. Which eye?"

"It's this one—the left. I was helping Mom at the store, carrying stuff around, and, I don't know, maybe I got something in it, and I began to rub it and it was sore. That was last night."

"Let's take a look. Mmm. Right. You've got a nice little pimple there. But I need help—wait a minute. *Joan! Cecilia! Somebody!* Joan, I need you. Take this light. I'm going to nick the top off this pimple here. Now, hold the light—that's right. Now then."

"Doctor! You're not going to *cut* it off! With that *knife!* Oh, *no!"*

"Be quiet, Cynthia. You won't even feel it."

"Can't you use like a needle or something? Oh, Doctor— *please!"*

"There—it's done. What's the matter with you, Cynthia?"

"I guess I'm just a rotten coward."

"For heaven's sake. I wouldn't hurt you, baby. You know that."

"I thought you were going to like carve your initials."

"Nonsense. I like your sarape, Cynthia—all that fringe. *And* all those beads. They're delicious. You look good in beads."

"Good. Now, Dr. Schmidt, *you* hold still. I want to see how *you* look in love beads. Wow—you look terrific."

"Hey—I do, don't I?"

"Promise me you'll wear them?"

"I solemnly swear. Now, get out. I've cured you, baby. Go home."

Dr. Schmidt lives on a quiet street of mulberry trees and watered green lawns on the south side of town. The desert begins at the end of his street, and the nearest oil and gas plants are a couple of miles away and to leeward of the prevailing desert wind. His house is a rambling brick house with a walled garden in back and a big mimosa tree overhanging the front door. The door was opened by a boy in glasses and a Boy Scout T-shirt.

"This is Paul," Dr. Schmidt said. "Paul is my No. 1 son. No. 2 is Philip, and No. 3 is Tim. They're probably around here somewhere."

"They're out," Paul said.

A slim young woman with golden-red hair came into the room.

"And this is my wife," Dr. Schmidt said. "I'm home, Ila Fay. And I hope to God we've got time for a drink before supper. I'm just a little . . ."

"There's time," Mrs. Schmidt said. "You-all go in and sit down and I'll—*Elwood!* What in the world have you got around your neck?"

"Love beads, ma'am."

"Wow!"

"Yes. They're a present from a grateful patient—from Cynthia Hurta. She was that glad she survived a little operation this afternoon."

"Well," Mrs. Schmidt said. "Oh, Elwood—did Mrs. You-Know-Who call you?"

"No—why?"

"She called you here around noon. She said she was in pain. It was the most urgent, most unbearable distress. She said she was in such agony she could hardly hold the phone in her hand. I advised her to call the office. Then I went down to the store. And guess who I saw going into Susan's Beauty Parlor?"

We had our drinks in a family room that overlooked the walled garden. It was a big, comfortable room with a table set for supper at one end and a fireplace laid with piñon-pine logs at the other. A mounted nine-foot sailfish hung above the fireplace.

"That fish up there is documentary proof that I had a vacation once," Dr. Schmidt said. "I caught it—*Fay* and I caught it—down in Mexico. I was able to get me a locum tenens. I got my good friend Dr. Orene Whitcomb Peddicord, of Kermit, to look after my practice, and Fay and I had four fun-filled days and nights in Acapulco. I'm not really complaining. I only mean that I'd like to be able to count on a day off every now and then. I truly enjoy my practice. I like taking care of Jal. I like being a G.P. I like the variety. I don't think I could stand the sameness of the specialties. I wouldn't want to look at hearts all day. Or urinary tracts. Or pregnant women. On the other hand, I know my limitations—in surgery, anyway. I'll do an appendectomy, if I'm satisfied it's necessary. I do cesarean sections and hemorrhoidectomies. I do tubal ligations. I've got a D. & C.—dilation and curettage—scheduled for tomorrow morning. I don't do hysterectomies. I know when to refer, or defer, and—knock on wood and other superstitions—I've never had any serious trouble. I've never even had a malpractice suit. I think I'm a good family doctor. I think I do my job. But, you know, I sometimes wonder who in hell is going to take my place. Another G.P.? Not likely—we're a vanishing breed of cat. So who? A pediatrician? An internist? An obstetrician? A general surgeon? A dermatologist?"

The telephone rang. There was an extension on a table at Dr. Schmidt's elbow, and he answered it. He frowned. Mrs. Schmidt came in from the kitchen and stood in the doorway. Dr. Schmidt listened and nodded and grunted, and hung up.

"That was the hospital," he said, and got up from his chair.

"Oh dear," Mrs. Schmidt said.

"I know," he said. "But it shouldn't take too long. It's one of the Lister boys. They brought him in from wherever he works, and his mother is there, and she says he's ruptured himself."

"Well," she said. "There's no harm done. I haven't put the chops on yet. Just let me know when you're starting back."

* * *

I could hear somebody moaning and groaning as we came in the hospital door. A nurse was standing in the doorway of the emergency room. She gave Dr. Schmidt a knowing look. We went into the room. A young man in work clothes was lying on an examining table, and beside him stood a woman in a gray pants suit, with an elaborate pile of blond hair. She was holding his hand. When he saw us coming, he closed his eyes and opened his mouth and groaned.

The woman had a stricken look. "Oh," she said. "Oh, Dr. Schmidt."

"Well, Randy," Dr. Schmidt said. "Can you tell me what happened?"

"He was lifting a great big sack of cement."

"Can you tell me about it, Randy?"

"I—I guess so. But it's like Mom says. I was lifting this sack of cement and, I don't know, I got this terrible pain, and then I blacked out, and—Oh, it hurts. It *hurts.*"

"Can you show me where?"

"Me?"

"Yes, Randy. Show me with your hand. I see. All across there? How about here? OK. Now—can you sit up?"

"Ohhh . . ."

"OK, Randy. That's enough. Well, what you've done is pulled a muscle down there. I don't believe you've got a rupture. I do believe you'll be all right. I'm going to give you a shot of Demerol to make you comfortable. That's just about all I can do."

"Are you going to keep him, Doctor?"

"You mean, admit him? Of course I'm going to admit him. He's hurt, and I want to be sure his trouble is what I think it is. Why?"

"Well, I'm just standing here thinking. You know, about the insurance. If he don't stay overnight, the insurance don't pay for any of this."

"I see. All right, Randy. The nurse will get you settled. I'll see you on evening rounds."

We walked back to the nursing station. There were two nurses there. One of them was an elderly woman in the Pink Lady uniform of a volunteer. Dr. Schmidt sat down at a desk and began filling out the admittance and order forms on Randy Lister. A teenage girl in jeans and a Jal Panthers football jersey came up the corridor.

"Dr. Schmidt?"

"Yes?"

"I'm Billy Will's friend—Billy Will Sharp?"

"Right."

"Yes. And Billy Will's hungry? He wants to know can I get him something to eat."

"Oh? And what's he hungry for?"

"He says he wants a cheeseburger."

"I see. And did he happen to tell you why I've got him here in the hospital?"

"Oh, sure. He's been having this pain in his stomach, and—"

"That's right. You tell him he can have a milkshake."

Dr. Schmidt went back to his forms. It was almost seven o'clock, and I was getting hungry myself. The telephone rang. The nurse answered it and looked at Dr. Schmidt.

"Are you here?"

"I guess so," he said, and took the receiver. "Hello? . . . Yes. . . . Oh—is that so? Mmm. Right. . . . Right. . . . OK." He handed the receiver back to the nurse. He shook his head. "Son of a bitch," he said. "Here's a man with nothing wrong with him except he's drunk by noon every day of his life and now his wife calls up—and call out the Marines! He's sick! He's got pains. He hurts. There are too many goddamned people in this town who think I'm like the light switch over there on the wall. Switch it on. Day or night. Rain or shine. And I'll come running. But I *ain't* a switch. I got rights. I'm a hooman bein'."

"What are you going to do?" I said.

"Do?" he said. "About the son of a bitch? Why, I'm going over to see him."

[1972]

9. The River World: Life on the Mississippi

The Lesta K., a square-nosed, diesel-powered towboat owned and operated by the Port City Barge Line, of Greenville, Mississippi, is pushing slowly down the Missouri River toward St. Louis behind a tow of big red hopper barges loaded with Nebraska wheat and Kansas flour. There are eight barges in the tow—each riding nine feet deep in the water under fifteen hundred tons of cargo—and they are lashed two abreast. They form a raft-like mass just about seventy feet wide and almost eight hundred feet long. At the head of the tow, where I am sitting on a coil of rigging near the bow of the starboard barge, there is the feel of a raft—a peaceful sense of drifting, a sense of country quiet. The only sound is the slap of water under the rake of the bow. I am alone and half asleep in the silence and the warmth of the mild midmorning sun. The river is empty. There is only the bend ahead and the bend behind, a sandy shore of brush and willows on the near bank, and a steep bluff crowned with cottonwoods a quarter of a mile away on the other— no towns, no houses, no bridges, no roads, not even another boat. Early this morning, after a night tied up in fog at Kansas City, we passed the mouth of the Big Blue River (originally La Rivière de l'Eau Bleue), where, one June day in 1804, the expedition headed by Meriwether Lewis and William Clark "saw a number of parroquets *(Conurus carolinensis)*, and killed some deer." There are no longer any parakeets along the Missouri River (or anywhere else in America), but its shores still look as wild as they were at the turn of the eighteenth century.

I was going to St. Louis, to Cairo, to Memphis, to Natchez, to Baton Rouge, to New Orleans—I was going down the river as far as I could go. I was going as far as I could find a towboat to carry me. The packet boat has vanished from America. It has gone the way the passenger train is going. It was too slow, too comfortable, too restful. But freight still moves on the rivers. The volume, in fact, increases every year. And one can sometimes arrange for accommodations on a towboat.

I had arranged to meet the Lesta K. at a grain-and-molasses dock some twenty river miles above Kansas City. That was late yesterday afternoon. A friend drove me out from the city, and I was waiting on the dock when the Lesta K. and its thrusting tow came into view, sliding downstream on a long crossing where the channel switched from one bank to the other. The Lesta K. was built in 1942, but its lines are still the standard lines for towboats on the rivers. I watched it lift into sight. First, a high white pilothouse with a narrow open bridge all around and a complex of whistles and fog bells and searchlights and radio and radar antennas on the roof above. Then an open texas deck. Then the boiler deck, with a small cluster of cabins forward and two faintly fuming smokestacks aft. Then the main deck, running the length of the boat (about a hundred and fifty feet), with a deckhouse almost as long. The main deck was just above water level—there was hardly three feet of freeboard—with two tall, bumper-like towing knees at the bow. The whistle blew. I waved. A deckhand with long, sandy hair and a horseshoe mustache waved back. He wore a T-shirt with a peace symbol on the front. The Lesta K. nudged gently against the dock.

The deckhand gave me a hand aboard, and took me up to a cabin on the boiler deck. Behind the ferocious mask of hair and mustache was a smiling, boyish face. And he wasn't a deckhand; he was the second mate, and his name was Johnny Avent. My cabin was at the bow, just under the pilothouse, and the roar of the engines was only a distant hum. There was a single bed, a chest of drawers, a chair and a desk, a *Playboy* calendar on the wall. An inner door opened on a bathroom with a sign above the washbasin: "Potable Water." I left my bag and followed Avent down and aft to the galley. It was six o'clock, and supper was just over. Supper is at five-thirty on the river. (So is breakfast, and dinner is at eleven-thirty.) We passed the last of the five-man forward watch—the six-to-noon and six-to-midnight watch—coming along the passage. None of them looked much older than the second mate. The remains of supper were still on the table: a platter with one surviving breaded veal cutlet; dishes of peas and carrots, lima beans, green beans, creamed corn, boiled cabbage, mashed potatoes, potato chips, chili con carne, cottage cheese, and combination salad; three big biscuits on a tray; half a poundcake; a bowl of whipped cream, a bowl of canned peaches; a pitcher of iced tea, a pitcher of Kool-Aid. The cook brought me a plate and a glass of ice. He was a big man with a big pale, worried face, and his name was Malone——H. L. Malone. "Or maybe you'd rather have coffee?" he said. I said I preferred iced tea. He nodded. "Yeah," he said. "Real fine." He sat down at the head of the table and gazed at a notice framed on the wall: "Pilot Rules for the Western Rivers & the Red River of the North." He frowned.

"They drink a lot of coffee on the river," he said. "Yeah——and the farther south, the more they drink. Now, I'm from Mississippi myself, but I give it up. I stopped last March, and I'll tell you something: no more heartburn. It cured it just like that. The same doctor told me to try corn oil for frying. He said it was a whole lot better. So I don't fry nothing no more in hog lard. Yeah——and another thing I learned. This was when I had me a little drive-in down home in Lexington. I used to sell a lot of pickled hard-boiled eggs. I sold dozens of them every week. But you know how hard a boiled egg is to shell. I spent half my time just peeling them eggs. Then the farmer I was buying from he give me a tip. Pip them, he said. Punch a little dent in one end before you cook them. And, sure enough, they peel just like a banana. But I don't grudge the fellas their coffee. I know they like it when they go on watch, and they like it when they come off watch, and they also like it in between. So I've always got a big pot on the stove. They don't allow no liquor on the river. That's the company rule. And no gambling, either. Coffee gives the fellas something to do. The only other thing is eating. The way it works, a fella works for thirty days straight and then he's off for fifteen days, and I try to keep them happy when they're on the boat. You know what they say: a full stomach makes a patient man. There's ten of us on this boat. There's the captain and his relief. There's the chief engineer and his relief. The rest are crew and me. I will say the company understands about food. They know it's important, and they allow me around a thousand dollars a month to work with. You wait till tomorrow. Saturday dinner is the high point of the week on the river. Steak——T-bone steak, with mushrooms. All you want. I broil a couple of dozen. I fry my chicken and my pork chops and my catfish, but I broil my steak. I've been on the river for nine years seven with Port City——and I've got my own way of doing things. I like it on the river. Of course, I don't have my wife anymore. She left me——after seventeen years of marriage. I don't think it was the river. These days, I could sleep in the morning till maybe four-fifteen, but I like to get up around three. I don't like to go right to work. I like to set around and drink tea and wake up good. I take my tea and go out on deck and set there. I like the dark and the smell of the river. And I don't let nothing bother me."

I climbed two flights of almost vertical stairs to the aerie of the pilothouse. The stairs were dark, and the pilothouse was dim with dusk and cigarette smoke. Jene Bills, the captain, was sitting there alone in the twilight at a console of levers and grips and gears and meters—a square-built man of about forty-five with smooth brown hair and a broken nose. His chair was a big leather armchair as high as a shoeshine chair, and it gave him a commanding view through the windows all around. I cleared away a pile of charts and maga- zines and sat down on a high wooden bench. The river spreading out ahead had a coppery sunset glitter. Bills craned his neck and grunted. "A lot of pilots cuss this time of day," he said. "I mean this doggone glare. But fog is worse. We've got radar—the screen is that box standing over there. We couldn't run at night without it. But radar ain't enough in fog—not on this river. The Missouri is too fast and too narrow, and the bends are too short. It's got a lot of bends that ain't but two miles long. You've got to do a lot of holding back—what we call backing up. I know a lot of pilots on the Lower River—on the Mississippi on down from Cairo—that are scared shirtless on this river. I've got a good feeling for it, but I will admit it can be trouble. It can be real hard work to go down. When you're moving along at eight or nine or even ten miles an hour and there isn't too much water in the channel, anything can happen. Like finding a bar built up on a crossing that wasn't there before. The most important tool we've got is the swing indicator. It's like a gyrocompass. It tells me if the tow is swinging out of line. It's a whole lot faster than my eye. I watch that machine as much as I watch the river. But the river is getting better, too. The Army Engineers have done a lot to stabilize the banks and maintain a decent channel. This channel used to change a couple of times a day. And the Coast Guard keeps the channel marked with buoys— like that red nun off to port. But this is still the trickiest river in the U.S.A. Coming up, it don't matter. You're poking along at three or four miles an hour. There's nothing much for the pilot to do but set back and read his Western magazine. No close work, and plenty of time to act if need be. I mean, when you cut your engines, the current is as good as a brake. But, going down, you can stub your toe pretty easy. When your tow is put together right, when you've secured your barges end to end and side to side and the stern of the tow is fast to the tow knees—when you've done all that, why, it's just like one big boat, and it steers like one. It don't act or feel much different. But you've got to remember one thing. It's one hell of a big old boat. You can't stop it or turn it like you would your car. Not unless you want to bust it up."

The sunset glare was fading from the river. The shadows deepened along the banks. Then the last of the light was suddenly gone, and the river was only a stir of paler dark. Three little running lights appeared on the faraway head of the tow. Bills turned on a searchlight. The beam reached out across the tow through a turmoil of white willow flies. It touched a bobbing black can buoy, then a ghostly finger of sandy shoal, then a bright-green jungle wall of trees. It felt back across the water and pounced on another buoy. "Another thing about this river," Bills said. "I think it's probably the cleanest. Up at Sioux City and all the way down to Omaha, it's as clear and blue as a lake. It's the prettiest, too. I guess I've been on most. The Upper Mississippi and the Lower. The Ohio. The Illinois. The Tennessee. If you want to know the truth, I've been on the river all of my life. I was born on a houseboat down at Memphis. And I guess you could say that the river was my salvation. I never had a father. I only had a stepfather, and when my mother left us, he raised me. He worked as a steeplejack when he worked. I done the rest—the cooking, the washing, the housekeeping, the woodchopping. That man never let up. He treated me worse than the meanest man would treat the sorriest dog. When I reached sixteen, I dropped out of school and run off down the river. I started out where everybody starts on the river—as a deckhand. That's the school for the river. There ain't no other. You learn to be a pilot by learning the river and watching the pilot work. Johnny Avent, the boy that brought you aboard, I'm teaching him right now. When you've made ten round trips on your river and can draw a map of its course and put in every bend by name and every light and every crossing, then you can take the Coast Guard examination. If you pass, you're a licensed pilot on that river. That's what I done. Those were still the steamboat days. I remember that long, lonesome whistle on those old steamers. It was a beautiful sound coming across the water. It was sad, but it made you feel good. There wasn't much else in those days that you'd want to brag about. Everything was different then. The river was just about the bottom of the gutter. Hell, it was the bottom. If you worked on the river, you were trash. People would walk away from you. But it gets you, the river. I had it in me too deep to let me quit, and I got my first license in 1950. Then things began to change. Business got better, and the pay and everything else got better, and they started crying for pilots. There still aren't near enough for the need. Last year, more than fifteen percent of all the freight that moved in this country was carried by barge, and it's going to be more this year. The reason is the rates are so low—three mills per ton-mile. The railroads, for example, charge the shipper fifteen. There's a lot of new people coming on the river now. We're even getting college men—fellas like Johnny. They're ambitious to learn and advance. Of course, we get the other kind, too. I mean that new kind of kid they've got these days. They don't know nothing, and they don't want to learn. They don't want to work. All they want is easy living. Eat, sleep, and make a payday. Then they're long gone. And do you know the pay a deckhand gets now? Twenty-two fifty a day. That's almost seven hundred dollars for the thirty days. And no expenses—no room, no board, no nothing. They make me sick. We call this here a bulkhead and we call what we're standing on a deck. They can't be bothered. They call it walls and floor. They call the bow the front end and the head the bathroom and the galley the kitchen. And they're not all kids. Some of them are grown men. I had a mate a while back who kept talking about the capsule. I asked him what the hell was that. He said, 'Why, that thing there.' And he pointed to the capstan."

Bills reached across the console and picked up a microphone. He pressed a switch. "Johnny?" he said, and his voice splintered out from a speaker on the bridge. "Polka Dots? One of you fellas. The captain wants some coffee." He glanced at me, but I shook my head and he put the microphone back. "Coffee gets to be a habit on the river," he said. "I seem to need it even when I'm relaxed at home. I sometimes wake up in the night and go out to the kitchen and make myself a cup. It drives my wife about crazy. But now I'm going to show you something pretty. We're coming into Kansas City. It's just around this bend, and, lighted up at night, it's the prettiest skyline on the river. I've seen them all, and nothing else can touch it." We picked our way through a crossing and into a tight hairpin bend. There was a glow above the riverside woods ahead. We came out of the bend, and there it was—an explosion of lights, mirrored in the dark of the river and diffused across the sky, climbing steeply up a terraced bluff to a soaring summit of flashing signs and floodlit towers. I looked up at Kansas City and thought of *Huckleberry Finn:* "The fifth night we passed St. Louis, and it was like the whole world lit up." So was Kansas City.

A voice from the pilothouse speaker called me back to the boat from my seat at the head of the tow. It was eleven-thirty and time for dinner. I walked back along the barges through a spillage history of past and present cargoes—wheat, rock salt, soybeans, phosphate rock, corn. I ate my T-bone steak (and five vegetables, baked potato, green salad, hot biscuits, vanilla ice cream) with the forward watch. They were Bills, Johnny Avent, the chief engineer, and two young deckhands—the one called Polka Dots, because he wore a red-and-white polka-dot cap, and another called Tear Drops, because soon after he came aboard the Lesta K. he received a shattering "Dear John" letter. Just beyond the windows at the end of the table, a long green shore of willows drifted serenely by. It was practically in the room. We sat at the table until well past noon. There was a somnolent feeling of Sunday. Afternoon is often an idle time on the river. The forward watch goes off to bed for its second installment of sleep. "What I like to do," Bills said as he pushed back his chair, "is get into bed with a good Luke Short or Frank O'Rourke or one of those, and the next thing I know, they're knocking on the door to get me up for supper." With nothing much to do, the after watch lie around on deck and smoke and talk and turn the pages of *Playboy* and *Cavalier* and *Penthouse*. Only the pilot—the relief captain—is fully awake and at work. Even the cook goes off to his room for a nap.

The pilot on the Lesta K. was a man named David Evans. He was a handsome, red-faced man of about thirty-five with long gray hair and with a heart tattooed on his thumb. When I came into the pilothouse, he was staring out at the river and whistling some tuneless tune. He had a mug of coffee on the console beside him, and a textbook—*The Hive and the Honey Bee*. "Beekeeping is one of my hobbies," he said. "It's an interest. I got three hundred hives down home in Mississippi—down in Choctaw County. I get a good hundred pounds of sweet-clover honey per hive. But there's so much poison in the fields these days you can't let your bees stray. You got to keep them close to home. The way you do that is plant good nectar sources nearby. The next thing I think I'll do is get me a herd of Black Angus cattle. And I want to build me a nice big home—a fifty-thousand-dollar home. But my real life is here on the river. I been on the river ten years, and I like it real fine. It's a world of its own. It's a world I feel comfortable in. The Missouri is the friendliest river. Everybody knows everybody else. Nobody wants to cut your throat. I got a first cousin who's a captain on the Lower River. His mother was a real Christian woman. I mean, she had the power of prayer. When we were all growing up, my cousin he cut his middle finger off. The blood was gushing out, but his mother she started praying and the bleeding stopped. I mean it stopped. I remember seeing it with my own eyes. But most of those pilots on the Lower River, they don't like it much up here. This

river is too fast for them. You know what they call the Missouri—
they call it the Big Muddy. They used to say it was too thick to run
and too thin to plow. But that ain't true no more. They've cleaned it
up. But it's fast. I've averaged twelve to fourteen miles an hour
going down with eight barges. That was high water—in May or
June. Of course, I've also busted up some tows. It's three hundred
and sixty-seven river miles from Kansas City to the mouth, just
above St. Louis, and one trip I busted up seventeen times. It made
a real long trip, chasing and catching and tying up those runaway
barges. It took me seven days instead of two or three."

Evans sat up higher in his chair. He reached for a pair of binoculars and trained them down the river. There was a dark spot on the
moving water far ahead. "Somebody coming," he said. "But we got
the right-of-way. The down boat always has the right-of-way." He
picked up a telephone and turned a radio dial. "Lesta K. to west-
bound tow coming into Wakenda Chute. Over."

A voice came out of a speaker: "Belzoni to Lesta K. How you
doing, Dave?"

"Real fine, old buddy. How's it look down there?"

"Had a little trouble in Bushwhacker. It's shallow, Dave. Real
shallow."

"OK, old buddy. I gotcha."

"Yeah. But, you know—no problem. How you want to pass?"

"I'll give you the bank. Port to port. One whistle."

"Gotcha, Dave. Say hello to everybody."

"Real fine, Skip. Will do. And the same to you."

I watched the Belzoni coming. It loomed slowly into shape. It
came creeping up along the shore on the left behind a tow of eight
barges. One of them carried a massive angularity of structural steel
—a section of a bridge. Evans pulled a single blast on the whistle.
The Belzoni replied. We came closely abreast, the Lesta K. moving
at what looked like breakneck speed. Evans jumped out of his chair
and stepped out on the bridge and waved. A man in a white shirt
with the tails hanging loose waved back from the bridge of the
Belzoni.

The river stretched bright and empty again. The green shores—
bluff and bottom, bottom and bluff—ran on and on and on. I
watched a flight of seven sandhill cranes flapping from shoal to
shoal. There was a volume of charts on the bench where I sat:
"Missouri River Navigation Charts: Kansas City, Missouri, to the
Mouth." Every bend, every crossing, every light was marked. I
turned the pages, following the names downriver. Like all place
names, they were a kind of poetry. Teteseau, Chamois, Cote Sans

Dessein, Creve Coeur, St. Aubert, Auxvasse, Gasconade, Bon-homme. Tamerlane, Amazon, Malta, Euphrase, Miami. Berger, Bernheimer, Hermann, Berlin. Slaughterhouse, Plow Boy, Bush-whacker, Rising Creek, Cowmire, Centaur, Pelican. The afternoon crawled peacefully away. Wilhoite, Lupus, Mullanphy, Diana.

I saw just three towns between Kansas City and the river mouth, below St. Charles. I had a passing view of the once premier port of Boonville (where in October of 1864 Price's Confederate Missouri-ans, marching victoriously up the river to Gettysburgian defeat in the three-day Battle of Westport, paused for a spell of roistering rest, one of them leaving behind an unfinished letter: "Wee hav plenty of corn bred and pore beefe to eat and sasafras tee to drink"); Jefferson City, the capital (with the lanterned dome of the State Capitol, the mansard roof of the Governor's Mansion, and the bat-tlements of the State Penitentiary strung along a landscaped bluff); and the tidy red brick waterfront of the old German town of Her-mann. We stopped at none of them, but a mile or two above Her-mann the Irene E., from Staude's Boat Supply Dock, came out to meet us. That was late Sunday afternoon. I stood with Malone at the galley door and watched the Irene E. approach. "Pete Staude is my grocery store," Malone said. "I give him an order on one trip and pick it up on the next. He's bringing me out just a few things now, but I got a big order for him. All the boats trade with Pete. He handles everything but liquor. He even does our laundry. And he's where we get our mail." The Lesta K. slowed to the speed of the current, and the Irene E. came alongside. Two after-watch deck-hands made it secure. We floated on together. A man in a business suit handed up a heavy crate and a bundle of mail tied with string.

"I hope for once you brought me the right kind of peas," Ma-lone said. "I mean them little ones, Pete."

"You got them, old buddy," Staude said. "And everything else you ordered."

"It better not be them big-as-chinaberry kind."

"I even got the Sunday paper for you," Staude said. "Now, who needs what?"

Somebody broke the string on the parcel and spread out the mail on the dining table. The crew, both watches—everybody but Evans, up in the pilothouse—crowded around. There were type-written bills and business letters addressed in pencil and big, thick letters in scented envelopes addressed in colored ink. The deckhand called Tear Drops had one of the scented letters, and he turned his back and stood in a corner to read it. Johnny Avent had three.

Before going down to bed that night, I went out on the bridge for a breath of river air, and heard a kind of music. It was a whining and whanging and thumping, and it came from the main deck, below. I leaned over the rail and looked down on Johnny Avent and two deckhands. Johnny was sitting on a box with the blade of a carpenter's saw bent against the deck like a musical saw, and he was tapping it with a hammer. The deckhands were dancing—stomping and whirling and clapping their hands. It gave me a curious feeling, a curious start of memory. I remembered a painting by the mid-nineteenth century genre painter George Caleb Bingham called "The Jolly Flatboatmen," which shows the long-haired crew of a river scow cavorting on deck to the music of a fiddler. I looked down at the whining saw and the capering deckhands, and wondered again at how little the river seemed to change.

After breakfast (pineapple juice, oatmeal, ham and eggs and grits), I walked out to the head of the tow to watch the sun come up. The sky overhead was black and clear and full of stars, but a layer of fog hung, boiling like steam, on the river. I sat and watched the stars fade and the sky go gray and the first spread of pink appear. It was still dark, it still had the feel of night, and then suddenly it was morning. The sun was up, and the fog was thinning and opening and drifting away, and the grass along the steep right bank was dappled with dewy cobwebs.

I heard somebody coming up the middle of the tow. It was Johnny Avent, hunched under a braided ball of two-inch rope the size of a bushel basket. Behind him came the deckhand Polka Dots with another. They hung one ball over the side of the starboard barge and the other off the port barge. Johnny came over and sat down on the deck beside me. "Them?" he said. "They're bumpers. We hang them out whenever we go through a lock. On the Upper River and up on the Illinois, they're hanging there all the time. The Upper Mississippi is nothing but locks. There's only one lock on this run—the Chain of Rocks lock, just above St. Louis." He gave his cutthroat mustache a pull. "I guess you've heard of William Faulkner," he said. "And Eudora Welty? And William Alexander Percy? And Shelby Foote? And Hodding Carter? Then you probably know they're all Mississippians—and so am I. I come from Greenville. My daddy is port engineer for Port City. I guess that's why I'm on the river. He used to be a chief engineer, and all I ever heard since I was a little bitty boy was the river. I didn't always act like it, though. I studied architectural engineering at college—at Southern Mississippi—and I had a rock band there. I play piano and organ, and like that. I gigged in high school and college both.

We played those long weekends. We'd play some college down in Louisiana and then cut over to Texas and come back by way of Alabama or Tennessee. I got me an ulcer, and my grades went down, so I finally quit. The other fellas, they're still playing, but my real world was always the river. I worked here summers, and I've been on the river full time since I got out of school last year. Captain Easy—that's what we call Captain Bills; there's another captain we call Captain Rough—he's teaching me to be a pilot. I like this peaceful life. It's peaceful, but it isn't lonely. I like the way you've always got somebody to horse around with and throw the bull with. And I like the money, too. I get twenty-seven eighty-five a day—that's the rate for a second mate—and it's all clear money. I mean, I haven't got anybody, and when I'm home I live with my daddy and mummy. I don't even smoke. It's nice to have that big old roll of money. You go in a local bar and start flashing a few fifties around, and those chicks, they kind of go for that. It's like being in the band again, the way those chicks come running, only better. You don't have to pack right up and drive to, like, Shreveport. I like money. But, thank God, I didn't sell my body that time. The medical school down at Louisiana State was offering three hundred dollars apiece for bodies to be claimed after death, and five of us drove down to New Orleans. We wanted that easy money for partying. But then we found out they were going to tattoo something on your heel for identification. I didn't like the idea of some girl getting into bed and looking down and reading my heel and thinking I'd been stole from some morgue."

I dropped the sports section of yesterday's St. Louis *Post-Dispatch* back on the pilothouse bench. I got up and stood at the window. "It looks like the river is getting a little wider," I said.

"Wider?" Bills said.

"I don't know," I said. "It just seems wider than it was."

"Yeah," he said. "Well, it *is* wider. It's just about twice as wide. But it's a different river. We come out of the Missouri at that big long bend back there. That was the mouth. This here is the Mississippi."

I left the Lesta K. on Monday afternoon at St. Louis. As we came out of the lock at Chain of Rocks, Bills received a radioed order to exchange his barges there for another tow and return with it upriver to Kansas City. The Port City Barge Line had made arrangements for me to continue my trip on another boat—the National Progress, of the National Marine Service, Inc., of St. Louis, H. P. Duplantis, captain. The National Progress was tied up just below the St. Louis waterfront, and the Lesta K. churned down there on its way to pick up its new tow—past the Eads Bridge (the first steel bridge built across the Mississippi, completed in 1874, built with arches high enough between the piers to clear the tall twin stacks of the paddle-wheel steamers), past the new soaring Saarinen wishbone arch, past the anchored replica of the Robert E. Lee, past the replica of the Santa Maria, past the five-deck excursion boat Admiral, past the floating restaurant Huck Finn, past the showboat Goldenrod. The National Progress stood offshore behind a tow of four shining doubletank refrigerated anhydrous-ammonia barges, flying the company's flag—a red beaver on a white background. We came alongside, and I stepped across the gap. A deckhand in bib overalls—a big, grumbling fat man—took me to my cabin and then on to the pilothouse. He climbed the steep stairs breathing hard and pulling at the seat of his pants. "I don't know about work clothes anymore," he said. "You can't get anything that will wear for more than forty-five minutes. I think the Mafia must have taken over the hole shebang."

The pilothouse was as loud and crowded as a cocktail party. There was Duplantis, a young Cajun with long black hair and bright blue eyes, sitting on the bench. There was the pilot, a young Mississippian named William McBunch, at the console. There was a refrigeration technician (anhydrous ammonia is ammonia liquefied by sub-zero cooling for safekeeping), a young Arkansan named Dennis Blackford. There was a deckhand from Texas making coffee at a little stove in a corner, and a deckhand from Missouri. The fat deckhand and I brought the number in the little room to seven. Everybody was smoking and drinking coffee and talking at the top of his voice.

" . . . and married a fella from Texas."

"It's a funny thing—you meet a fella from Texas, and if you call him Tex, he kind of preens. But you meet a fella from Arkansas and you call him Arkie—well, you got a fight on your hands."

"You ask me, I'd rather have a sister in a whorehouse than a brother in Texas."

"I don't know why they call a Cajun a 'coon-ass.' I never ate coon in my life."

"The way I heard it, every time you mention Missouri, a jackass will kneel down and pray."

I sat down on the bench, and one of the deckhands brought me a cup of coffee. It was black and strong, and sharp with chicory. The deckhand leaned on the arm of the bench.

"That's coon-ass coffee," he said. "That's what they call it. And we make it drip. But every captain on this line has his own idea about how to make his coffee. One captain has me make it one spoon of Luzianne and then one spoon of Community, then another spoon of Luzianne and another one of Community. And so on. And it has to be just right or he gets as mad as a mule."

"I remember one time," Duplantis said. "We took a new cook on at Memphis. One of the deckhands came running up here to the pilothouse and he said, 'Oh, Jesus, Duke, you won't believe it but that new cook she's a girl.' Well, I'd heard of women cooks on the river—a few old widows. But he was right. She came up to report, and she was a young girl. Good-looking, too, and built real nice. She said she had an aunt who had cooked on towboats. She said she had taken home economics in high school, and her aunt had taught her the rest. The aunt had told her about the different watches and when they ate and the kind of food, and about accommodating the crew. I said, 'The what?' The men, she said—about going to bed with the men. However, she said, her aunt had told her not to play any favorites. That could only cause trouble. She would take the fellas in turn when they wanted her. But she had one rule. Nobody but me was to know her last name or where she lived on shore. And that's the way it was. She accommodated the fellas—practically the whole boat. But then the trouble began. It was just what she had tried to avoid. Dissension. They all of them fell in love with her, or thought they had, and in no time at all everybody—even the married men—was unhappy and jealous and snarling at everybody else. So when we got up to Marseilles, Illinois, I had to put her ashore. She was a real nice girl—real likable, and a good cook, too. But she was strange—real strange. I remember her name. It was Shirley."

"It was Shirley Ann," the Missouri deckhand said.

I had supper that night with the after watch (fried country ham and redeye gravy, sweet potatoes, succotash, okra, banana cream pie) and then sat for a while on the texas deck, and watched a new moon rise. I saw what the early Victorian novelist Captain Frederick Marryat had seen before me—had seen almost a century and a half before: "I did not expect that the muddy Mississippi would be able to reflect the silver light of the moon; yet it did, and the effect was very beautiful. Truly it may be said of this river, as it is of many ladies, that it is a candle-light beauty." I went down to bed before nine. The nights are short when you are called for breakfast at five o'clock. My cabin was over the engine room, and I awoke a dozen times to the grinding roar of the engines backing and braking, but only for a moment. The usual engine sound—the steady forward thrust—was a soporific hum.

Duplantis was alone in the pilothouse but was talking on the telephone when I climbed the stairs after breakfast. I stopped at the door that opened onto the bridge. The river was unmistakably the Mississippi now. It stretched a mile wide and infinitely on ahead. In the thin white early-morning light, it might have been a lake. But the banks were still riverbanks—sandbars and willow flats, willow slopes and high cottonwood bluffs.

"Yeah," Duplantis said on the telephone. "I gotcha, man. I'll just keep paddling." He hung up, and turned. "There's fresh coffee there on the stove. Or if you'd rather have a Coke, there's some in the refrigerator underneath. And you can pour me some more coffee while you're at it." He was wearing dark glasses, and his long dark hair hung down across one eye. "That's Pond Lily Light over there on the Missouri side. We made good time last night, in spite of a lot of fog—better than sixty miles a watch. We're past Cape Girardeau and we're getting close to Cairo. It's interesting there, the way the Ohio comes in. A lot of pilots think the books have got the rivers wrong. You can see it here on this chart. The Mississippi comes in from the west and the Ohio comes down from the north, and after they meet you can see how the Mississippi bends and runs due south. A lot of the pilots think the Ohio is the main river and the Mississippi is the feeder—the tributary. I think they've got a point. And here comes the fella I was talking to."

The tow came distantly into view, hugging the high Missouri shore—a tiny white pilothouse rising behind an acreage of barges. It came close enough for me to make out the head of the tow: it spread five barges wide. I took up a pair of binoculars and read the name on the pilothouse: Theresa Seley. Duplantis pulled the whistle twice, for a starboard-to-starboard passing. The Theresa Seley replied in confirmation, and came slowly up and slowly abreast and past. Duplantis raised a hand in the ritual greeting. I counted the barges. The tow was five barges wide and six barges long—a total of thirty barges. It *was* an acreage. It was five acres of barges. And, at fifteen hundred tons per barge, it carried thirty-five thousand tons of cargo. It was more cargo than could be moved by rail on a freight train of three hundred cars.

"Fellas new on the river are scared of certain cargoes," Duplantis said. "It scares them to handle oil or petrochemicals—chemicals of any kind. Those things are dangerous. Anhydrous ammonia is dangerous. So you have to be careful. You have to follow the safety rules. But the kind of load that scares me most is something else entirely. If you noticed that boat, the Theresa Seley, he had a couple of deck barges loaded with river sand. That wet river sand is real unstable. It shifts. Even a gentle turn can shift the load, and a shift of fifteen hundred tons of sand—all that weight, with the buoyancy all underneath—it can turn you right smack over. I've never had any trouble. I've never even come close, except once when I tried to keep from running down two measly little ducks. I've never had anything like a fire or explosion, but I had a tow one time where it would have been kind of interesting. That was up on the Upper River. I picked up a tow at St. Paul of eight barges of popping corn and a jumbo barge of soybean oil. All the way down to St. Louis, at every lock and every bend, I kept thinking, What if something happened? What if something exploded? What if we got hit by lightning? My God, the whole Middle West would be knee-deep in buttered popcorn!"

I left the National Progress around ten o'clock that morning off the village of Hickman, Kentucky, just north of the Tennessee line. The circumstances were much the same as those that had moved me to the Progress from the Lesta K.: an order had been telephoned to Duplantis to meet another National Marine Service towboat there— the National Gateway, Victor Wood, captain—transfer his tow to her, and return upriver to Hannibal. Arrangements had been made for me and the refrigeration technician, Blackford, to continue aboard the Gateway, destination Baton Rouge. The Gateway, built in 1966, was bigger and finer than the Progress, and my cabin was a guest stateroom—twin beds, a deep leather armchair, a reading lamp, a tiled bathroom hung with big, thick towels. Across the passageway was a lounge for the crew, with a sofa, comfortable chairs, a television set, and a table piled with paperback books (including *Ada*, by Vladimir Nabokov, and Saul Bellow's *Herzog*) and copies of the Memphis *Press-Scimitar* and Hodding Carter's Greenville *Delta Democrat-Times*. The boat gave a shudder. I looked out the window. We were under way—behind a seven-barge tow of anhydrous ammonia and caustic soda, with red metal danger flags standing stiff on every barge. I found the stairs to the pilothouse and went up. Wood—thirty-eight, green-eyed, tousle-haired, unshaven, sockless—was at the console. A gray-haired deckhand with a sunken jaw was sitting on the bench.

" . . . seniority," the deckhand said. "That's what they say. Thirty minutes of kissing ass will do you more good than thirty years of seniority."

"Yeah?" Wood said. "Well, I tell you what. How about you going over there to the stove and pouring everybody a nice little cup of coffee?"

We moved around an overgrown towhead island and into a long starboard crossing. The Missouri shore loomed and lifted, and through the trees I could see the slope of a field of stubble corn. A congregation of crows was busy among the rows. "My home town isn't far from here," Wood said. "It wouldn't be more than thirty miles for one of those crows. Sikeston, Missouri—my daddy was a cotton farmer there. I never meant to go on the river. I guess I'd have to call it just an accident. But once I got started, I was hooked. It's another kind of life. It's like one of those drugs. There ain't no future and there ain't no past. There's nothing but the river. That's the way you get to feel. But the river has been good to me. There's enough here to keep you going. You start in decking, and if you've got enough smarts you try to climb. I'd come up to the pilothouse in my off-duty hours and watch the captain. The old man made a pilot out of me. He went back to the old river days when you could chew a man out, when you could make him feel like nothing—when you could kick him all over the deck. But he wasn't that kind of man. I learned everything from him. Any man is welcome in my pilothouse. He can come up and set and talk and enjoy the scenery any time his work is done or his watch is over. But I expect him not to abuse it. He's got to behave himself. There was a time when the river was my only home. I worked nine straight months on a boat without putting foot on shore. Me and another pilot bought a towboat and went into business on our own. I didn't have no children then, and my wife travelled with me most of the time. She really rowed the boat. She could have passed my pilot's license easier than I did. I kept at it for eight years, but it was hard work, running the boat and running the business, too. So one day I sold my share to my partner and went back to working for somebody else. But I come out ahead—I come out with my house paid for, and a nice little farm down in southern Missouri, and a couple of dollars in my pocket. The best thing about it was my wife got to understand the river. So she and I, we kind of understand each other. We don't have the trouble some fellas have. I wake up when I'm home at about 3 A.M.—I can't sleep no more. And my wife gets up and puts on that little housecoat and makes up a cup of coffee. The only thing she grumbles about is when I've got to have that little nap in the afternoon."

"My old lady won't let me sleep," the deckhand said. "When I'm at home, we don't do nothing but go."

"Yeah?" Wood said. "I don't even go to church no more. That preacher we got, he's always stopping me and telling me I have to come to church. I told him no sir. People think you're isolated here on the river. They mean isolated from the world, and that's true. But you're not isolated from yourself. You get close to yourself, you get to know your thoughts. I told that preacher, 'If you believe in a Supreme Being—and I do—you're closer to Him out here than in any old Baptist church.' The preacher don't bother me. I know what my own mind tells me. I don't have to have somebody tell me if I'm doing wrong. I'm a grown man. I know right and I know wrong, and I know it all by myself."

The cook on the National Gateway was a thin, stern, bald-headed man from Texas named W. B. Wimberly. He was a country cook, and the galley was a big room with the feel of a country kitchen. There was always a view through a double door that gave on the low main deck—a framed and changeless view of a slowly passing countryside: the lift of a grass-grown levee, a skiff pulled up on a mudbank, willow thicket and cottonwood grove, cattle grazing in a field. There was a big refrigerator, never locked, with iced tea and milk, with grapefruit juice and orange juice and tomato juice, with cold meat and cottage cheese and a bowl of hard-boiled eggs. There was a big table set for eight in the middle of the room with a crowded tray of condiments. All the usual things were there (ketchup, mustard, French dressing, chili sauce, peanut butter, steak sauce, jelly, honey), but there were also other delicacies—Frank's Red Hot Sauce, Bruce's Banana Peppers, Evangeline Gumbo Filé. I went down to dinner that day with the chief engineer, the technician Blackford, three deckhands, and the pilot, a gray, quiet Louisianan of fifty named Pierre Bourgeois. We helped ourselves from the stove and a buffet counter. Nobody talked and everybody ate. I watched one of the deckhands eat a bowl of chicken fricassee, an inch-thick slab of pot roast, mashed potatoes and gravy, lima beans (spiced with Frank's Red Hot Sauce), carrots, spinach, two wedges of corn bread, combination salad, and a dish of butterscotch pudding. There was a bowl of hard-boiled eggs on the table. He ate one egg with his chicken fricassee and two more with his pot roast, and he washed it all down with two glasses of cherry Kool-Aid. Wimberly sat in a corner and smoked and turned the pages of the National Insider ("How Jackie Lives When Nobody Is Looking") and sternly watched us eat.

We finished and made way for the forward watch. The engineer went back to the engine room, Blackford went out on the tow to check the refrigeration, the deckhands went off to sand and paint the texas deck. Bourgeois went up to the pilothouse, and a few minutes later I joined him there. He reached under the console and handed me a big, floppy copy of *Flood Control and Navigation Maps of the Mississippi River: Cairo, Illinois, to the Gulf of Mexico*. "This river is famous for its crazy bends," he said, "and the one we're coming to is just about the craziest. See where it's marked Kentucky Point on the chart—where the river goes into a horseshoe bend that takes a big nipple out of the Missouri side. That's the bend we're coming into now. That's the famous New Madrid Bend. This is where they had that earthquake back in the Daniel Boone days—back there in 1811 and 1812. They tell me the New Madrid earthquake was the worst we ever had in this country. The river turned red and twisted around and ran upstream. It made the famous Reelfoot Lake, over there in Tennessee, and it made this New Madrid Bend. It's a real mixup. Our left bank right now is Tennessee and the right bank is Missouri, but up ahead about a mile the left bank is Kentucky again. It's nineteen miles from where we are, just coming into the bend, to where we come out, but if I was to drop you off at the neck up there you could walk across to the other end in probably fifteen minutes. It ain't much more than a mile. Some people say why don't they make a cutoff, dig a canal across the neck, save a lot of time? I say they better not. They better not fool around with any of these bends. The bends make the pressure that keeps the water level up. If you dug a straight channel from here on down to the Gulf, you wouldn't have nothing but a ditch. The water would run right off, like water off a rock. The only thing I've got against these bends is that's where you meet the traffic. I know of two tows right now that are coming up this bend. It's like they *like* to bunch up."

Bourgeois reached for the telephone, and I reopened *Flood Control and Navigation Maps of the Mississippi River*. I looked again at Kentucky Point and its transplanted piece of Kentucky, and then leafed on through the book. Kentucky Point was only one among many such geographical confusions. The turnings and re-turnings of the Lower River have undone boundary lines all the way down to the Gulf. Part of Tipton County, Tennessee, now finds itself on the Arkansas side of the river, and part of Mississippi County, Arkansas, is on the Tennessee side. Part of Tunica County, Mississippi, is embedded in Lee County, Arkansas, and a good part of Lee County is over in Tunica County. Part of East Carroll Parish, Louisiana, has shifted across to Mississippi, and there is much of

Mississippi isolated here and there along the Louisiana shore. I thought of Mark Twain's account of this phenomenon in *Life on the Mississippi*. "The town of Delta," he reported, "used to be three miles below Vicksburg: a recent cut-off has radically changed the position, and Delta is now *two miles above* Vicksburg." I found Delta (Louisiana) on my map. It is now—almost a hundred years later—neither above nor below Vicksburg. It is directly across the river from that city, and two full miles to the west. It was long after dark when we came into the harbor at Memphis. We took on supplies and mail from another floating ship chandlery, and Bourgeois went ashore to fly home for his fifteen days of leave. He was replaced by another Louisianan, a man named William Reeves. But I slept through all this and first heard about it from Wood the next morning, after breakfast. "Only that ain't what we call it," he said. "We don't call Memphis by its name. We call it Big Shelby. Shelby is the name of the county it's in. I don't know what the reason is. It probably goes way back to the very early days. There's a lot of traditions like that on the river. There's a crossing down near Battle Axe Bend that the chart calls Bordeaux Crossing. But what we call it on the river is Boodrow Crossing. And coming into Baton Rouge there's a point named Free Nigger Point. That's always been the name, and it don't mean nothing at all. It's just a name. But last year they changed it on the map to Free Negro Point. That made me kind of laugh. It made me think of our church back home. It was built back in my granddaddy's time. He was the town doctor and also the Baptist preacher, and he got the church built cheap out of slabs from that little sawmill they had. So everybody called it Slab Shanty Church. Then back when I was growing up—back in the nineteen-forties—the congregation raised some money and built a nice big new brick church. They named it the Union Grove Baptist Church. But you know what everybody calls it? Even the preacher? They call it Slab Shanty Church."

I went out on the tow that afternoon with Blackford. Unescorted idlers are not permitted on red-flag barges, and I went with his permission and equipped (as regulations require) with a life jacket. We walked along the echoing metal decks between the high-humped anhydrous-ammonia tanks. "It's easy enough to explain," he said. "All you got to do is maintain the temperature in the tanks at minus twenty-eight degrees. That keeps the ammonia liquid and under control. When the temperature rises, it begins to vaporize. We run the vapor through the refrigeration unit and it liquefies again. I like this kind of work, and I like it on the river. I like those fifteen days on shore, too. I don't have a family. But I like to get cleaned up and move into a motel and go partying around St. Louis. But by the time my leave is over, I'm just about ready to come back. I'm like homesick for the river." Blackford left me at the head of the tow. He turned back to check his refrigeration units, and I sat down in the sun below a drooping company beaver flag and watched the river spreading and bending on ahead. And the traffic. There was a tow approaching now at almost every bend. We passed the Sebring (on two whistles) with four oil and chemical barges. We passed the Sarah Jane (two whistles) with nine hopper barges. We passed the William Barnes (one whistle) with ten petroleum barges. We passed the Ole Miss (two whistles) with twenty hopper barges. We passed the Franklin Pierce (one whistle) with four petroleum barges and five jumbo hoppers. The sunlight began to dim. There were clouds building up to the west and south. Blackford came up and sat down and smoked a cigarette and carefully ground it out, and then we walked back to the boat. The clouds had gathered overhead, and the river looked dark and heavy. The banks looked far away.

We were eating supper when the rain began. It was almost dark, and the air was very still. It was a thin, drifting, drizzly rain, and it hung in the air like mist. "That was the forecast," Wood said. "There's some kind of depression down in the Gulf. But there aren't many pilots that enjoy a rainy night on the river. Rain makes everything hard. If it's bad, it knocks the radar out, and if there's a lot of wind, it's worse. It kicks up a chop so you can't hardly see the buoys. It's almost as bad as fog."

"You ever been up there on the Ohio, Cap?" one of the deckhands said. "Where they got that Haunted Hollow Point? They say you're coming along on a bad night and you'll see the running lights of a boat. But you get just so close and they disappear on you."

"Yeah?" Wood said. "Well, if that ever happened to me, I'd give him a whistle and plenty of room. I wouldn't take no chances on him being a ghost."

The rain dripped down all night, and it was drizzling at breakfast on Thursday morning. But we were still moving. We were due in Baton Rouge sometime that night, and we were more or less on schedule. Then, around eleven o'clock, the drizzle stiffened into rain, and the wind began to blow. The rain drummed down on the open decks and blew in at the windows in sheets. I was watching it from the bench in the pilothouse just after dinner when a message came over the radio from the company office in St. Louis: "Attention, National Gateway. There is a storm moving into Louisiana from the Gulf. We do not want you to go past Natchez. Do not go past Natchez until further notice. Repeat. Stop at Natchez."

The relief captain, Reeves, was at the console. He was a big man in his middle fifties, with a big belly and big, rough, smiling face. He acknowledged the order in a slow, untroubled voice. He hung up and reached for a cigarette. "You hear that?" he said. "Well, I was just thinking the same myself. I didn't think this was any ordinary squall. I thought it looked kind of bad. But I know a good place to tie up at Natchez. That is, if somebody else ain't already beat me to it. And if I don't stub my toe getting there. I don't know. Look at that son of a bitch out there—that's what I call choppy water. We passed a tow just before you come up here that said they'd had some trouble down around Rifle Point, and that's exactly where we're coming to right now. I don't know it we're even going to make it. Just look at that rain. I can't hardly see a goddam thing. Look at them buoys, the way they're jumping around. You can't tell red from black. Well, I know one thing—I'm sure as hell not going down through Natchez. I sure don't want to run that bridge down there today. The place I got in mind is the upper end of town. It's on the Louisiana side. But what if somebody's got it? I sure don't see no traffic. And there's a fella tied up over there. It looks like everybody is already tied up but us."

Reeves put out his cigarette. He picked up the binoculars and gazed out through the streaming glass. He put the binoculars down and lighted another cigarette. "Well, it won't be long now," he said. "That's Magnolia Bluff beginning over there. That's where those kids found all that money that time. They were playing along the shore and they saw something laying in the water and they fished it out and it was a coffee can full of silver dimes. Son of a bitch— you know what I think? I think I'd better start looking right now for a tree to tie up to. I got a feeling my place is took. I don't see a tree that will hold me. I don't see no trees at all. I don't see nothing but willow sprouts. And I sure wouldn't lay up like that fella over there at that towhead. He'll have some trouble getting off. But it ain't as bad as it was. See how that bluff has cut off the wind. But I don't know. There just ain't no real trees. And—son of a bitch. What did I tell you? There's my place and there's a fella in it. You know something? I'm going to have to try and run that goddam bridge."

I stood up for a better view. An old brick building appeared low down on the Mississippi shore. A street climbed up the bluff behind it. There were rooftops showing along the top of the bluff. That was Natchez. We came around a bend. A bridge loomed up through the rain. The channel markers led between two middle piers. The gap didn't look much wider than our tow. But Reeves didn't head for the channel. He pulled the head of the tow far off to the left, angling toward the Natchez shore, running straight at a string of barges moored along the face of a wharf. The bridge widened and rose higher overhead. An orange trailer truck was moving slowly across the bridge in the driving, blinding rain. Then the string of moored barges began to swing away—swing off to the left, and suddenly out of sight behind the big stone face of a pier—and we were back in the channel and sliding under the bridge and plunging out on the other side.

"Son of a bitch," Reeves said. He reached for another cigarette. "We made it. We got through there real fine. But I have to thank that Natchez bluff. I'd never made it with that wind hitting me. But goddam it—I still got to find me a place to park. I can't keep rolling along half blind like this. But I don't know. Everywhere I see a likely-looking tree there's a fella already tied up to it. No, sir. I ain't never had this kind of trouble trying to find a place to tie up. There's nothing on this left bank—nothing open, anyway. I wonder should I go over there to the right bank and take a look? I sure can't see from here. Maybe if I got real close—But I can't. It's too shallow. See that black buoy. It's all of it shoal over there. There's nothing to do but keep going. I never saw anything like this in my whole damn life. Every tree got a barge tied to it. And where there ain't any barges there's nothing but levee bank. I don't know where we're going. I don't know what we're going to do. And we got a fifty-mile wind coming at us. Look at them trees, how they're bending. I swear to God, I just don't know. They told me stop at Natchez, and here we are still going. Goddam—there's Destruction Landing over yonder, and that's St. Catherine Bend just ahead. We're way below Natchez. We're fifteen miles below. I got to do something soon. I think I'll try right now. I sure would hate to have this tow bust up. What I'm going to do is go into that right bank there. I don't think much of the trees, but it's deep enough, and it even looks like it might be a little bit slack. I do believe I've found me a place. I do believe I have." He picked up the intercom microphone. "Angelo? Frank? All right, fellas—let's go."

We moved into a right-hand crossing, back toward Louisiana. The only visible buoy was a red buoy a hundred yards or so from shore. Beyond it was a kind of cove, a little indentation in a bank of crumbling mud, and above the bank was a grove of tall, feathery willows. The trees were thrashing, bending almost double. Three deckhands in hooded yellow slickers came humping out on the main deck down below. They ducked across the deck, heads down and slickers flapping, and up a ladder to the stern of the starboard ammonia barge, and on to a coil of heavy mooring line. The sound of the engines changed to the vibrating roar of reverse. Reeves was standing now, leaning across the console, peering. We slid—every deck and bulkhead clanging against the wind and the current—half broadside into the bank. The deckhands ran out a wooden gang-plank. They went down the plank, hauling the line, and into the mud and up the bank to the trees. The trees leaned flat in a wilder gust, and two of them splintered and broke. The feathery top of one lifted high in the air. It sailed away like a gull. The deckhands struggled back aboard and broke out another line. The engines turned gently over in a slow, braking reverse. The rain came down and the mudbank melted and crumbled and the willows thrashed in the wind. But we were out of it now. We were out of the current, out of the pull of the river, sitting safe on a sheltered shore. Reeves turned away from the console. He walked back to the stove and picked up the coffeepot. "I'm going to have some coffee," he said. "How about you?"

The storm was almost over by the time I went down to bed that night. The rain had ended and the wind had dropped, and I could see the new moon racing through the last of the clouds and the deep-blue sky opening up beyond. But the river still looked and sounded rough, and we were still moored along the mudbank. I lay in the dark and listened to the river and the sound of the engines still clanking away in reverse. A voice in the passageway said, "Five feet on the gauge at St. Louis." I dozed, and suddenly awoke. It was still dark—I had dozed for only a moment—but the engines had a different sound. I sat up and looked out the window. The mudbank was gone. We were well out on the river, and moving. I was in no hurry to get to Baton Rouge. But life on the river is movement, and it was good to be moving again. I rolled over and went back to sleep.

[1972]

10. Some Ladies in Retirement: Mt. Lebanon, New York

Between the Revolution and the Civil War, at least a hundred communistic societies were set up in this country. Most of them were of an energetically unorthodox religious character, and all were humble, agrarian, and generally unpopular. Few of them lasted very long. Of the less than a dozen societies that gathered sufficient momentum to survive both the deaths of their founders and the Civil War, only one is still in existence. That is the United Society of Believers in Christ's Second Appearing, the members of which are usually called Shakers.

The United Society was the first American communal organization, and it was always the largest, the richest, and the most austere of the lot. It is composed of celibate men and women, who live under the same roof—though carefully segregated—in more or less self-sufficient groups, or "families," several of which, situated within walking distance of a community meetinghouse, traditionally comprise a "village." Its members abjure pork, alcohol, tobacco, doctors, instrumental music, and architectural and sartorial ornamentation. The theology of the order is, perhaps as much as anything, a chilly derivative of Quakerism and seventeenth-century French millennialism. The sect got its start in England in 1747, during the course of a Quaker revival, but it did not acquire much vitality until nearly a quarter of a century later, when one of its members, a thirty-four-year-old Manchester millworker named Ann Lee, underwent a spiritual experience that gave her such a fervent abhorrence of the weaknesses of the flesh that she was chosen to lead the group. Gradually, the doctrine was evolved that Christ was female as well as male and that He had been reincarnated in Mother Ann, as the leader became known to the believers, thus fulfilling the promise of His Second Coming. In 1774, four years after Mother Ann was selected to head the sect, a revelation persuaded

her to lead her eight most loyal followers—six men and two
women—to America. They landed at New York, where Mother
Ann lived for two years in miserable poverty while her disciples
spread out over the countryside, asserting her divinity and pro-
claiming her belief in a communal life and isolation from world
distractions. Mother Ann, who, like her followers, had recurrent
trouble with puritanical authorities suspicious of the sect's claim to
celibacy, subsequently moved to a farm near Watervliet, New York,
where she died in 1784, exhausted by evangelism, privation, and
frequent jailings. Shortly thereafter, the United Society of Believers
in Christ's Second Appearing was organized. The first Shaker settlement, which was named Mount Lebanon, was established in
1787 about twenty-five miles southeast of Albany, in Columbia
County, by Joseph Meacham, one of Mother Ann's original disciples. The society reached its greatest strength during the eighteen-
fifties. At that time, it owned well over a hundred thousand acres of
fruitful land, had a membership of some five thousand, and main-
tained eighteen villages, each of which contained at least two large
families, in seven states—New York, Maine, New Hampshire,
Massachusetts, Connecticut, Ohio, and Kentucky.

Shakerism is moribund now. There have been no converts to it
in the past forty years, and since conversion is naturally the sole
means of perpetuating a continent order, the membership is rapidly
dwindling. Fewer than fifty members are left in the entire society.
Only four villages remain—Hancock, in Massachusetts; Canter-
bury, in New Hampshire; Sabbathday Lake, in Maine; and Mount
Lebanon. Mount Lebanon once had eight families, but, like the
others, it is now down to one. This, as I found when I drove up
there one brilliant summer day, consists of six women and one
man. The youngest of them is sixty and the oldest is ninety-two.
They live together—lonely, retrospective, and gently backslidden
—in a house that was built for a family of seventy-five or more.

Mount Lebanon, despite the implication of its name, is tucked
away in a deep pocket in the Berkshires, near the Massachusetts
line. A gravel road, cut into the face of a wooded hill, leads down
to it from the Albany-Pittsfield highway, which winds through the
uplands. I turned into this road a little after noon on the day of my
visit, dropped precipitously for a couple of hundred feet, rounded a
sharp bend, and came abruptly upon the settlement. It was a subdu-
ing sight—a phalanx of seven big, raw-boned, white clapboard
buildings of indeterminate purpose, all rearing up among towering
elms and maples. The largest, a broad, six-story structure, stood
within a few feet of the road. The others, some of three stories and

some of four, were ranked behind it at the bottom of a slope, symmetrically arrayed in two parallel rows. To one side and at some distance from the large building, was a mammoth gray stone barn, built on the slope, with an upper entrance on the road and another, at the opposite end, leading into a barnyard far below. There was no sound or sight of life, but the six-story building, unlike the others, looked as if it might be occupied. A strip of weedy lawn in front of it had recently been cut, and its windows, though uncurtained and coldly staring, were immaculate. I pulled up in front of it and got out. The house had two identical front doors, about a hundred feet apart. The day was bright and bland, but both were tightly closed. As I hesitated, wondering which door to approach, the one on my left opened a crack, and a woman of advanced but incalculable age, with a dark, wrinkled face, peered out. "I like to see what's going on," she remarked, apparently addressing me. Before I could reply, a voice behind her called, "Now, Sarah, you know you haven't got your wrap." The old woman gave a shrill, mischievous laugh. "I'm as tough as a pine knot," she cried, and vanished, slamming the door.

Then the other door opened and a somewhat younger woman came out. She was short, plump, and pink-and-white, and she wore a long, plain, full-skirted blue dress. I learned later that Shaker women have always worn dresses of this design, which was current in the eighteenth century, in emulation of Mother Ann, who favored it; the clothes of Shaker men have tended to keep more in step with the times. The woman smiled at me with friendly curiosity. I walked over, introduced myself, and asked if I might look around the place. "You're very welcome here," she said. "I hope you didn't mind Sister Sarah Collins. Poor Sarah is ninety-two, and sometimes she acts a little queer. We're always glad to have good people call on us, and I'd enjoy showing you what there is to see." She closed the door and came out on the lawn. "I suppose you know that the North Family, is what we're called, is all that's left of Mount Lebanon. Everything else in the village, even our meetinghouse, has been sold, and most of the buildings have been torn down or moved away. But one Shaker family is a lot like another. We believe in uniformity. The rest of the village was on down the road a ways. The reason we're called the North Family is that we're at the north end. Shaker families are named for their location. But I haven't told you *my* name yet. I'm Sister Jennie—J-e-n-n-i-e— Wells. It isn't J-e-n-n-y, because I'm no mule." She laughed merrily. "Shakers don't approve of mules, you know. We've never had any. We think they're unnatural."

An expression of intense concentration appeared on Sister Jennie's face. "I'm trying to think where to begin," she said. "Most of our visitors these days are antique collectors, and all they're interested in is buying up what little fine old handmade Shaker furniture we have left. Why, those people would grab the chairs right out from under us if we'd let them. Our furniture is very fashionable all of a sudden, you know. I understand it's called modernistic." She gave me an amused glance. "Maybe that proves just how far ahead of the world Shakerism is. We don't make furniture—or anything, for that matter—now, but when we did, we made it exactly like the furniture the first Shakers made. We're always being told how beautiful our things are. I don't say they aren't, but that isn't what they were meant to be. Shakers aren't concerned with anything as frivolous as beauty. All our furniture was ever meant to be was strong, light, plain, and, above all, practical. It is, too, as you'll see when we go inside. But I want you to see the rest of the place first. Then we'll come back here to the dwelling house. That's our name for the house a Shaker family lives in. No matter how large a family got in the old days, and some of them got close to a hundred, it never had more than one dwelling house. When this house was finished, in 1812 or around then, it was four stories, but the family grew so fast that two more had to be added a few years later. Well, that's one problem we don't have to worry about anymore. There are only seven of us left in the North Family, and our house has eighty-one rooms."

"How does it happen to have two front doors?" I asked.

"It has two back doors, too," Sister Jennie said. "And also two center halls on every floor. You might say a Shaker dwelling house is really two houses. The men live in the left half and the women in the right. We each have our own parlors, and everything. The only room that we share is the dining room, but we eat at separate tables. Shaker men and women aren't even permitted to shake hands with each other. My stars," she added smiling reproachfully, "I hope you didn't think that we actually *lived* together!"

I assured her that I hadn't, and we started up the road in the direction of a flagstone path that led down between the dwelling house and the barn to the other buildings. After a moment, she said, "I'm sure there's no need for me to point out our barn. You couldn't very well miss it, could you?" I replied that it was probably the biggest barn I had ever seen. "I'm sure it is," she said, beaming. "I don't want to sound vain glorious, but it's the biggest stone barn in the whole United States. It's fifty feet wide and it's two hundred and ninety-six feet long and, as you can see, it has five floors. That's very unusual. It was built in the eighteen-fifties, and it's as sturdy now as the day it was finished. At that, it's the newest building in the North Family. The others are considerably over a hundred years old. The Shakers always built for permanence. We say that Shakerism can't be told; it must be lived. Still, you can learn a lot about it just from that barn.

"We're very practical people," she went on. "There's no foolishness about anything we do. Our barn was made the length it is for good reason. The men wanted to have room enough for a dozen or more loaded wagons on the floor at the road level, in case a sudden storm came up during haying. That doesn't mean much now, of course. We don't raise much hay. Our stock is down to ten milch cows and four horses, which is just a fraction of what we used to have. We've sold or rented out most of our land, too. The North Family farm was good-sized once—nearly a thousand acres—but now it's not much more than two hundred, including pasture and wood lots, and we have to hire two men to do the work. About all we're able to do ourselves is housework. But no matter. Another thing about the barn is that it's wide enough for a big team and wagon to turn around in. The reason it's built on a slope is so hay can be hauled in at the top floor and pitched *down* to the mows. Then it's pitched *down* from there to the stock stalls below. In most barns, you know, hay has to be pitched *up*. A good many Shaker barns are built like ours. Shakers have never seen any sense in fighting against gravity." Sister Jennie looked at me earnestly. "Not that we mind working hard," she assured me. "We believe in it. Even our elders and eldresses are expected to do their share of manual work. They're our leaders, you know. Every family is supposed to have two elders and two eldresses. We have only one eldress now, and we haven't had an elder in years. Anyway, as I was saying, there aren't any loafers in a Shaker family. Loafing and communism just don't go together. Mother Ann said, 'Hands to work and hearts to God,' and that's our guiding rule. I wish you could have come to see us forty or fifty years ago. A Shaker farm was a busy place in those days."

As we walked down the path, I asked Sister Jennie how long she had been a Shaker. "Practically all my life," she said, with satisfaction. "I'm seventy years old, although I may not look it and I certainly don't feel it, and the Groveland Shakers, up near Rochester, took me in when I was just four. I was a half orphan, with a cruel stepfather, and my mother thought I'd be better off with the Shakers. Back in those days, you know, there weren't many good orphan asylums. The Shakers occasionally adopted poorly situated children or children who had no parents, and educated and looked after them until they became of age. Every Shaker family had its own school, and they were very good. They had to be. We don't admire ignorance. When a Shaker child was twenty-one, he was free either to go out into the world or stay and be gathered into the Church as a convert. Four of us here at Mount Lebanon came to Shakerism as children. That's merely a coincidence, though. Most Shakers have been converted from the world. We've converted Jews, atheists, and all kinds of Protestants—everything but Catholics. There were still a few converts coming in when I was a girl, before the world got too strong for us. I must say I never dreamed that Shakerism would turn out the way it has. We've been victims of circumstance, I suppose. But we don't need to go into all that."

Sister Jennie shrugged and went briskly on to say that Groveland was abandoned in 1892, when she was fifteen. Most of its members had become too feeble to work. Groveland was the third of the society's communities to go under, and five others soon followed it. As was customary, the Groveland people moved to the nearest surviving Shaker village, which was one that had been established at Watervliet after Mother Ann's death there. It was at Watervliet that Sister Jennie reached twenty-one and elected to enter the order. She moved to Mount Lebanon in 1930, eight years before the Watervliet village was given up. "The North Family here needed somebody young and active," she told me, with a faintly challenging look. "I might as well admit that I do most of the work here—the marketing, the meal planning, the cooking, and in the winter I even tend the furnace. The truth is, I'm about the only one who can. That's in addition, of course, to making all my own clothing. Most of the others buy their clothes, which is contrary to custom, but they are no longer able to make their own, so it can't be helped. Also, I keep an eye on things in general, except for finances. What little money we've accumulated over the years, mostly from the sale of property but partly from selling the things we've made, is handled by a more business-minded member, over at Hancock. I think most of it's invested—in A.T.&T. and R.C.A. and stocks like that. If you're wondering how we got our land in the first place, it came from converts. In the early days, a good many of the converts were farmers. They gave us whatever land they owned, and if it wasn't conveniently near one of our villages, we sold it and bought some that was. That's how Mount Lebanon got started, from a gift. Our rule is—perhaps I'd better say was—that a convert must pay all of his worldly debts and settle any other obligations he may have outside and then make over to the community he chooses to join whatever money and property he has left. The agreement—or Covenant, as we call it—that a convert must sign before he is gathered in is very legal. Signing the Covenant is the final step in becoming a Shaker. An applicant must spend six months with us as a novice first. Nobody has ever been forced to become a Shaker or to remain one. Any one of us is free to return to the world at any time. The only thing is that if you leave after signing the Covenant, you're not allowed to return. And, of course, you can't reclaim your gifts."

The path had brought us down to a broad walk that ran between the dwelling house and the first of the two rows of buildings and there was another walk between the rows themselves. Just beyond the second row was a meadow in which several cows were grazing. Knee-high grass bordered the walks. The six buildings were at least thirty or forty feet apart, and they all looked even bigger, gaunter, and emptier than they had from the top of the slope. They made me feel uncomfortable. In spite of their size, or perhaps because of it, since it gave them a curiously urban look, they didn't seem quite real in this setting.

Sister Jennie gazed up at the buildings admiringly and sighed. As we strolled along the walk in the direction of the barn, she said, "If this were the old days, we wouldn't even be able to hear ourselves think. These buildings were about the busiest workshops you ever saw then. They were all workshops except that one over there. It used to be the novices' dwelling house and the infirmary. That's where Sister Sarah and Sister Sadie—Sadie Maynard, that is, who is getting a little queer, too—would be living now if we weren't so reduced in our circumstances. Sister Sarah used to be very good at making tape chair seats. Sister Sadie made bonnets. I couldn't begin to tell you how many different trades were carried on in these shops. The North Family did weaving, dyeing, tailoring, hatmaking, shoemaking, broommaking, soapmaking, blacksmithing, metalwork, carpentry, woodworking, seed drying, and goodness knows what else. Practically every family did a lot of different things. And, of course, all the families did a good deal more than just take care of their own needs. The different families in a village used to make things for each other. They all made things to sell to the world, too. We had to carry on some trade with the outside, because we couldn't very well raise everything we needed. We didn't like to do it, though, and we never tried to make more than a fair profit. The North Family's specialties—most of the families had at least one—were brooms and packaged seeds. I'll tell you something that you probably don't know. The Shakers here at Mount Lebanon were the first people in the United States to sell seeds in little packages—you know, the kind you can buy for a dime now in any grocery or hardware store. I mean vegetable seeds, of course. You may have noticed that there aren't any flowers around here. Shakers have never wasted time on useless things like flowers."

We had reached a gate that opened on the barnyard. At Sister Jennie's suggestion, we turned back toward the dwelling house. "I haven't lived seventy years without learning my own strength," she said cheerfully. As we were passing one of the former shops, a man in overalls suddenly came around the corner of it. He was squat, stoop-shouldered, big-eared, and white-haired, and he was carrying a pail of chicken feed. When he saw us, he stopped, looking startled and uneasy, as if he were not accustomed to encountering strangers. Sister Jennie greeted him with kindly warmth. "This is Brother Curtis White," she said to me. "He keeps me supplied with stovewood, and he's wonderful with chickens. Brother Curtis is sixty years, and he's the youngest member of the family." Then she told Brother Curtis that I was interested in Shakerism. He cleared his throat. "Place was alive forty years ago," he said glumly. "You liked to work here then. I came here as an orphan when I was eleven. Started out sickly, but work made me well. Used to be I'd milk twenty cows and cut a cord of wood every day. I'd cut a cord in three hours—times I've done it in two. Been cutting wood over forty years and I've lost only two toes. Wasn't my fault neither time. Both times, my ax had been ground by somebody else." He nodded to Sister Jennie and then to me. "Ground wrong," he added, and walked away.

Sister Jennie and I continued on to the rear of the dwelling house. A fat, slate-colored cat was sitting on the doorstep of the entrance to the women's side, watching us expectantly. Sister Jennie chuckled. "Old Moses is too polite to scratch or whine when he wants in," she said, opening the door. "He just waits." The cat ducked spryly between my ankles and through the doorway. We followed him into a dim, musty passage, full of sharp turns and lined with closed doors. "We're all very fond of Moses," Sister Jennie said. "He came to us twelve years ago, and we converted him. Shakers aren't supposed to have pets, but cats have always been allowed, because they're useful. They fight mice. Old Moses is going on twenty now. Shakers live forever, even Shaker cats. I suppose you've heard about the longevity of Shakers?" I confessed that I hadn't. "Well, it's a fact," she said. "You almost never hear of a Shaker dying until he's very, very old. We're almost never sick, either. Elder Frederick W. Evans, of this village, who was one of our greatest intellectuals—why, he even corresponded for a while with Tolstoy about cooperative farming and spiritual matters—used to say that no Shaker had any business being sick until he was past sixty. I agree with him. When you lead a pure, disciplined, non-competitive life, like ours, you just don't have the worries and anxieties that cause illness." She smiled, and added, "People didn't start calling us Shakers because we were all sick and trembly."

"How did the name originate?" I asked.

"Oh, the world's people made it up back in Mother Ann's time, to ridicule the way we worship," she said mildly, halting with her hand on the knob of one of the closed doors and turning to me. "I guess I might as well tell you that our meetings aren't like ordinary church services. They're mostly singing and marching. If you ever saw a Shaker meetinghouse, you'd probably say it looked like a ballroom or a gymnasium. We never had pews or anything like that—just benches around the wall. At the start of our services, there would always be a very short sermon by one of the elders. Then he would call out, 'Go forth and march!,' and the real meeting would begin. Six or eight good singers would form a group in the middle of the room and start a hymn. The rest of us would parade around them, marching two or three abreast. We had to march in step and we had to beat time with our hands in a certain way. Some of the marches were slow, but most of them were fast and lively. We really had to step. We'd keep going for an hour or more, and the faster we marched, the harder we'd be wrestling against the powers of evil. Sometimes, our struggles made us twist and turn. Well, that's what our enemies called shaking. At first, they called us Shaking Quakers, and then just plain Shakers. I don't know how we started using the name ourselves. It wasn't anything to be ashamed of, so I guess we just got into the habit. Besides, Shakerism is a whole lot more than a name." Sister Jennie opened the door abruptly. "We had our last meeting here in Mount Lebanon in 1933, just before we sold the meetinghouse," she said. "We're all too old now to march anyway."

We entered a broad, bare, white-walled foyer, with a steep staircase leading from it to the second floor. Through an open doorway, I caught a glimpse of what was apparently the women's parlor—a large, cheerless room crowded haphazardly with ladder-back chairs. The foyer was furnished only with a long refectory table, above which hung several lurid watercolor views of Venice and Naples, and a rigid but graceful wooden settee, on which three elderly women were sitting, looking like chaperons at a prom. They smiled at us with a kind of sedate excitement. One of them was Sarah Collins. Sister Jennie introduced me to her and to her companions—Eldress Rosetta Stephens and Sister Grace Dahm. Eldress Rosetta, who wore a sombre gray Shaker gown, is a tiny, sweet-faced woman of eighty-six. Sister Grace is in her middle seventies, small and round, with short, curly white hair. She was wearing a giddy green-and-lavender housedress. They all had risen upon being introduced, and Sister Sarah, whose dress, though of Shaker cut, was a rich crimson and made of a material that resembled velvet, greeted me with a jovial wink.

"I like a new face," she said.

"We've been watching you through the window," Sister Grace said. "We saw you talking to Brother Curtis, and everything."

"Dear Brother Curtis," Eldress Rosetta said. "He never seems to be doing anything, but he's a great help to us. I remember him when he was a little boy. I'm one of the ancients of this city, you know."

"Eldress Rosetta is English," Sister Jennie told me. "She was born in England."

Eldress Rosetta confirmed this modestly. "America is a noble country," she said, "but I grew up in London. My father kept an Aerated Bread shop on the Waterloo Road. Elder Frederick Evans brought me to Mount Lebanon when I was eleven. We met in England, where he was doing missionary work. My father had great respect for the Shakers, and my mother had died, so he let me come with Elder Frederick. We crossed the Atlantic Ocean on the *Great Eastern* in 1872. That was the ship they laid the Atlantic cable with, you know. It was a most magnificent ship. Europe had been combed for costly engravings to decorate it with. It was so grand that none of us children on board were allowed to go about unattended. They were afraid we might damage something, you see. I remember everything about the *Great Eastern* so vividly, more vividly than things that happened only a few years ago. Isn't that strange?"

"Well, I remember Groveland almost better than I do Watervliet," Sister Jennie replied.

"Watervliet was where I lived before I came here," Sister Grace said. "I remember it very well. It was nice there, and we had good friends in Albany."

Sister Sarah grinned at me. "I do like a new face," she said.

"We all do," Sister Jennie said gently.

There was a prolonged introspective silence, and then Sister

Jennie said that perhaps we had better continue our inspection of the house. "It's almost time for me to start getting supper ready," she explained. "We eat at five-thirty."

We excused ourselves and started for the stairs. "I think I'll just go along with you," Sister Grace said. She got up and joined us, and the two others settled contentedly back on the settee. As we passed the refectory table, I glanced at the watercolors above it. "Please don't look at those things," Sister Jennie said. "We're getting more and more lax here, I'm sorry to say. Just because someone gave those pictures to us, we had to put them up. Pictures were never permitted in the old days. Mother Ann always believed that they were distracting, and she knew that they are terrible dust catchers. That's the reason we don't have carpets, either. Tidiness is one of our principal rules. Mother Ann said, 'Clean your room well, for good spirits will not live where there is dirt. There is no dirt in Heaven.' And, look, here's another of our rules." We had reached the stairs, and she placed her right foot on the bottom step. "This is the way we must go upstairs," she said, glancing sharply at Sister Grace. "Some of us are getting out of the habit now, but the rule is always the right foot first. That's for discipline and uniformity. We are also supposed to put our right stocking and shoe on first."

There was no furniture at all in the second-floor hall. Sister Jennie opened a door at one end of it. "Well, this is my room," she said. "We each have a room to ourself now, but the rule used to be two to a room, sometimes three. First of all, I want you to notice that transom." The transom, which was open, was a wooden panel fixed on a vertical center pivot. "Most of our rooms have them," she said. "They're much more sensible than ordinary transoms, of course, because they create a real draft. They're something special with Mount Lebanon." Sister Grace and I followed Sister Jennie inside. It was a corner room, over twenty feet long and at least fifteen feet wide, with white plaster walls and two large windows, but it was so full of furniture that it looked small, cramped, and dark. In it were a narrow, cotlike bed; a big, square table with drawers; a built-in cabinet with drawers, which covered most of one wall and rose nearly to the ceiling; a three-step ladder stool; a chest of drawers; a sewing table; a small, octagonal table; a Morris chair; a ladder-back rocking chair; and three ladder-back straight chairs. Two of the straight chairs were hanging side by side against one wall, suspended from pegs by the upper slats in their backs. "That's the way Shakers keep chairs out of the way when they're not in use," Sister Jennie said. There were no pictures on the walls,

but there were two unframed cards with maxims printed on them.
One read:

> A man of kindness to his beast is kind.
> Brutal actions show a brutal mind.
> Remember: He who made the brute,
> Who gave thee speech and reason, formed him mute;
> He can't complain, but GOD'S omniscient eye
> Beholds thy cruelty. He hears his cry.
> He was destined thy servant and thy drudge,
> But know this: his creator is thy judge.

The other read "Shun idleness. It is the rust that attaches itself to
the most brilliant metals—Voltaire." "Sister Catherine Allen
of Mount Lebanon wrote that poem," Sister Jennie said, ignoring
Voltaire. "There used to be a copy of it posted in every Shaker
barn."

I picked my way around the room, with Sister Jennie sidling
along informatively at my elbow and Sister Grace watching us from
just inside the door. Except for the Morris chair and the octagonal
table, Sister Jennie assured me, all the furnishings were of classic
Shaker manufacture. They were made of dark-stained wood and
they were as ruthlessly severe and functional as a folding chair,
though considerably more handsome. "There isn't a thing in this
room that I'd let one of those greedy antique collectors lay a finger
on, except over my dead body," Sister Jennie said happily. "Especially that rocker. The Shakers invented the rocking chair, you
know, and mine—or, I should say, that one—is probably the oldest in this family. The less said about the Morris chair, the better. I
won't deny, though, that it's very comfortable. The octagonal table
was made by a neighborhood carpenter and given to us as a gift.
We took it in the spirit in which it was given, but it's all wrong. In
the first place, it's doodaddy, and in the second place, if you notice,
it's made of curly maple. Curly maple is the only wood that the old
Shakers never used. They thought it was too ornate."

Sister Grace moved a step or two into the room and gave a timid
cough. Sister Jennie looked at her inquiringly. "Would it be all right
if I showed him _my_ room?" Sister Grace asked eagerly. "I'd like for
him to see it, if it's all right." "Why—" Sister Jennie began, but
Sister Grace, cutting her short, turned to me and went on in a rush,
"There's some very nice furniture in my room, too—and besides
I've got a parrot named LeRoy that's over sixty years old and can
talk, and a music box that one of the world's people gave me that

plays 'A Bicycle Built for Two.' If you could come in for just a minute, I'd give you one of LeRoy's pretty feathers, and you could wear it in your hat."

I glanced at Sister Jennie. Her expression had become a trifle fixed. Then she smiled. "Well, I guess we've seen everything there is to see in here," she said, "so I don't see why not."

AUTHOR'S NOTE:

I must have been one of the last visitors to an inhabited Mount Lebanon. Soon after my visit, the surviving members were moved to a community in Hancock, Massachusetts. It, too, has long ceased to be a living Shaker village; it has, however, survived in the form of a museum. The big, bare, beautiful buildings that once housed Mount Lebanon's eight families stood empty for some years, but they, too, have been preserved. They now house the Darrow School, a preparatory school for boys.

[1946]

11. Rapido: *Into Italy*

I went to Italy some months ago—to Venice, to Florence, to Rome. It was my first visit, and I saw most of the sights that most first visitors see. I saw St. Mark's Square and the Doges' Palace, the Bridge of Sighs, Harry's Bar. I climbed the steps to the Piazzale Michelangelo. I saw the Duomo, the Pitti Palace, Harry's Bar. I climbed the Spanish Steps. I saw the Sistine Chapel, the Colosseum, the Trevi Fountain, Harry's Bar. But I also saw some sights that tourists these days seldom see. I did all my travelling by train.

I began my Italian travels in Switzerland, in Geneva, up two long flights of deserted steps in the marble monumentality of the Gare de Cornavin, at six o'clock on a rainy morning. I had spent a couple of days in Geneva, chiefly at the headquarters there of the World Health Organization, and when my business was finished I decided to give myself a holiday; being still barely convalescent from my transatlantic flight, I decided to take the train. My train was the daily Paris-Venice Express, leaving Geneva at 6:07 A.M., with stops at Lausanne, Domodossola (at the southern end of the Simplon Tunnel), Stresa (on Lake Maggiore), Milan, Brescia, Verona, Vicenza, and Padua, reaching Venice at 4:20 P.M. I stood on the glassed-over platform at Track No. 3 in the loom of a string of darkened passenger cars, with a heavy suitcase and an empty stomach, with a dozen words of French and three or four of Italian, and waited for somebody to tell me what to do.

A businessman with a briefcase came up the steps.

"Parlez-vous anglais?"

A stare. He went on.

An elderly couple came up the steps.

"Parlez-vous anglais?"

A stare. *"Non."*

178

A man in a blue uniform (porter? trainman? clerk?) came along the platform.

"Parlez-vous anglais?"

He stopped and looked at me. He shrugged. I pointed up and down the string of standing cars.

"Venice?"

He looked me carefully over.

He said, *"Première classe?"*

I nodded.

He took me lightly by the arm and led me up the platform. He stopped at the third car. A small sign near the entrance read "VENE-ZIA." I thanked him from the bottom of my heart. I climbed aboard, and the lights went on. It was a car much like an American Pullman bedroom car, with a row of compartments opening on a narrow windowed aisle. The compartments were glassed in and contained two facing settees upholstered in orange fabric, each divided by armrests into three seats. I found my designated compartment and my designated seat, a window seat facing forward. I stowed my suitcase in an overhead rack and sat down and looked at my reflection in the window. The car gave a little stir. I took that to mean that we were now joined to the Paris-Venice Express. The compartment door opened, and a man came in—a short, stocky, bald-headed man in tan suède shoes, dark trousers, a pale-gray jacket, a striped shirt, and a bow tie. He put his luggage on the rack, smiled and nodded, and sat down in a facing seat near the door. He opened a copy of *La Suisse*. My empty stomach rumbled.

"Pardon," I said. I pointed fore and aft. *"Wagon-restaurant?"*

He shook his head. *"Non. Pas de wagon-restaurant."*

I looked sick.

He smiled. He gestured toward the aisle. He made a motion suggestive of pushing a cart.

"Le mini," he said. *"Café. Croissant."*

I pointed to my watch.

He nodded. *"Bientôt."*

The train gave another stir. It began to move. We slid silently through the station, into the dusk of dawn. It was still raining. Buildings passed in the gloom. Steep, tree-lined streets climbed up and away. A conductor appeared. He held out his hand for our tickets, gave them each an absentminded punch, and withdrew. I looked out the window. Geneva had vanished. There were no outskirts; there was the city, and then there was open countryside—hillside vineyards, hilltop groves of pine, plunging, foaming waterfall streams. A cart came trundling down the aisle. *Le mini!* I jumped to the door.

I held up a finger. *"Café au lait."* I held up another. *"Crois-sant."* I held out a handful of little Swiss coins.

I went back to my seat with a steaming container of coffee, a little container of milk, a packet of sugar, a croissant wrapped in wax paper. The croissant was almost the size of a small loaf of bread. It was neither hot nor cold. There was no butter. I took a bite. It was fresh and flaky. It was perfection. I all but rolled my eyes. I took a swallow of coffee. Oh, my God! I couldn't believe it. I took another swallow. And it was true. It was the richest, the coffee-est coffee I had ever tasted. It was a masterpiece to match the croissant. It was the kind of coffee that one might hope to find in a four-star restaurant. A five-star restaurant. And I had found it on a snack cart on a train.

The morning slowly brightened. There were long, low, hill-hugging farmhouses here and there among the climbing vineyards. Through the compartment door, through the windows along the aisle, I could now make out the lake—the Lake of Geneva, Byron's inspiring Lake Leman. The waters were dark and choppy. They stretched darkly away, beyond the horizon, to France. It didn't look much like Byron's depiction in *Childe Harold:* "Lake Leman woos me with its crystal face." It looked more like the North Atlantic.

The train began to slow. It gently stopped: Lausanne. I looked out at a wall, a muddy flower bed of salvia, an old woman in black. The compartment door opened, and a young woman in a Burberry raincoat came in. She had long blond hair and three-inch heels, a Vuitton carryall, and what looked like a French paperback edition of an American gothic. She looked at me and then at the bald-headed man. There was a rapid exchange between them in French. She heaved her bag and her raincoat up onto the rack and took the seat at the opposite end of my settee. She opened her book. She read intently for a good two minutes. Then she looked at me again.

"I think you are American," she said. Her English was almost without accent. "I am right?"

I said she was. And how did she know?

She laughed. *"Oh là là!* There is no difficulty. You have the buttoned-down collar and the jacket with one vent. In Europe, it is two vents or none."

I asked about her excellent English.

She shrugged. "It is necessary to my job. I am a courier—a tour guide. I have English, German, Italian, and, of course, French. I am Swiss. I have known many Americans on my tours. I am interested in how different they speak. Some like you. Some not. I love America. I hate Switzerland. I am unhappy in Switzerland. It is because I know so many other countries. I go now to meet a tour in Milano. I think I will live in Italy. Or maybe France. Or America. How I would love to live in America! It is my dream. Look!" She brought out a package of Marlboro cigarettes. "I smoke nothing else." So, in fact, did almost every other smoker I observed in the course of my trip. The exception was an American girl at a table next to mine in Madonna, in Venice. She was smoking Player's. A long-expatriated American I dined with in Rome confirmed my observations. "It's that Marlboro cowboy," he told me. "Marlboro was just another cigarette in Europe until they came up with that guy with his big hat and all those horses. Europe is very macho— men and women both. Marlboro fits right in with the bluejeans and the boots and the big, hand-tooled leather belts. It's part of that everlasting romance with the Wild West."

The courier went back to her book. The bald-headed man was still deep in *La Suisse*. I went back to my window—to the vineyards, the leaping alpine streams, the rain. A town appeared: Vevey. Then a village: La Tour-de-Peilz. Then another: Clarens. Then a town: Montreux. Associations surged: Rousseau, Byron again and Shelley, Charlie Chaplin, Nabokov, Simenon. I looked, too late, for the Castle of Chillon. Then the lake was gone, and we were in the depths, the deeps, of the valley of the Rhône. The hills rose into mountains, into rock and fir and a distant glimpse of snow. The mountains climbed, mile after mile, always changing always the same. This was no mere scene. This was Scenery.

The compartment door opened, and a man in a blue uniform came one step in. He stopped and stood almost at attention. He extended a hand. *"Passeports, s'il vous plaît."*

The scene, the Scenery—everything—vanished in a total blackness. The bald-headed man looked up from his paper. The courier looked up from her book. She gave me a professional smile. "Simplon," she said in the voice of a guide. "The famous tunnel."

I knew the statistics. It was twelve and a half miles long—the longest tunnel in the world. It lay at an elevation of around twenty-three hundred feet. And—I felt a little twitch of not quite uneasiness—we were piercing the very heart of the Lepontine Alps. The roof of rock above us was seven thousand feet thick.

My companions went back to their reading. I sat and waited. There was no sense of motion, almost no sound. We seemed suspended in space. The bald-headed man turned a crackling page. The black at the window began to pale. I could make out the rock of the tunnel wall. We burst out of the tunnel into light—into light that was more than mere daylight, into a dazzle of brilliant sunlight. We had left the rain in Switzerland. We were in Italy. We were still in mountains. But it was a different scene, a different Scenery. The sun made all the difference.

The compartment door opened, and a man in a pale-blue uniform stepped in. He inclined his head, he smiled, he held out his hand. "Passaporti, per favore."

The mountains began to diminish. They shrank to foothills, to hills, to broad, vineyarded slopes, to an occasional tilted, stubbled cornfield. Houses, then buildings appeared, and a railroad station with flower beds and trees: Domodossola. We moved abruptly on. I closed my eyes and dozed. I awoke to a softer countryside. It had a sun-swept, pastel, almost Mexican look. No, not Mexican. It was a landscape painted by Pissarro. The farmhouses were square, solid, rooted, tinted pale yellow, pale orange, with red tile roofs and green shutters. A man in rags stood in a doorway eating an apple. I looked at my watch. It was only a little after ten, but I had breakfasted lightly and long ago and in another country. I began to think about lunch.

I asked the courier about a restaurant car for lunch. She seemed to reflect, then spoke to the bald-headed man. She turned back, smiling.

"You will eat after Milano," she said. "The *wagon-restaurant* is added there, at Milano."

"And when do we get to Milan?"

"Just after noon," she said. "At twelve-twenty."

I said I only hoped that we were on time.

"On time?" she said. "I do not understand. The train is always on time."

It was on time, precisely, to the minute. Then we sat there, in the huge, glass-roofed shed of the Stazione Centrale, flanked by track after track after track, by standing strings of passenger cars, by waiting trains (one with a restaurant car full of people eating and drinking), by trains coming and going, by platforms surging with uniformed porters, uniformed police, travellers of every class and kind, for thirty-five minutes. It was a scene that tugged sadly at memory. It made me think of Grand Central Station in New York some thirty years ago.

Our compartment now was almost full. The courier had departed to join her tour, but the bald-headed man still sat in his corner seat. Her seat was now occupied by a young Italian in a dark three-piece suit with dark circles under his brooding eyes, and in the two seats opposite me were two Germans, men in their late thirties—one dark and one fair, and both in tight, flared trousers and glossy and pungently leather-smelling leather jackets. The fair one sat writing slowly, thoughtfully, in a book-size diary. His friend sat smoking, chain-smoking, Marlboros. The Italian sat erect, lightly tapping his foot. I already missed the courier—her company and her English. The train gave its gentle stir, and we gently began to move. We moved through a maze of tracks, past warehouses and factories, through slums. They were dreadful slums, old and crumbling, but they were not the kind of slums I knew. They were not American slums. They had the sour and grimy look of poverty but they also had an alive-and-kicking look. There were flowering plants on every windowsill, and every back yard, every tiny, angular patch of unpaved ground, was a garden green with lettuce and cabbage and spinach and the last of the season's tomatoes, and every fence or wall was strung with grapevines.

A man in a starched white coat came along the aisle, opened the compartment door, and handed out a kind of menu. The Swiss declined his. The Italian took his but didn't look at it. The Germans took theirs, folded them neatly, and put them in their pockets. I took mine and read it with total concentration. It was headed SER-VIZIO RISTORAZIONE." The rest was printed in Italian, French, German, and English versions. The menu in English read:

IN CAR BUFFET-BAR OF THIS TRAIN

Meals at Fixed Prices
Lunch or Dinner
Pasta asciutta
Meat or Poultry
Vegetable-Cheese-Fruit
(Drinks not included)
L. 7.400
Service and taxes included

There followed a long list of drinks of many kinds, with their prices. Coffee was L. 350. Wine (quarter litre) was L. 900. Mineral water (half litre) was L. 500.

I got up and moved out the door. The waiter was headed forward. The buffet-bar, then, would be aft. I found it two cars back. It was a standard dining car, with tables for four flanking a center aisle. I was shown to a window seat across from an elderly Italian woman with a thin bun of white hair and thick black eyebrows. We were joined by a bearded Italian in a leather jacket and a tall, blond, thin-lipped German woman of around forty. There was no conversation. This wasn't America. I glanced at the German woman, and she looked instantly away. The other woman sat with her eyes on her plate. She might have been saying grace. The bearded man fidgeted, looking up and down the car, drumming his fingers on the table. The car filled up, was finally full. The performance then began. And it was a performance—a deft, practiced, precision performance.

A waiter rolled a drink cart up the aisle. *"Vino rosso? Bianco? Minerale?"* The two Italians and I chose wine: a quarter-litre bottle of Chianti. The German woman ordered mineral water.

Close behind the drink cart came another. This was the pasta cart. It drew abreast of our table. One, two, three, four—we each received a giant dollop of pasta asciutta. It was shell-shaped macaroni in a thick, hot sauce of garlic and tomato. I ate with appetite and pleasure. The two Italians ate as if famished. The German woman frowned and picked. I still had a couple of bites to go when the next cart appeared. I finished just before my plate was snatched away. Another plate and another dollop—two dollops. One was a chunky veal stew in a rich brown sauce. The other was a giant helping of buttered zucchini. And a big hard roll. My appetite had dulled a little, but I ate again with pleasure. The Italians were still famished. The German woman continued to pick. A measured interval passed. I could see the next cart waiting in the wings. The performance was rising to its climax. I finished my stew, my zucchini, most of my wine. The ultimate cart arrived: a big bowl of fruit (apples, pears, grapes) and little, individual, foil-wrapped discs of Bel Paese. And, for those who wanted it, coffee—tiny cups of *caffè espresso*. The cheese was sweet and creamy. The pear I chose was a perfectly ripened Bosc. The coffee was my first Italian *caffè espresso,* and a revelation. It bore almost no resemblance to American *caffè espresso.* It was like comparing my earlier snack-cart coffee with American coffee-break coffee. I paid my bill (it came to the equivalent of about ten dollars) and went back to my car, my compartment. The aisles were crowded with passengers waiting for the second seating, the second performance. I almost envied them. I would have enjoyed an encore. It had been a bravura production.

* * *

I found the bald-headed Swiss alone in the compartment. The others, apparently, were out to lunch. The Swiss had brought his own. He was eating from a paper bag what looked like a pâté sandwich, and on a little ledge at his elbow were a plastic cup and a half-litre bottle of Beaujolais. We exchanged a companionable smile, a significant nod. We were the originals, the natives, here. The compartment for the moment was ours again. I stretched out in my seat. We were leaving a city, an industrial city: Brescia. And, as usual, there was almost no urban sprawl. There was city, then country—a lovely, soothing countryside of vineyards and crop-land, wandering rivers and distant hills, and the often decrepit but always beautiful foursquare pastel farmhouses. I gazed at it in peace and contentment.

The countryside ended, another city began. We slowed and floated to a stop: Verona. There was a movement in the aisle. The young Italian plunged in, wrestled his luggage off the rack, plunged out and away. Gazing out the window, I saw him emerge onto the platform. There was another surge of movement. He was charged, encircled, embraced by a shrieking young woman, by three small children, by a teen-age girl, by an elderly couple. They herded him triumphantly away.

The Germans came back, smelling of beer. The diary-keeper fell instantly to sleep. The smoker smoked his Marlboros. The countryside briefly returned. Then another city, another station: Vicenza. I sat up. *Vicenza!* The home of Palladio! The treasure trove of Palladian architecture! But all I could see was Track 5. I tensed, and waited. We moved on. I craned this way and that—out my window, out the window on the aisle. It looked like any Italian town. The usual countryside began. There was a hill in the distance, a scattering of trees, a slope of green. There was the sugges-tion of a building on the summit. It was much too far away to make out. But I saw it clearly in my mind's eye: a stucco facade, a double porch with Ionic and Doric columns, a sculptured pediment, a colonnade. A Palladian villa. A Palladian masterpiece.

The Germans got off at Padua. The train moved on. The end of a journey is always swift, always sudden. There was another moment of countryside. Then the cranes, the storage tanks, the refineries of Mestre—the industrial fringe of Venice—loomed across the plain. We glided across the causeway (the Austrian bridge, built in 1846 to the outraged cries of Ruskin and other traditionalists) and into the station: the end of the line. I followed the Swiss along the aisle and out to the platform. He stopped there, put down his bags, and extended his hand. He smiled. *"Au revoir."*

I smiled. "Goodbye." We smilingly shook hands.

He turned away. I lost him in the crowd. I walked up the platform and through the station and out onto the great porch to the long steps leading down to the Grand Canal and the ferries and taxis moored at the quay. I started down. A cowled figure sat on one of the steps. It was a woman with a tragic face and an infant nursing at a long, pale breast. She held out a hand. *"Bambino!"*

I found a couple of hundred-lire coins. She raised her head and smiled. *"Grazie."*

She couldn't have been past her middle thirties. But she had no upper front teeth, and only one below.

I stood at the crowded coffee bar in the Venice railroad station with a cup of *cappuccino.* I had spent three days in Venice, and now I was travelling on, to Florence. I listened to the talk around me, to the high-speed babble of Italian, and wondered why the Italians (and the French) seemed to talk so fast. English by comparison, even English English, was a drawl. Was it race? Was it linguistics? Or was it simply because to me it was a babble? A louder, more urgent babble filled the room from somewhere overhead. I didn't know the language, but I knew the voice. It was the international voice of the loudspeaker—a microphoned announcement. I listened with a touch of anxiety. Was I missing something I should know? I finished my coffee and picked up my bag and went out into the great sunstriped shed that gave on the spread of tracks and platforms. I walked along and found what I wanted: "INFORMA-ZIONE." I went in and up to a counter. A woman clerk raised her head.

"Rapido per Firenze?" I said. I knew I would never again even inwardly smile at someone struggling with English.

"It leaves at eleven-twenty-eight."

"Binario?"

"You wish to know the number of the track?"

I said yes.

"That *rapido* has the name Freccia della Laguna—Arrow of the Lagoon. It will be on Track No. 16. It is all seats reserved. You have your *prenotazione?* Your reservation?"

I said I did, and thanked her.

"OK," she said.

* * *

My car was a gleaming, spotless coach. There was an off-center aisle, with sections of facing double seats along one side and a row of facing single seats along the other. My seat was one of the tête-à-têtes. The car was quickly filled. Voices were raised, tickets were waved, people were evicted from their seats, the conductor was appealed to, the evictees moved on to evict others, luggage was heaved from rack to rack, cigarettes were lighted, outraged fingers were pointed at no-smoking ideograms. The train made its effortless start and began to move. A fresh-faced man in his middle twenties—jeans, tweed jacket, turtleneck jersey—came down the aisle. His seat was the one facing me. We smiled and nodded. The causeway began. I looked back at the last of Venice. The babble gradually stilled, like a theatre audience waiting for the curtain to rise.

My companion gave me a tentative look. *"Parla inglese?"*

I knew the accent. It was my own.

"Yes," I said. "I speak it all the time."

He almost jumped in his seat. "Hey!" he said. "Terrific! Hey, that's great. I mean, Jesus, I haven't talked to another American, to anybody that really spoke English, in almost two weeks. It was getting so I felt like I couldn't breathe or something. Like I was, you know, all bottled up. Where're you going—Rome? Oh? I thought about Florence, but, Jesus, I've been so many places, and I've got a friend that I think is still in Rome. I'll tell you something. I never knew it was going to be like this. I don't mean I've had any trouble getting along. No problem. I started out in Madrid. Then I flew up to Paris. I've been in Brussels and Munich and— uh, Amsterdam. And Genoa and Milan and Venice. And, you know, everybody at the hotels and the restaurants and all like that, they all speak English. But I haven't had a single conversation—I haven't, like, talked to a single soul. And it's a funny thing, I never thought I was any great big talker. I mean, I was never the kind of guy that did all the talking. So this is terrific, I mean meeting you like this. I'm from Philadelphia. Where are you from? Eastern Long Island? I've been out there. My roommate in college's parents had a place out there. It was near Southampton. Is there something called Water Mill? Right, that was it. Hey, how did you like Venice . . ."

It was almost noon. A steward with gold epaulets on his starched white jacket came along the aisle. There was a hungry stir in the car. My companion took a slip for the first seating. I decided to

wait. I had had a late breakfast. And enough talk. I sat and watched
the familiar countryside slide past—the plantations of feathery
poplars, the endless vineyards, the tidy little apple orchards, the
tinted houses. I knew I was seeing only a surface. I knew there was
a darker reality. But I saw what I saw, and I saw only beauty and
pastoral peace.

The early lunchers began to drift back. I got up and moved against
the tide. If I passed my Philadelphia friend, I didn't see him. The
design of the restaurant car was much like that of my coach. There
was the same off-center aisle, a row of tables for four, a row of
tables for two.

"*Solo?*"

I nodded, and the steward led me to a table occupied by a priest.
He gave me a benedictory nod. There was a menu at my place. It
was another fixed-price meal. The car was slow to fill up. I had
forgotten that the performance began only when every table was
taken. I looked at my watch. It was already well past one o'clock,
and we were due to arrive at Florence at two-thirty-five. I remembered the courier: "The train is always on time." I sat and waited.
The steward strolled by. I caught his eye, and pointed to myself.

"Firenze!"

He smiled, and raised a calming hand.

I relaxed for a moment. But my car, with my luggage, was three
long cars away. The steward came strolling back. He gave me a
fatherly look. Then he turned and spoke what sounded like a
parade-ground command. The drinks cart appeared. The steward
pointed to a table for four up ahead. "Firenze!" The cart trundled up
to that table. The steward pointed again. The cart shot forward.
Then it was my turn. The priest looked patiently on. I ordered a
half-litre bottle of Chianti. The cart moved along to the next Firenze. The pasta course this time was noodles, creamy with melted
butter and topped with freshly grated cheese. The meat was slices
of roast veal in a brown sauce, and the vegetable was spinach—the
spinach for which Florence is famous. The cheese was again Bel
Paese, but this time the waiter cut it from a wheel—a slice almost
as big as a slice of cake. My fruit was another Bosc pear. The *caffè
espresso* was, as before, two tiny swallows of perfection. I finished
and paid my bill. It was five minutes after two. The steward gave
me a pleasant smile. It was also an I-told-you-so smile.

We were coming into Florence. I got down my bag and my
raincoat. My companion's seat was still empty. I headed down the
coach. My companion was standing at the last section of seats,

bending over a brown-haired girl in a green suède suit. She was smiling an intoxicating smile. As I came up, she was saying, "Oh, Rome's different. You'll really love Rome. I mean, you really will—"

She looked up and broke off, and he followed her look.

"Hey," he said. "Oh, that's right. You're getting off at Florence. Well, it was real great talking to you."

"I enjoyed it too," I said.

"Great," he said. "And *ciao*."

My last meal in Florence was lunch, and I had it at the big, comfortable station *ristoratore* near the Santa Maria Novella. It was a bar-buffet, and a good one. The loudspeaker babbled its urgent babble, but I heard it this time undisturbed. I knew what I needed to know. The *rapido* I was taking on to Rome was again the Freccia della Laguna, and I could see across the sweep of the train shed the empty, waiting track (Binario 12) as I ate. I got my lunch—two sandwiches of thick-sliced baked ham on little round buns—at the buffet (by pointing), and carried it over to a window table. A waiter brought me the usual half litre of Chianti and, later, a *caffè espresso*. When I saw the Freccia della Laguna pull in, I gathered up my things and went unhurriedly aboard. I had, as before, a tête-à-tête seat, and I shared it with an ample woman in her fifties with rimless glasses and a copy of *La Nazione* turned to the crossword puzzle. The section across the aisle was occupied by a French couple with a teen-age daughter and a younger son. The father wore bluejeans, the mother smoked Marlboros, and the daughter wore her hair pulled back through a hand-tooled leather ring. The tooling depicted a galloping horseman and the legend "Pony Express: First with the U.S. Mail."

I resumed my window-gazing of two or three days before. After the overflowing sidewalks and the death-wish traffic of Florence, I was ready for immersion in another Post-Impressionist countryside. It was a countryside now of rounded hills and steepening vineyards and vivid hilltop silhouettes of cypresses or umbrella pines and an occasional cluster of walls and rooftops surmounted by a campanile. Houses that I took to be trackworkers' houses appeared at intervals of several miles. Each of them had its garden and a terrace in the shade of a grape arbor. They were solid two-story, square-built stuccoed houses, built for function and endowed with beauty, and as I watched them pass I felt a stir of memory. They made me think, in their practical simplicity, in the instinctive artistry of their design, of the little foursquare, stone-built houses along the Potomac River on the towpath of the Chesapeake & Ohio Canal, which were built by a tightfisted nineteenth-century capitalism to house the tenders of the locks.

A highway swept down from the hills and swung parallel to the railroad tracks. It was the Autostrada del Sole, one of the principal roads that lead to Rome. Traffic by American standards was light, and it looked, even by Italian standards, fast. But it wasn't fast enough. I watched as we overtook each speeding truck, each rushing car—overtook and passed and left far behind. The Freccia della Laguna was truly *rapido*. We could hardly have been moving at less than a hundred miles an hour. I thought of the Long Island Rail Road and the three long, jolting hours it takes to cover the hundred miles from my village of Amagansett to the Pennsylvania Station in New York.

Somewhere south of the aerie hill town of Orvieto, in a rocky pasture bounded by vineyards, I saw a flock of sheep. The sheep were the first livestock I had seen in Italy, and I gave them an interested look. They didn't really look like what I thought of as sheep. They were much too small for sheep; they were lambs. But they were small even for lambs. I watched the flock of tiny creatures out of sight and wondered. A day or two later, in a restaurant in Rome, at the suggestion of my expatriated American friend, I ordered one of the specialties of Roman cuisine, *abbacchio arrosto* —roast leg of baby lamb. It arrived on a little platter—a whole leg of lamb. It was about the size of a chicken leg.

I came out of the Termini at Rome and into the immensity of the Piazza dei Cinquecento. I had been blocked and buffeted all the way from the train, and there were a hundred people ahead of me at the official Yellow Taxi stand.

A short young man in a fringed leather jacket fell into step beside me. He gave me a winning smile. "Taxi?"

I looked at him.

"What hotel you go?"

I told him.

"Buono!" he said. "Ten thousand lire."

I shook my head.

"Eight thousand." I shook my head. He made a gesture of abject capitulation. "Six thousand."

I knew the price was probably still exorbitant. A gypsy cab is

never less than exorbitant. But it was getting dark. And there was
the almost motionless line at the official stand. I said OK.

"OK," he said. "Now quick." He pointed far across the piazza.
"The Mercedes."

We crossed the piazza at a half trot. He opened the trunk of his
car and flung in my bag. He moved around and held open the
right-rear door. I ducked my head and started in—and felt his hand
on my arm. He gently drew me back. He had a slumped, apologetic
look.

I said, "What's the matter?"

He slightly turned his head. A tall, young, fierce-looking policeman was standing at his elbow. The driver moved quickly
around the car and unloaded my bag. He handed it to me with a
shrug.

The policeman stared at him for a long moment. Then he stared
at me. He pointed back across the piazza to the taxi stand. "Only
the Yellow Taxi," he said. "Only the Yellow." He pointed to the
driver. "Not allow!"

The driver stood with his head down. I hoisted my bag and
trudged back across the piazza. I joined the line at the taxi stand. I
watched the little yellow Fiats come and go. I glanced back toward
the Mercedes. It was still there. The policeman had disappeared. I
gazed around, and saw a familiar back, a familiar fringed jacket.
The driver was coming out of the station, keeping quick step with a
heavily laden elderly couple, smiling an ingratiating smile, waving
an expressive hand.

[1981]

12. Trans Europ Nuit: *Copenhagen to Paris*

I was checking out of the Hotel d'Angleterre in Copenhagen one afternoon some weeks ago when another American arrived to check in. He spoke American and he looked American. In his late fifties or early sixties, he was of medium height, he had long gray side-burns and curly gray hair, his trousers were skinny bluejeans, his jacket was a quilted down vest, his shirt was checked and buttoned with snaps and his belly hung heavily over his belt, his shoes were tan snakeskin cowboy boots, and his hat was a big, elaborately curled and dented Stetson. I studied him out of the corner of my eye, and wondered. Texas? Oklahoma? Nebraska? I finished my business and moved away, and sneaked a look at his registration form. I couldn't make out his name, but I glimpsed his place of residence: New York City.

I had spent four enjoyable days in Denmark, in Copenhagen. I walked in the Tivoli gardens. I strolled the mile-long pedestrian Strøget, the city's sumptuous version of the Via Condotti in Rome, and I drank the peerless Danish coffee at several of its many pave-ment cafés. I strolled the Nyhavn waterfront, and noted a sign in one of its many tattoo parlors: "I Tattooed Your Dad." I gazed at the lovely old house there (at number 20) where Hans Christian Andersen wrote his first fairy tales, and the house (at number 18) where he died. The doorman at the Angleterre pointed out to me, across the parklike Kongens Nytorv square, the house in which Sören Kierkegaard was born. I climbed the corkscrew ramp of the seven-story Round Tower (which Peter the Great of Russia is said to have climbed on horseback) and looked down, as from the top of the Empire State Building, on the whole of the city. I ate the best fish I've ever eaten at the *fiskekaelderen* (fish-cellar) restaurant Den Gyldne Fortun, and I ate delicate reindeer medallions at the Egois-ten. I never saw a piece of litter (I watched a man—a young man

—walk fifteen feet out of his way to drop a Coca-Cola can in a trash basket), and I never saw a uniformed policeman, or even heard a siren. I liked everything about Copenhagen except the almost continuous wind. But I had awakened that morning ready to pack and move on. Now, looking at my fellow-American, my costumed fellow-New Yorker, I was more than ready; I was eager to be on my way.

I was going to Paris, and I was going by train. I am one of those who have a fondness for trains—almost any kind of train—and, having never spent a night on a European train, I had booked a sleeping compartment on the *lyntog,* the Danish express to Paris that leaves Copenhagen every afternoon at the comfortable hour of four-forty-five. The Angleterre doorman called me a cab (the customary gleaming Mercedes), and the driver (who, as is usual in Copenhagen, spoke English and had a brother in the United States) drove me, in the Roman style of horn and brake and drag-race plunges, to the red brick, turn-of-the-century magnificence of the Central Station. He opened the door for me and got my luggage out of the trunk and carried it into the entrance hall. I paid him and thanked him (there is no tipping in Denmark), and found my track (Spor 7) and sat down on a bench to await the boarding call. The concierge at the hotel had got me a timetable, and I looked up my train. It was No. 397, with stops at Hamburg and Liège and a connection at Hamburg for Munich. There were also some asterisks and some footnotes in Danish. I had a companion on the bench—a young woman, blue-eyed and with hair the color of wood shavings, in a big Icelandic sweater. I cleared my throat.

"Do you speak English?"

"Yes," she said. "A little."

I held out the timetable. "I wonder if you can tell me what this means."

"Oh," she said. "I fear not. I only visit here. I am Italian."

There was a sudden surge—a gathering into orderly ranks as if for some sort of parade—toward Spor 7, toward the stairs leading down to the tracks. The Italian girl was up and away, and I surged along behind her. There was a waiting train on Spor 8, and there were people placidly massed along its length. Spor 7 was empty. The Italian girl had disappeared. I asked a man with a briefcase which direction my train would come from. He shook his head. No English. I asked a woman with two shopping bags. She smiled and pointed to Spor 8. I was clearly out of the tourist zone. I stood with my luggage and watched the commuters—I supposed they were

commuters—standing and waiting, and thought of the free-for-all
on the Long Island level of Pennsylvania Station. The crowd began
to melt away, and the train on Spor 8 stirred. Behind me, there was
a hiss like a giant sigh, and a black-and-red locomotive marked
"D.S.B." ("Danske Statsbaner") and a string of shiny black cars
came gliding almost surreptitiously along Spor 7. The first cars
were coaches, the next were couchettes, then—marked in white
"*TEN: Trans Europ Nuit*"—came the sleepers, each with a little
sign near the door: "Hamburg," "München," "Liège," "Paris." I
found my car and my compartment. I stowed my luggage on an
overhead rack, and sat down at the window end of the long, upholstered seat that would open into my bed. There was a kind of table
in the window corner with a top that lifted to disclose a washbasin.
There was an ideogram in red indicating that the tap water was not
potable. There was a mirrored cabinet on the wall above the washstand stocked with three glasses, a decanter of drinking water, two
folded hand towels, a package of highly perfumed soap (compli-
ments of Compagnie Internationale des Wagons-Lits), and a packet
(ditto) with a label that began with "*Gebrauchsanweisung*" and
ended with "Instant Shine." There was a little door at the base of
the washstand, and I opened it. Out came a little white china
chamber pot. There was another red ideogram on the windowpane.
It showed a bottle slashed by a big black X. It seemed incredible
that a Dane—one of the people who made Copenhagen the cleanest
city I had ever seen—would throw a bottle out the window, but if it
didn't mean that, it meant no drinking in the compartment, and that
(to judge from the flow of akvavit and Tuborg beer in Copenhagen)
was even less credible.

The train moved, was moving. It moved as silently, as
smoothly, as naturally as a ship under sail. The platform slid away.
In a moment, in half a moment, we were moving at speed, racing
—out of the glare of the sheds and into a dusky daylight, through
spreading railroad yards, past factories and warehouses, past blocks
of apartment houses, past a deserted suburban station, past another
spread of apartments. Then we were in an open countryside of
fields, pastures, hedgerows, an occasional mannered plantation of
pine or white birch. Denmark is a small country, and Copenhagen
is on two tiny islands, but I had a sense of space that was almost
Kansan. There wasn't a house as far as I could see. Then, suddenly
there were six or eight houses clustered together along a narrow
street—little square houses like doll houses, with steep, red-tiled,
pyramidal roofs. American farmers live on the farm. In Denmark,
farmers live in the village. The enormous countryside began again.

It was a landscape made for snow, for blizzards, for raging winds. The dusk deepened. There was a spark of light in the distance, a spidery glint of water, and then it was dark.

The sleeping-car steward appeared in the doorway. He was a stocky young man in a brown uniform, with a ruff of taffy-blond hair curling out from under a pillbox cap. He took my ticket and my passport, and gave me a French customs form to fill out. He spoke a functional, singsong English. I looked at my watch: it was almost six o'clock. I asked him when the restaurant car would be open.

He shook his head. "No," he said. "On this train there is no *wagon-restaurant*."

"No restaurant?" I said. "No place to eat?"

"No, no," he said. "You eat. There is a bistro on the ferry. We go from Denmark across the strait to West Germany on the train ferry. The bistro is good, is like . . . " He smiled, and made a gesture. "You have a tray. You move in line. You take care of yourself —take this, take that, take what you like to eat. Good food."

"And wine?"

"Oh, I think," he said. "Also beer and *snaps*."

I was getting hungry, and thirsty. "When do we get to the ferry?"

"One hour," he said. "Then one hour and five minutes on the ferry. Plenty of time. The strait is big—twenty kilometres. And when you come back your berth is made up."

The steward moved on, to the compartment next door. I heard an exchange in French—a man's voice, a woman's voice, the steward's voice. His French sounded better than his English. It had the curl of real fluency. And that reminded me. I unfolded the customs form. Like most government forms, it was full of ambiguities and seeming irrelevancies: if I had been a woman and married, I would have been obliged to state my maiden name. I duly listed my moneys—my dollars, my francs, my remaining kroner. I refrained from declaring one Danish coin, a tiny brassy coin about the size of a shirt button. It had come to me somehow in change, and I showed it to the hotel concierge. He said, "Five øre. One hundred øre make a krone. It is nothing." I asked what I could do with it. He said, "Throw it away."

I finished the form and sat back at the window. The countryside had vanished. The window gave me only my reflection. Then I noticed the windowsill. Fixed to it were six little brass plaques. The first one read, *"È pericoloso sporgersi."* The next read, *"Ne pas se pencher au dehors."* The next *"Nicht hinauslehnen."* Then *"Es*

peligroso asomarse." Then *"È perigoso debruçar-se."* And then
"Do not lean out." I looked up at the ideographic bottle. Don't
throw bottles out the window! I glanced again at the plaques. Don't
lean out the window! Well, defenestration was one problem that we
didn't have back home. We settled that a generation or more ago.
Modern American trains, like modern American buildings, have
windows that are made not to open.

I was tired of sitting. I got up and went out into the corridor to
stretch my legs. The door of the next compartment was open, and a
man of around forty, in a sleeveless sweater and an open shirt, was
standing there smoking a cigarette. He gave me a nod and a smile.

"Moving right along, aren't we," he said. His English was
American English. "And I haven't felt a bump. These European
trains! The steward tells me we'll be averaging around a hundred
and thirty kilometres an hour when we get into Germany."

"Is that right?" I said. I looked at him. "I thought you were
French."

"Oh?" he said. "Well, I am. More or less—I'm French-Canadian. I learned my English in the States. Most of it, anyway. I did
graduate work at Iowa State. But you ought to hear my wife's
English. She had three teachers—me, an English friend in Mon-
treal, and a woman we know from Alabama. She has an accent all
her own."

The French-Canadian rolled down the window and defenes-
trated his cigarette. There was a rush of chilly, damp air—salt air.
The Baltic Sea! The train began to slow. Lights appeared, and a
wilderness of tracks. A platform, a station shelter drifted up. A sign
loomed: "Rødby Faerge." The train stopped, stood, then slowly
backed up the way we had come. The platform, the station, moved
away. We stopped again. There were voices somewhere out in the
night. It was raining, a mysterious, drizzling, Baltic rain. We
moved again—back, then forward—gathered speed, slowed. A
man in a wet brown uniform, with a pipe upside down in his
mouth, stood hunched in a fall of foggy white light from somewhere high overhead. There was a clanking and grinding, a sinking
and swaying, a settling, a steadying. The steward came along the
corridor.

"Now we ride the ferry," he said. He pointed a finger aft. "The
bistro is that way out. Take your money, your valuables. I lock all
the compartments. There are always thieves."

* * *

I followed a stream of fellow-passengers down off the train and onto a metal deck. There was only a faint sense of motion, a regular dip and sway. A scant step or two from our track, a wall, a bulkhead, rose twenty feet or more. The ferry looked a good block long. I counted six cars in the shadowy light, but there may have been more. The locomotive had been left behind. A couple pushed past me—a youngish couple. The girl was short and chunky with raccoon eyes, and she wore a pair of bib overalls. The man was taller and chunkier and wore red-white-and-blue running shoes, sweat pants, and a gray sweatshirt with a number on the back and "University of Memphis Training Camp" across the front. I thought of the West Side cowboy at the Angleterre, and willingly got out of their way. I let them get well ahead, and then walked along beside the cars—past another "Paris" and a "München"—to an open doorway in the bulkhead. I went up three ringing flights of stairs. There were windows along an outer wall, but all I could see was the black, wet night and a lacy boil of white water far below.

The bistro was a large room furnished with long wooden tables and folding chairs, and there were two cafeteria counters back-to-back down the middle. I got my tray, I moved in line, I took care of myself. The food was an opulent assemblage of *smørrebrød*—big open-face sandwiches of many combinations of many kinds of cheeses and cold meats and fish on the inimitable rich, grainy Danish bread—and yogurt and fruit and pastries. I took a *smørrebrød* of thinly sliced ham, decorated with an almost floral design in mayonnaise and parsley and shavings of cheese, and another composed —an almost Beaux-Arts edifice—of tiny shrimps. I hesitated over a choice of tea or coffee, beer or akvavit, or wine. I took a half-litre bottle of Sichel le Cellier, *vin de table, rouge*. The currency at the cashier was kroner. Most of the tables were full: the ferry is not merely a train ferry but also carries trucks, cars, and foot passengers. I looked carefully around for the Memphis trainee. I found an empty chair at a table of jovial Danes (or Swedes or Finns or Norwegians), and watched them become more and more jovial over akvavit chased with beer and, every now and then, a round of liqueur chocolates.

A couple arrived at the table adjoining mine, and I lost interest in the Danes. The man was around thirty, and he was tall, dark, and handsome in a Mediterranean mode. His shoes were suède, his suit was silvery gray and double-breasted, his shirt was lavender with a white collar, his cuffs were fastened with heavy gold links, his

necktie was the color of his suit, and a lavender silk handkerchief
plumed from his breast pocket. The girl—she looked about twenty
—was slim and blond and beautiful. She wore emerald silk or satin
knickerbockers, green stockings, a rosy-pink brocade jacket, and a
grass-green blouse unbuttoned down to out-of-sight, and her right
hand blazed with an emerald ring. Her shoes had three-inch heels
and seemed to be made of three or four strands of stainless steel.
They sat down with their trays, and the man leaned back. The girl
opened a screw-capped litre of wine and filled his glass. He took a
listless sip, and began to eat. She ate with one eye on his every
move. He finished his *smørrebrød* and his wine. She refilled his
glass. There was a banana on his plate. The girl reached over and
quickly peeled it, quickly cut it into neat little discs. He drank his
wine and ate his banana, and she ate and watched. He finished, and
took out a package of cigarettes. I had to look away, and then had
to look back. She was leaning across the table, holding out a flaming cigarette lighter.

I woke up almost thinking I was back with the jovial Danes. But
this wasn't the ferry—this was the train, and we were standing in
the pitiless, piercing glare of a metropolitan station. I craned my
neck: "Hamburg." And the joviality was coming from the next
compartment—not the French-Canadian compartment but the
other, the one just beyond my ear. I thought I heard a guitar. I heard
shrieks and roars of laughter. I heard glasses and bottles and what
sounded like somebody dancing. I looked at my watch: it was almost midnight. I looked out at the station again. There were plenty
of people about—walking, waiting, waving, embracing. And a variety of uniforms: brown, blue, green. Two youths were sitting on a
bench, gazing at the train, eating ice-cream cones: it might have
been noon in a park. They suddenly slid away. We were moving,
but moving backward. We moved out of the station, past pillars,
past stairs, past benches and people, past signs for Marlboro and
Coca-Cola in German, and into a yard, past a string of freight cars
on a siding. They were painted bright red, and on each, in white,
was the name "Blue Star Lines." The joviality next door continued.
The train stopped, waited, and moved forward again. We pulled in
to a platform—a different platform. A woman sat on a bench,
slumped in sleep, a cat in a box at her feet. We waited, we moved,
we slipped away backward again. I dropped onto my pillow. There
were footsteps, running footsteps, in the corridor.

* * *

It was morning. I lifted the window shade. A lush green pasture
flew past. Three black-and-white cattle appeared, and vanished. We
were flying. My watch said seven-thirty. We were due to arrive at
the Gare du Nord at eight-forty. At this rate, we could be there
almost any minute. I got up and jumped into my clothes.

I was shaving when there was a knock on the compartment
door. It was the steward with my passport. I said something about
our speed—that we seemed to be making very good time.

He nodded. "Very good," he said. "I think we are now only
twenty minutes late."

"Late?"

"We left late from Hamburg—more than one hour. There was a
mistake."

"I thought we did a lot of waiting there," I said.

"Yes," he said. "The conductor comes to me. He says, 'How
many passengers do you got in this wagon for Munich?' He says
Munich! I say, 'I got eleven passengers in this wagon for *Paris.*
This is a Paris wagon.' And he says, 'This is the Munich train.' I
don't know who made the mistake. But except for me we would all
be now in Munich."

"Well," I said. "Good for you."

"No," he said. "Not good for me. Good for you. But I get paid
only when I work. If we were now in Munich, I have more hours
work, more money."

I finished shaving and packed my things, and went out into the
corridor. The steward was knocking on a door three compartments
away. The door of last night's joviality was ajar, and I caught a glimpse
of a man with a beard and of what looked like a matronly back. I
watched the countryside of France fly past—the little, hedged-in
fields, the narrow, hedged-in roads, the tiny, crowded, citylike villages. If Denmark was Kansas, this was Connecticut. The French-
Canadian came out of his compartment. He was still wearing his
sleeveless sweater, but he had added a navy-blue blazer and a necktie.

I said, *"Bonjour."*

"Hi, there," he said.

"The steward tells me we almost went to Munich."

"Vous plaisantez!"

We were in the Gare du Nord, stopped and standing at the platform,
and I was filing down the corridor within a minute or two of nine. I

wondered what would have happened if we hadn't got hung up in
Hamburg. The steward was waiting at the foot of the sleeper steps,
handling luggage like an American Pullman porter of twenty years
ago. Tipping is not strictly forbidden in France. I gave him the last
of my kroner, and added for good measure my little five-øre button.
I followed the crowd up the length of the train and into the station.
There was a big, plain bar-buffet just off the main room. It was
furnished with rows of tables for two and a service bar, and it was
crowded. I found a place, a table to myself, and ordered. Most of
the people around me were drinking coffee and eating rolls, but a
good many others were drinking wine; I watched a man across the
room finish off a glass of red wine and wave to a waiter for another. My waiter was back in a minute, shifting through the tables
and singing to himself, and served me a cup of coffee with milk, a
bowl of brown-sugar lumps, and a basket of five or six croissants.

I was enjoying myself—enjoying every sip and every bite—
when I saw the University of Memphis trainee and his companion
come in. They were still in their full regalia. There was an empty
table no more than a foot away from mine, and I saw them see it. I
saw them come up and sit down. I occupied myself with my coffee.
The trainee gave a satisfied grunt, a sociable grunt, and I sensed
him looking my way. I waited. But he only looked; his face was
blank. He turned back to his companion and said something that I
couldn't understand. Except that he said it in German.

[1982]

13. En Vitesse to Rome

I had occasion some weeks ago to make a trip to Rome, and for reasons of self-indulgence I took an overnight flight to Brussels (the shortest transatlantic experience of cramping crush and midnight babble and penny-pinching pretentious food that I could find) and made the rest of my journey in easy stages—Brussels to Paris, Paris to Lyon, Lyon to Nice, Nice to Rome—by train. All the trains I rode were clean and comfortable, and one of them, the new Paris-Lyon T.G.V. express, is the fastest train in the world.

But first I rested, convalesced. Jet lag is the chief malaise of the contemporary traveller, and its only cure, like that of the hangover, is time. Brussels is rich in therapeutic diversions. I took long, recuperative strolls around the cream-and-gold-and-gray baroque magnificence of the Grand' Place, and shared a sidewalk café table there one afternoon with a Nigerian businessman: "Oh, Brussels is a beautiful city. Oh, yes. It is a beautiful city for business, too. But the people—the Belgian people—are cold. Oh, so cold. They are as cold, I think, as the Liberians." I climbed up through the formal gardens of the Mont des Arts to the Patrimoine des Musées Royaux des Beaux-Arts and saw the stunning collections there of Pieter Bruegel and René Magritte. I sampled some of the numerous beers that are the Bordeaux and Burgundies of Belgium, and ate the delicious deep-fried roasted peanuts at the bar of the Hôtel Amigo. I lunched at Aux Armes de Bruxelles on the locally ubiquitous *moules et frites*, and dined at La Maison du Cygne on its twice-cooked (boiled, then sautéed) goose called *oie à l'instar de Visé*. And, at the suggestion of my Nigerian acquaintance, I rubbed for good luck the hand-polished brass right arm of the bas-relief, just off the Grand' Place, of the fourteenth-century Brabantine hero Everard t' Serclaes.

* * *

The Étoile du Nord *(1ère classe à supplément spécial)*—the express on which I was booked to Paris—leaves the Gare du Midi in Brussels at 11:43 A.M. and arrives (it is almost never late) in Paris, at the Gare du Nord, at 2:11 P.M. making the trip of roughly a hundred and sixty-five miles at an average speed of around sixty-five miles an hour. I was waiting on the platform high above the street (the Gare du Midi is one of the few railroad stations I know in which one *ascends* to the tracks) when the Star of the North—its stainless-steel flanks reflecting everything in sight—backed in, and it looked to me as if every other car was a restaurant car. I passed two of them on the way to my car, and in both there were people already at table. I found my compartment and stowed away my luggage and sat down. There were places for six passengers in the compartment, but I had it to myself. Along the aisle, there was much movement, but only in the direction of the restaurant car just aft. The train began to move. The industrial reaches of Brussels slid slowly, briskly, rapidly by. I decided that I, too, was hungry. I got up and followed the crowd. The restaurant car had tables for four along one side and tables for two along the other, and most of both were occupied. I stood and waited. The steward approached—a big man with flowing white hair and an elaborate white mustache who wore a stiff white uniform trimmed with gold braid. I held up a finger.

"*Bonjour, Monsieur. Avez-vous une réservation?*"

I showed him my *supplément* and my compartment ticket.

He shook his head. He pushed my ticket away—thrust it away. He fired a rapid rebuke and turned impatiently back up the aisle. I stood there.

I felt a hand on my arm. A woman's voice, an American voice, said, "Maybe I can help." I looked down at an attractive woman, a faintly smiling woman of about forty. She was seated with two older, sterner women and a much older man.

"Yes," I said. "Have I done something wrong?"

"No, not really. But the seating here is all by reservation. You make it in advance—at the station. I call this train the *déjeuner* special. Most people don't bother with a compartment. They just eat their way to Paris. But he told you not to worry. What he actually said was 'Be tranquil.' He said to wait—he would find you a place."

I thanked her with feeling, and waited. I watched the waiters swaying up and down the aisle with wine and beer and Pepsi-Cola. The steward gravely beckoned. He pointed me into an aisle-side chair at a table for four. My companions were all men—a tousled young man in a gray suit with vest beside me and, facing us, two heavy men of fifty or more in vested navy blue. All three of them had begun their two-and-a-half-hour lunch. The tousled young man was sipping Evian water and eating a plate of prosciuttolike ham; the men in blue were eating pâté and drinking Kronenbourg beer. They seemed totally unaware of my arrival. I looked at the menu: two or three choices for every course, and the courses were appetizer, entrée, cheese, and dessert. And *"Le café vous est offert."* The *déjeuner* of the Star of the North was too much like *dîner* for me, and I ordered à la carte: an avocado stuffed with the tiny North Sea shrimp called crevettes; cheese; and a half-bottle of Muscadet.

There was a sudden loudspeaker squawk. A parade-ground voice said *"Attention!"* Then came a tumble of French. Then: "Ladies and gentlemen. Please have your passports or identity cards ready for examination by the Belgian and French authorities." I got out my passport, and the tousled young man, craning his neck, took notice.

"Pardon," he said. "You are American?" He smiled an apologetic smile. "I thought you perhaps were English. I am a doctor, and I hope to go to America—to the great university of Johns Hopkins. I have correspondence with Dr. Bennett there. You know him, perhaps? The Americans are so different from the English. I have noticed that. I go to many international conferences. Like now, I am going to Toulouse. The English are so cold. You know? They are colder even than the French."

"You are Belgian?"

"Yes," he said. "But I am of Ostend. I am Flemish. So I grow up with two languages. First Flemish, then French. Now I am learning English. It is the language of science today. So I am pleased to talk in English for my practice. You like our crevettes? It is a specialty of my home. We have much good fish in our sea. Ah, look! See how the countryside has changed. The architecture of the farmhouses—the old ones not the new. There are now a different roof. We have left Belgium. We are in France. . . ."

Four figures in navy-blue uniforms appeared at the end of the car. The two Belgians had narrow red stripes on their trousers. The French were a man (with wide red stripes) and a woman—a young black woman—in a skirt and a little round hat with a red band. It was she who looked at my passport, and she handed it back with a wide, warm smile. The Flemish doctor and the two businessmen across the table each briefly flashed an identity card. The businessmen were now eating steak and drinking wine.

The doctor took a bite of sole and nodded down the aisle. "Germans," he said. "German tourists. The clothes are tourist clothes. It is interesting, the Germans. They are the only people of Europe who take their holidays in every month of the year. They have no tradition of August. That is why there is so many of them to see. But they are not bad. It is only the way they look. . . ."

The businessmen across the table moved on to cheese and ordered a second bottle of wine. The Flemish doctor chose a bunch of bright-green grapes from a passing trolley and ordered tea. I sipped my coffee. The doctor spoke of his wife, his children, his student years in Brussels. I spoke of my wife, my son, my student years in Missouri. I watched the passing countryside—the sugar-beet fields, the rows of poplars, the little farmhouses with their steep tile roofs. The businessmen were finishing their wine and an assortment of pâtisserie. I looked at my watch: it was almost two o'clock. Buildings appeared, a platform, a station, a sign: "Saint-Denis." The businessmen were sipping cognac in tall, slim glasses. The doctor looked intently out the window. He straightened his necktie and pulled down his vest. *"C'est Paris,"* he said.

I moved with the crowd down the aisle to the vestibule and down the steps to the platform in the Gare du Nord. The American woman, my benefactress of the restaurant car, was just ahead of me. She was carrying a big pocketbook and an attaché case. She caught the eye of a porter, and he came hustling over.

"Oui, Madame. But you have more luggage?"

"Oh, yes," she said. "It is coming."

"Oui. And how many pieces?"

"Forty-three," she said. *"Quarante-trois."*

"Madame?"

"I have a group," she said. "A tour."

I walked the streets and bridges and quais of Paris, and ate and drank and walked, and went to the races at Longchamp (where I saw the first bowler hats I had seen in years), and walked and ate and drank, and got lost in the Louvre (where I checked my raincoat under a sign that read, "We ask to the visitors to take off their bags and packets of the cloakroom before 4:30"), and on the morning of the fifth day I took a taxi to the Gare de Lyon and was directed to Quai 8 for the eleven-fifteen T.G.V. (Train à Grande Vitesse) for Lyon, scheduled—almost guaranteed—to arrive there, some two hundred and sixty-five miles to the southeast, at 2:10 P.M. I saw my T.G.V. from almost a block away—a dozen orange-and-white striped cars, brilliant even in the gloom of the station, and an orange-

and-white locomotive streamlined as for a leap into space. I found my car *("1ère Classe/Voiture 3/Non-Fumeur/Lyon")*, climbed aboard, and deposited my luggage in a shelved compartment *("Bagagerie")* in the vestibule. An automatic door opened into a car with seats in pairs along one side and single seats across the aisle. The seats were notably wide and were upholstered in some heavy orange fabric, and there were matching orange curtains at the windows. My seat was one of the single seats. I settled myself and got out that morning's *International Herald Tribune*. By the time I had reached Ann Landers, the car was full, and a moment later we were in motion.

The T.G.V., I had read, has a *grande vitesse* of two hundred and thirty-eight miles an hour. It cruises at about a hundred and sixty-five miles an hour. Even that is almost twice the speed of the fastest American train. Its speed is made possible by a combination of power and a newly engineered roadbed and track: deep ballast, concrete crossties, almost no curves. ("It is built like a highway," a railroad man told me later in Lyon. "There is no need to worry about grade. The train has the power to maintain speed on a three-and-a-half-percent grade.") This new roadbed, however, is not yet complete. It extends from Lyon only about two-thirds of the way to Paris (or did at the time of my trip), and we were moving now on a roadbed much like that between Paris and Brussels, jogging along at not much more than a hundred miles an hour. I watched a strangely familiar suburb of green lawns and blue swimming pools and ivy-covered houses drift up and away. The houses thinned out, truck gardens appeared, then grain fields, then a scatter of staring white cattle in a pasture. Then a grove of white birch. Then a peaceful stretch of river (or perhaps a canal) with a system of locks and an approaching barge, and two fishermen in berets standing on the bank. Then fields and pasture again. And then—a Kansas grain elevator. Then, in the distance, a Nebraska windbreak. Then a dump. Then a weedy, rust-streaked community of mobile homes. And that was too much. I went back to the *Herald Tribune*.

There is no formal restaurant car on the T.G.V. But one can eat, and eat well. One can, by prearrangement, be served a full-course meal at one's seat, on a folding table much like those on airplanes. Or one can walk through a car or two to a little bar-buffet. I was to dine with a friend in Lyon that night, at Léon de Lyon, and I lunched at the bar. Le Bar du T.G.V. is no snack bar. It offered both *spécialités chaudes (pizzas, quiches, croque-monsieur, tartelettes à l'oignon)* and *restauration froide:* sandwiches of Norwegian salmon, Parma ham, or goose pâté, all served on bread *(Tartine de pain Poilâne)* baked by the celebrated Parisian bakers Pierre and

Lionel Poilâne. I ordered an onion tart and a bottle of Beaujolais-Villages (from a list that also offered Côtes de Provence, Côtes du Rhône, and Saint-Émilion) and ate at a window counter. I ate and watched the passing scene. The countryside had recovered itself and returned to what I expected of France. There were narrow roads lined with poplar trees. There were little patchwork fields enclosed by squared low hedges that had been trimmed and shaped by hand. A village sprang up, a station platform, a little station with a sign: "Saint-Florentin." The patchwork fields flowed back. But something seemed to have changed. The hedges had lost their neatness, their trimness, their shape. They looked shaggy, almost blurred. And then I realized. They *were* blurred. We were on the new track and moving into our *grande vitesse*. We were moving as fast as any traveller has ever moved on earth.

I got a cup of *café express* at the bar and carried it safely back to the counter. I drank it without event. I walked easily through the two long cars to my seat. There was no unusual sense of motion. There was only the rush and blur of the countryside. I don't know what I had expected to feel—a sense, perhaps, of exhilaration. But speed, like everything else, has not only its value but its price. The window was no longer a real train window. It was a window without a real view. I had finished the *Herald Tribune*. I got out a book. T.G.V. wasn't all that different from T.W.A.

I read and napped and, in spite of myself, looked out the window from time to time. It was a habit hard to break. There were hills, almost mountains, on the left. There were the remains of what looked like a Roman aqueduct, but it was gone before I could actually see it. There was a dry-stone wall that might also have been Roman. There was a long, long tunnel. And another. And another. There was a wide river. We were on a bridge. We were crossing the Rhône. And then we were ambling past a tumble of old buildings overgrown with ailanthus trees and into the Lyon-Perrache station. The time, by my watch, was two-twelve.

I waited my turn at the taxi rank. A cab finally came. The driver murmured the usual *bonjour,* took my bags, and stowed them away in the trunk. He gave me an inquiring look.

I said, "Hôtel de Bordeaux et du Parc."

The driver stared at me. Then he turned and opened the trunk and took out my bags and put them on the sidewalk. He turned again. He pointed down a little slope of roadway and sidewalk to a clump of trees and a big, five-story yellow building with big black lettering across the upper facade: GRAND HÔTEL DE BORDEAUX ET DU PARC.

"*C'est là,*" he said.

I picked up my bags and crept away.

There was a café on the corner with rows of tables and white wicker chairs along the sidewalk and a green awning overhead: "Le Bistrot Perrachois." And a hanging sign: "*On Boit. On Mange. On Sympathise.*" I went over and sat down at a table and ordered a coffee. It had been an unusual day, and I wanted to savor it for a moment. I had travelled on the fastest train in the world. I had met an honest taxi-driver. And now I had found a café that offered not only drink and food but also sympathy.

I walked back up the slope to the Gare de Lyon-Perrache a couple of mornings later and located my train and went down to the platform. My journeys were getting longer. I had spent less than two and a half hours on the train from Brussels to Paris, and almost three on the T.G.V. My train today was number 1551 (*"Valence/Avignon/Arles/Marseille/Toulon/Nice"*), departing at 11:50 A.M. and arriving in Nice at 6 P.M. I waited on the platform in an ever-thickening crowd, almost a commuter crowd, and fought my way aboard the car marked "Nice." My seat was again a single seat, and I found it midway down the car. It was occupied by a tall young woman in a slouch safari hat. I summoned up my pidgin French.

"*Pardon,*" I said. "*Mais c'est ma place.*"

She got up without a word and walked away.

I made myself comfortable, and looked around. There was a priest asleep in the seat in front of me, and an elderly, pink-cheeked couple in the seats across the aisle. There was a man of around thirty in a business suit and with a flowing breast-pocket handkerchief in the aisle seat in front of them. He was reading a colored comic book. The woman in the safari hat was standing at the end of the car with the vacant look of a straphanger. A little boy in gray flannel shorts came trotting down the aisle. His eyes were wide and his lips were moving. I caught his voice as he passed: "*Oh là là, oh là là . . .*"

Lyon is the third-largest city in France, but we were already in open country. We were moving at a reasonable speed—a window-gazing speed—down the rugged valley of the Rhône. Even the valley floor was steep, and there were steeper wooded hills in the distance. And then, almost suddenly, there were vineyards—long strings of vines growing on narrow terraces buttressed with old stone walls. Many of the walls were whitewashed, and some of them served as signs—great billboard proclamations of vineyard or *propriétaire*. One of them, the only one I could read clearly, was

"Paul Jaboulet Aîné." It wasn't a name I knew, but I knew where we were. This was the famous Côtes du Rhône. I could have been looking at the birthplace of the wine I had drunk last night—the wine I would make a point of drinking at lunch. I looked at my watch: the time for lunch was now. I knew there was no restaurant car on this train, and no T.G.V. lunching at one's seat. But there would certainly be a buffet-bar. I found one just one car back. There was a small bar, attended by a man in a red jacket, a red-and-white striped shirt, and a red necktie. Facing it was a row of banquettes and tables. I ordered my wine and a *croque-monsieur*, and sat down at a corner table. A *croque-monsieur* is the robust ancestor of the anemic grilled-ham-and-cheese sandwich of America. The ham is plentiful, the cheese is real cheese, and the bread has texture and flavor. A couple approached, hesitated, and joined me. The man was blond and bearded, the woman was dark, with coal-black hair and eyes, and she had a ring on every finger. Both were in their middle forties. They settled themselves.

"You American?" the man said.

I said I was.

"I thought so," he said. "I heard you at the bar. So are we. For many years. But I am born European, in Germany. My wife is Latin-American."

"El Salvador," the woman said. "So poor. So sad a country."

"Where you from?" the man said.

"I live in New York," I said. "And you?"

"We live in paradise," he said. "A paradise on earth. Santa Ana, California."

"It is beautiful," the woman said.

"We have everything we want," the man said. "We have just been to Munich, where I have family. They tell me I have changed. They say I am materialist. I say, 'Of course.' They say I do not feel for the poor. I say, 'Why should I?' I came to America at age nineteen. I had twenty-five cents in my pocket. Now I have a beautiful home. I have a Jacuzzi. I have a Porsche—the fifty-thousand-dollar Model 928. I drive that on the weekend. I drive to work in a Mercedes-Benz. My wife has her Audi. When we travel, we stay only at the best hotels. Four stars."

"So comfortable," the woman said.

"Before America," the man said, "I worked in Lyon. I went back yesterday to see my old boss." He took a sip of beer and smiled. "He found me changed."

"I love Lyon," the woman said. "It is the real France. It is the most French of all French cities. More French than Paris. The people of Paris—I don't know. I think they are cold."

"Totally," the man said. "They're as cold as the Swiss."

On the way back to my car, I passed the boy in the gray flannel shorts, skipping up the aisle. The man in the business suit was still reading the colored comic book. The pink-cheeked couple were drinking wine and eating lunch from a brown paper bag. The man looked up and gave me a warm, winey smile. The priest was still asleep. The young woman in the safari hat was sitting in my seat. I stopped and stood a moment. She was staring intently out the window.

I said, *"Pardon, c'est ma place."*

She got up without a word and walked away.

We had left or lost the Rhône. We were moving through an arid landscape of rolling hills and brush and stone. But it was still a landscape of vineyards, and some of the vines were growing in an almost cobblestone soil. We flew through a tiny, clustered village. There was open country again, and then the beginning of a town. We began to slow, slowed, and stopped. There was a platform and a bustle of people. People moved down the aisle and off. People came aboard. I craned my neck, and made out a sign: Avignon. Avignon! I was looking at the ancient seat of the papacy in the fourteenth century, the home of Petrarch and Laura. But all I could see of it was a station platform and a poster advertising "1664 de Kronenbourg" beer.

South of Avignon, the countryside seemed brighter, sunnier. Of course—this was Provence. This was Monet's "magic light." This was the light—the clear, soft light—that so bemused van Gogh, the light that animated the terra-cottas and siennas and piney greens of Cézanne. I looked out at van Gogh cornfields and sunflowers, at Cézanne hillsides and olive trees. We passed, at speed, through Arles. The pink-cheeked man across the aisle leaned out and tapped the arm of my seat. He beckoned me in his direction and pointed out his window, pointed to a widening strip of silvery gray. *"La mer,"* he said. *"La Méditerranee.*

We moved into Marseille, past glimpses of the harbor and oil refineries and storage tanks, funnelling in toward the Marseille Saint-Charles station through a spreading network of tracks. There were tracks and sidings and waiting trains and moving trains and

switches and signals, but there were also wide strips of lawn between the tracks, and hedges, and rows of flowering oleanders. It
all had an oddly suburban look. The garden strips gave way to
platforms, a great glass roof closed overhead, we came to a gentle
halt. I watched the familiar bustle. Time passed. We backed slowly
out of the station, and moved slowly in again. We waited, and
moved again—and this time in earnest. We gathered speed. A man
with a trolley came trudging down the aisle—Pepsi, Kronenbourg,
Perrier, *jus d'orange, jus de pamplemousse*. I stopped him. I
wasn't particularly thirsty, and I wasn't particularly fond of grapefruit juice. But I couldn't resist that ridiculously pompous name.
"Une pamplemousse," I said.

The Marseille express was now a Côte d'Azur local. Aubagne.
Toulon. Hyères. We were moving through mountainous hills, high
and rugged inland, lower and broken along the coast. Through the
breaks I could see an occasional sweep of a truer and bluer Mediterranean. There were vineyards again. There were fields of roses—
seas of roses. There were palm trees. I got up and went to the
W.C., and came warily back. I looked down the intervening rows
of heads. It was almost disappointing: my seat was empty. The train
toddled along past old hotels and rising condominiums, from one
fashionable name to another. The loudspeaker crackled on and off
—Saint-Tropez, Saint-Raphaël, Cannes, Antibes, Cagnes-sur-Mer.
Then Nice—only, the announcer didn't pronounce it in French. He
pronounced it in Italian, almost to rhyme with "pizza."

I walked down the aisle and along the platform and up the stairs
to the station. At the taxi rank, the taxi that pulled up for me was an
Alfa Romeo. My taxis in Brussels had all been Mercedeses, my
taxis in Paris and Lyon had all been Peugeots. At a restaurant that
night, I asked the waiter for a *café express*. He nodded. *"Un caffè
espresso,"* he said. I thought about all this, and the next day, at my
hotel bar, I asked the bartender about it.

"Nice is French," he said. "Naturally. But it is also Italian. But
the people of Nice!" He shrugged. "We are ourselves. We are
Niçois."

I was travelling overnight from Nice to Rome. My train (Trans-
Europ-Nuit) was scheduled to leave at eight o'clock. It would arrive at eight the next morning. "Listen," the concierge at my hotel
told me after confirming my reservation. "The train is always waiting on the track by seven o'clock. Sometimes more early. Why
wait? Go aboard and be comfortable."

I did. I had an early dinner near the station and walked across the street and went down to the track. The train was there. I found my car: *"Voiture 97/Schlafwagen: Nice-Roma."* The steward stepped down to meet me and took my bags and led me to my compartment. "In the morning," he said, "I bring you *caffè?*"

I undressed and got into bed with a book. There was movement and voices in the corridor. I read my book. At eight o'clock, we began to move. We moved for what seemed no more than four or five minutes, and stopped. I looked out the window: Beaulieu. We moved on, and stopped: Monaco—Monte Carlo. I watched a smiling young couple coming along the platform. Then an older couple, wooden-faced. Youth and age? Or winners and losers? We moved on, and stopped: Menton. We moved on again, and stopped: Ventimiglia. There was movement again in the corridor, and a knock on my door. *"Passaporti, per favore."* A glance, a nod, and he moved on. I got back in bed, and turned out the light.

I woke up to another, less peremptory knock. It was the steward (*"Buon giorno"*) with a cup of coffee on a tray. It was a little past seven. By the time I had shaved and dressed and packed my bag and finished my coffee, we were gliding into Termini Station in Rome.

[1983]

14. Janine: By Barge to Dijon

I flew to Paris not long ago, travelling at the now humdrum, though almost supersonic, speed of six hundred-odd miles an hour. From Paris, I took a train—the T.G.V. (Train à Grande Vitesse) express —to Lyon. The T.G.V. is the fastest train in the world, and it made the trip of three hundred and seventeen miles in just two hours. From Lyon, I travelled to Dijon, a distance of around a hundred and sixty miles, and it took me six days and six nights. I travelled by boat—by barge.

There is good reason to visit Dijon. It is a beautiful town of eighteenth-century boulevards and squares and dark medieval alleys and byways, and its center is small enough to comfortably comprehend on foot. It was the seat of the powerful fourteenth-century Dukes of Burgundy, and the birthplace of Jean-Philippe Rameau and of Gustave Eiffel. There is a thirteenth-century Gothic church (with an eleventh-century Roman crypt), an art museum (housed in the former ducal palace) whose collection of Old Masters has been favorably compared with that of the Louvre, and a once-residential square designed by Jules Hardouin-Mansart, the architect of Versailles. It is the home of the combination of white wine and crème de cassis that takes its name from an ardent admirer and onetime mayor of Dijon named Chanoine Félix Kir, and of the world's most celebrated mustard. It has many fine restaurants (among them, most notably, Le Chapeau Rouge and Les Caves de la Cloche), whose cellars are agreeably stocked with such wines of the region as Brouilly, Morgon, Chiroubles, Fleurie, Moulin-à-Vent, Chénas, Pouilly-Fuissé, Gevrey-Chambertin, Clos de Vougeot, Richebourg, Vosne-Romanée, Nuits-Saint-Georges, Aloxe-Corton, Pommard, Volnay, Meursault, Montrachet, and Beaune. There is also good reason to travel there by boat. The water route—up the river Saône (which joins the Rhône at Lyon) and through the nineteenth-century Canal de Bourgogne—marks the eastern boundary of Beaujolais and Mâconnais and the Côte d'Or, whose hundreds of tiny vineyards produce those renowned and relished wines. One is often told in Lyon that the city is bathed by three rivers—the Rhône, the Saône, and the Beaujolais.

The barge that carried me to Dijon was a beamy, low-slung vessel, a hundred and twenty-six feet long, with accommodations for two dozen passengers, in twelve cabins (each with toilet and shower) not much bigger than the sleeping compartments on a European train. It was one of several such passenger barges owned and operated by Floating Through Europe, Inc., of New York City, and it was called Janine. In Lyon, the usual berth of the Janine is at the Quai Fulchiron, on the west (or steep and stony old-town) bank of the Saône, just upriver from its junction with the Rhône, and I and my fellow-passengers—twenty of them, all fellow-Americans— boarded it there around three o'clock on a hot, blazing Wednesday afternoon.

The Janine has an open forward deck (furnished with white iron garden chairs and matching parasoled tables), which opens into a red plush salon, a small bar, and a dining room with six tables, each of them seating four. Aft of the dining room (I later learned) is the galley, and aft of that, up some steep steps, is the pilothouse. The cabins are below—at the waterline, in fact—and all of them have names reflective of the region. I was assigned to Beaune. There were two small, head-high windows (with the river lapping almost to the sills), two narrow bunks, arranged foot-to-foot in an L formation, and a small closet. There was a plastic bottle of Évian mineral water in the washstand, a red rosebud in a vase on a shelf, and three framed reproductions of lifelike fruit and flower arrangements by Redouté on the walls. I stowed away my luggage and went back up on deck. Most of my fellow-passengers were already there sitting or standing and chattering cocktail-party talk. Two or three idlers watched with interest from the street above the seawall and the quay. A pretty, dark-haired, blue-eyed, hugely smiling French girl (named Bernadette) passed among us with a tray of tall glasses of kir.

By the time I had finished my kir (and wondered at its popularity as an apéritif), my shipmates had begun to sort themselves out. All of them appeared to be in their fifties or sixties. There was a clique of four couples from Texas, a clique of four couples from Westchester County, a couple from California, and two women from Michigan. By this time, too, the Texans had switched to

Scotch, and the New Yorkers had switched to Martinis. The cock-tail-party chatter climbed to a higher pitch.

"I'd appreciate your not breathing while I'm smoking. . . ."

"I feel sorry for people who don't drink. When they wake up in the morning, that's the best they're going to feel all day. . . ."

"Well, somebody told him that the airlines were required by law to accept a musician's instrument along with the musician. And this was in Switzerland, you know. So he went out and bought himself a twenty-five-foot alpenhorn . . ."

We were moving. We had cast off and were sliding away from shore. The party chatter faltered. The Saône at Lyon is a beautiful river, and I stood and watched it reveal itself as we reached mid-stream and gently chugged upriver through a green *allée*, between orderly rows of leafy plane trees that lined the gray stone quays. Beyond the trees were rows of apartment houses—dusty yellow and faded orange, with tall windows flanked by faded blue shutters —in the formal style of the middle nineteenth century, and rising beyond the apartments were the delicate towers and spires and bel-fries of churches. The party chatter began again. We crept under a bridge. A racing scull appeared in the distance. It came skimming closer. And closer. And suddenly darted for shore, to sit there bucking and bouncing in our wake. The women from Michigan smiled and waved. The oarsman hunched his shoulders and looked away. The sky to the west brightened into a sunset blaze. A star came out. Up ahead, on the left, a patch of pale-blue neon shone through the trees: "PAUL BOCUSE." One of the New York women saw it, too.

"Oh, look! We had dinner there last night. And it was the great-est. It was just the greatest ever. And Paul Bocuse himself came over to our table and autographed my menu."

A slim young Englishwoman (named Kirsty), blue-eyed and sandy-haired, came out on deck and announced that dinner was served.

The chef on the Janine is a young Flemish Belgian (named Geert), and his sous-chef is an Englishwoman who is also Kirsty's mother. Her name is Shirley. Neither he nor she is Paul Bocuse, but they *are* chefs. And we dined formally, leisurely, and well. The entrée was turbot à la meunière in a white-wine sauce, around which were arranged slices of sautéed bananas. With it we drank a Chablis. The main course was roast lamb with tiny green beans (no thicker than strands of spaghetti) and dauphine potatoes. With it we drank an Aloxe-Corton. That course was followed by a green salad and a variety of local cheeses. The dessert was raspberry sorbet and a white cake layered with chocolate, whipped cream, and hazel-nuts. We sat down at eight o'clock, and it was around ten-thirty when we had our coffee. One of my tablemates—I think it was the man from California—finished his coffee and sat back with a groan.

"You know what they say about gastronomy," he said. "They say it's the only vice that grows stronger with age. I'm feeling very old tonight."

There is no night traffic on the Saône. Its several locks all close at seven-thirty in the evening. When I came up from my cabin at around seven-thirty the following morning, we were still moored where we had spent the night—alongside an old stone quay below an invisible village called Trévoux. Three of the Texans were sitting at a table in the dining room. Two were drinking coffee. The other was drinking a Coke. I stepped out on deck. It was a mild morning, with a wispy fog still sparkling in the trees above the quay. A young woman was standing near the bow. She was a member of the crew whom I had only glimpsed the day before. She was dressed in black—black jeans, black jersey, black sneakers—and her hair was long and black. She wore dark glasses, and silver earrings in the shape of lightning bolts. Her sleeves were rolled up to the elbow. There was an elaborate tattoo on her left forearm, and the nail of the little finger of her left hand was a good inch long and painted black. She had a cigarette in her mouth.

"Hullo," she said. "My name is Angie." Her English was British English. "I hope you slept well."

I said I had, and asked her about her job.

"Oh," she said. "I'm the deckhand. We'll be casting off any moment now. We're only waiting for Geert—for the chef. He went up to the village bakery to get our bread. He should—I mean, there he is now."

A slight young man with a pale mustache came wobbling along the quay on a bicycle, steering with one hand and clutching a bag of three-foot baguettes with the other. He passed us with a nod and jumped off the bike and trotted up a gangplank and into the pilot-house.

I went in to breakfast. There was a buffet. I helped myself to orange juice from a pitcher and to coffee, and carried them over to a table. The chef had brought back more from the village bakery than those baguettes. The basket on my table also held fresh crois-sants and fresh sweet rolls. But it was the bread that mattered most. It was the lightest French bread I had ever tasted, and the crustiest.

The center was feathery, almost gossamer, and the crust was almost an inch of crisp and crumbling thickness. And, spread with good sweet butter (from Normandy), it was a rapture of gastronomic vice.

I climbed the steep steps to the pilothouse. It was a window-walled room with a clear view up the length of the barge to a sighting pennant on the tip of the bow. There was a spoked wheel, a console, a shelf of charts, and a wide leather-covered bench. A little white Jack Russell terrier was asleep on the bench. The captain was standing at the wheel. He was a big young Frenchman—black-haired and black-bearded, and with eyes the color of green olives —named Luc Malfoy. His uniform was a Yale-blue running suit (with "Janine" lettered over the heart) and white running shoes. "No," he told me. "I am born in Brittany." His English was British English. "But I am three years on this river. And I have been on the rivers of Holland and England. I always prefer to go upstream on this river. The current is strong, and maybe eight miles an hour is the best we can do, but it is better than running down. That can be trouble at the bridges. This is a good river. The dredges work every day on the channel. It is clean—very clean. It is maybe the clean-est river in France. Sometimes in hot weather, we stop and the guests go swimming. And the fishermen you see along the shore— they are not like some others, like the fishermen in Paris. They catch fish. Good fish to eat. Pup-pee? No, he is not mine. We are good friends only. He is own by Shirley. And that is his name— Pup-pee. And he is the good sailor. Watch him when you see him on deck. See how he runs."

Lunch on the Janine is served at one o'clock. But Bernadette, by popular request, opened the bar before noon. The Texans drank Scotch, the New Yorkers drank Bloody Marys, the Californians and the women from Michigan drank white wine. I tried, at Berna-dette's suggestion, an apéritif called Suze. It was a lemony yellow in color and it had an odd, bittersweet flavor. It tasted as if it might have been distilled from some familiar weed—purslane, perhaps. But I liked it well enough. Lunch was a cold buffet. There was bread and wine (Chablis), and a dessert of frozen Grand Marnier soufflé. The main dish was a glazed whole salmon—two of them, in fact—returned to mock life with scales of cucumber crescents and garnished with hard-boiled eggs, sliced tomatoes, and truffles. Kirsty called us to the buffet and handed a big fish knife to one of the Texans. He handed it back. "No, Ma'am!" he said. "I'm not going to be the one to destroy a work of art."

The bus, a big blue-and-white Renault, was waiting for us on the esplanade above the Quai Lamartine at Mâcon. Kirsty got us aboard and seated, and exchanged a vehement greeting in French with the driver. She said to us, "We shall make two visits this afternoon. We go first to an important Mâconnais vineyard. Then we go to the famous Abbaye de Cluny. At the vineyard of Georges Lardet, we shall meet our guide. She is French, but English-speaking. Her name is Françoise." The bus moved off. Several of those who had most appreciated the salmon and the Chablis immediately fell asleep. There were three or four blocks of hysterical, almost Parisian traffic, and then we were in a westward-rising countryside of vineyards and scattered tiny stone-built, tile-roofed villages. The road was a well-kept blacktop, but it wasn't much wider than the driveway at my home, on eastern Long Island. The driver had a radio going, and we were entertained for a mile or more by what sounded like a French version of "Old MacDonald Had a Farm." We turned off just before the village of Leynes, crawled down a winding hill, and stopped between two fields of vines. Kirsty marched us out. An attractive young woman with cropped brown hair came up from a huddle of old stone buildings to meet us. She wore a brown jacket, knickerbockers in a bold tan-and-brown check, green stockings, and high-heeled ankle-strap shoes.

"Bonjour," she said. "Good afternoon. I am Françoise. I welcome you to the vineyard Saint-Véran. Saint-Véran is a new *appellation*. It was created by law in 1971. Before that, it was Beaujolais *blanc*. Pouilly-Fuissé is our region's best wine. Saint-Véran is second, but good. Very good. And, too, less expensive. You will wish to know about our vineyards. You will observe that the slopes face east or southeast. That is for the morning sun to dry the dew. Dew can cause disease. You will observe how stony is the ground. That is good. The stones will hold the good heat of the day. And our soil. It is so valuable that the grower before he leaves the vineyard will wipe it off his boots. You will observe also that there are many grapes left on the ground between the rows. They are discard. We choose at harvest only the best. And now here is M. Lardet. But he is always called Jo-Jo."

M. Lardet—Jo-Jo—smiled. *"Bonjour,"* he said. He had no English, but he had presence. He was a big, mustachioed man in a flowing black apron and a big black hat with a wide sky-blue band. A silver, porringerlike *tâte-vin* hung on a chain around his neck and

"Cru Saint-Véran" was lettered in sky blue across his chest. Françoise took his arm. "So now we visit the *cave*," she said. "You will taste for yourself the goodness of Saint-Véran." She started off, down a cobblestone ramp. We passed through a courtyard. We descended a flight of damp stone steps. We came into a cellar lined with huge casks. M. Lardet equipped himself with a *pipette-tâte-vin* and approached one of the casks. Françoise and Kirsty passed out little *tâte-vins*. Françoise waited with a smile until the last of our cups was filled. "This is the vintage of 1980," she said. She brought her cup up to her eyes. "You will observe the color. We call it golden green. Next, you will observe the aroma. There are those who find here the fragrance of hazelnuts. And now—the tasting!"

We drove through a steeper countryside. We passed a butte-like hill that separates the villages of Solutré-Pouilly and Fuissé. There were vineyards on the eastward slopes, and white Charolais cattle, and sometimes black-faced sheep and brown goats, on the slopes facing west. There were fields of rape. There were stone walls and rows of plane trees and poplars and geometrical plantings of pines and, at many of the crossroads, rainbow gardens of dahlias. Every village had its dogleg Rue de la Liberté or Rue de la République, its Place de la Gare, and its unvarying signs: "CAFÉ." "AUBERGE." "BAR-TABAC." "PEUGEOT-TALBOT." "MOBILE." "ELF." Every house had its window boxes, and every window box was bright with geraniums. Somewhere in one of the villages we swung off a narrow street and through a massive archway and into a massive courtyard giving on a massive complex of gray stone: the Abbaye de Cluny. Françoise told us its history. It was founded by the Benedictine order around 910 A.D. The abbey church was begun around 1088 and was completed in 1130, and for some years it was the largest church in the Christian world. Its style was Romanesque and early Gothic, and there was even a suggestion of the East, brought back from the First Crusade. It is today a school—the École Nationale Supérieure des Arts et Métiers. Nothing remains of the original architecture but an arm of the transept and a bell tower. "The abbey was destroyed in the eighteenth century, in the Revolution," Françoise told us. "What we see today is of the nineteenth century. The Revolution was, you know, the enemy of religion. The Revolution suppressed the Benedictines and destroyed the abbey. It was a total collapsation. The stones were carried away in all directions. Some were used to build a stud farm. We will see a view of it in our walk."

*   *   *

The Janine was still moored at Mâcon. Shirley was walking Pup-pee on the quay. The bar was open. The salon soon filled. There were complaints about the quality of the ice. ("I've never seen ice that melts like this. I think it's something new. I think it's *hot* ice.") But then we were called to dinner. It began with a soup: a mussel bisque. The main course was roast veal with a sauce au poivre. There was a green salad with a port-wine vinaigrette, and a selection of cheeses. Dessert was two Bavarian creams, apricot and vanilla, with a purée of whortleberries. With the roast we drank a Côte du Rhône. The white wine— golden green and smelling faintly of hazelnuts—was a Saint-Véran. When I went down to my cabin, I found a bedtime snack on my pillow: a chocolate thin-mint.

There was a tier of bookshelves along one wall of the dining room. I went over for a look while I was waiting for breakfast. The shelves were crowded with more or less battered hardcovers and paperbacks—books left behind by generations of travellers, a library by accretion. There was something for every taste. *Inland Waterways of France. Ulysses. La Petite Fille au Tambour,* by John le Carré. *The Great Gatsby. Cujo,* by Stephen King. *Acceptable Losses,* by Irwin Shaw. *Le Livre de la Jungle,* by Rudyard Kipling. *Histoire de Mâcon et du Mâconnais. Maigret Meets a Milord.* I took M. Simenon down. I glanced at the opening page: "At that time, in the port above Lock 14 . . . the *Providence* was moored in front of the Café de la Marine, behind the Éco III . . ." That was enough. I carried it over to my table.

Bernadette came up the aisle with a plate of what looked like very thick fried bread. I stopped her on the way back and asked her what it was.

"That?" she said. "Is called French toast."

"*You* call it French toast?"

She laughed. "Oh, no. Is called in France *pain perdu.* You wish?"

Pain perdu. Lost bread. I decided that that was a little too Proustian for so early in the morning. I ate a croissant instead.

I finished breakfast and went on deck. The Janine was still sitting in Mâcon. There was talk of waiting for a refrigerator repairman. There was a rumor that the quality of the ice would improve. It was announced that we would have lunch ashore, in Gevrey-Chambertin, at La Rôtisserie du Chambertin, a restaurant of multiple stars. I made myself comfortable in the sun and read about murder in the rain on the Canal de l'Aisne à la Marne. There were other readers, and games of backgammon and double solitaire. I went ashore and walked on the quay and climbed a dozen or more worn stone steps to the leafy walk above. There were big wrought-iron planters spaced along the seawall, with geraniums and begonias in brilliant bloom. There was a large park with gardens and shade trees. Across the Saône I could see another old stone seawall and an orderly mass of forest. Mâcon is not a village. It is a town—an industrial town—with a population of almost forty thousand, and it has been an important river port for centuries. Walking under the trees and past the flowering planters, and looking out at the bright-green water, I thought of the river towns I had known at home, and their dingy and desolate waterfronts.

We travelled to Gevrey-Chambertin by bus (a red-and-white Renault this time), and with a guide—another young English-speaker —named Colette. Colette had long dark hair, and she wore tight slacks and high-heeled pumps. She introduced the driver with a merry laugh, and told us that we would rejoin the Janine in the late afternoon at Tournus, the next big town upriver. She then sat down on a little seat up front and began an animated monologue to the driver. We passed through a countryside much like that of the day before. The place names, though, were rather more impressive: Nuits-Saint-Georges, Flagey-Échézeaux, Vougeot, Chambolle-Musigny, Beaune, Morey-Saint-Denis, and Gevrey-Chambertin. Chambertin, for all its fame, turned out to be not much more than a crossroads—two or three narrow streets, a few tall houses behind high stone walls, and La Rôtisserie du Chambertin. It, too, sat behind a high stone wall—a creamy-white stone building with a steep roof tiled with an astonishment of pink and green and baby-blue tiles. Colette and the driver led us through a low front door and down a long stone hall and into a big stone room with high black beams and a fireplace at each end. One of them was equipped with an ancient iron rotisserie. The other fireplace was laid with logs a good ten feet in length. There was a long table set for us in the middle of the room. Colette took the chair at the head. The driver sat on her left. The rest of us sat where we could. Our lunch began with a round of kirs. The entrée was a trout soufflé in a dark wine sauce. The main course was veal braised in a brown sauce with fennel. There was the usual array of local cheeses. There was a black-currant sorbet and assorted petits fours. We drank three wines. One was white, a Montagny, and the others were red Chambertins. Colette stood up as the first Chambertin was poured. "I will tell you something interesting," she said. "Chambertin is a wine of great fame. It was the wine most favored by Napoleon. And its name has also interest. The first to grow it was a peasant named Bertin. *Champs* is meaning 'fields.' Now, this first Chambertin we drink is young. It is the vintage 1980. It is pleasant. But the other is the vintage 1976. There is a saying: 'The wine when young is foolish, like the children are. With age it becomes wise.' You will find the difference is true."

We drove into Tournus at a little past five. The bus let us off at the main quay of the town. There was a gravel barge on the farther shore, and two sand barges moored near a bridge downriver. But that was all.

"*Où est le bateau?*"

"*Ce n'est pas ici.*"

There was a moment of silence.

"*Où est le bar?*"

"*C'est là—tout droit.*"

"*Voilà!*"

We crossed the street to the Café de la Marine. There were tables and chairs on the sidewalk, and a sheltering awning overhead. We were sitting there in ease and comfort, listening to a bedlam of starlings hidden in the trees, when the Janine, tricolor flying and horn howling, finally came poking under the bridge.

There was some feeling that night that the ice was a bit colder than the ice of the night before. Dinner, Kirsty told us, would be a simple buffet. She hoped that after our big Burgundian lunch a buffet would be sufficient. We sat down to a country pâté en croûte, to sliced country sausages, to céleri rémoulade, to a salad of tomatoes and cucumbers and corn, to cheese from the Cistercian abbey at Cîteaux, to baked Alaska (or omelette à la norvégienne), to Chablis and Beaujolais. I heard no complaints of unsatisfied hunger.

There is an outdoor market every Saturday morning in Tournus, on a narrow street behind the Café de la Marine. The Janine was not scheduled to cast off until around ten-thirty. I and several others went ashore for a look at the market. It was mostly a farmers' market, of fish and meat and fresh produce and cheeses and breads and pastries. There were one or two surprises and pleasures. The different varieties of fish were separated from one another by sprays of what looked like laurel leaves. I saw shallots the size of lemons, and an onion that looked like a thick red banana (*oignon banane rouge),* and rabbits skinned and gutted and with the feet removed but otherwise intact, including the head, and even the eyes. One of my companions managed to ask the seller the reason for that. The man shrugged. *"Comme ça, vous sauriez que ce n'est pas un chat,"* he said. We took that to mean that there are unscrupulous types who will try to pass off a cat as a rabbit.

The Saône between Tournus and Chalon-sur-Saône is wide and wandering and there is no prettier stretch on the river. Chalon-sur-Saône was our next port of call, our mooring for the night. I sat on the bow with *Maigret Meets a Milord,* but I didn't do much reading. It was difficult here on the sunny Saône to keep my mind on the dismal Canal de l'Aisne à la Marne. There was a feel of deep and peaceful country, but it was country ordered by man. The rows of plane trees, the poplar *allées,* even the patches of woods and the meadows of grazing sheep, had a look of arrangement, of traditional design. There were swans floating here and there along the riverbanks, geese grazing in the sheep meadows. A heron flapped from shore to shore. A flock of some cootlike ducks dived under our bow. A couple on horseback — a man and a woman in immaculate riding clothes — appeared on the left bank and cantered away on a path among the poplars. A village appeared on the right: thirteen stone houses, some long and low, some tall and thin, but all of them the color of yellowy autumn leaves, all of them with faded blue shutters, all of them roofed with rusty-black tiles — strung out in a tight little row behind a column of shapely plane trees, above a long stone quay. One building had a sign along its facade: "CAFÉ DE LA MARINE." One of the New York couples had joined me at the bow. The woman gave a little sigh. "Those houses," she said. "Those trees. Everything looks as if it ought to have a frame around it. Everything looks like those wonderful Impressionist paintings you've seen in some museum." It was not, perhaps, a stunning observation. But it was the simple truth.

The approach to Chalon-sur-Saône from the south is dominated by an island with a climbing, prowlike headland. I watched it nearing and rising. The headland became an acre or two of garden, of red and white and yellow and orange and purple flowers, set off by lawns and surmounted by a colonnade of poplars. We came closer: the garden became a great floral bunch of grapes, flanked by a floral wineglass and a floral barrel of wine. Chalon-sur-Saône is a gateway to good eating. "In Chalon-sur-Saône," Alexis Lichine writes in his classic *Wines of France,* "begins the famous food and fabulous eating for which Burgundy was always famed. . . . Just to the south is Charolles, from whose deep green pastures comes the famous Charolais beef . . . snails from the vineyard hills." We tied up at the Quai Gambetta, and I went for a walk before dinner. I walked no more than a dozen blocks, but I passed half a dozen restaurants that looked to be of some quality. Dinner on board that night was an affirmation of M. Lichine. The entrée was escargots de Bourgogne, and the main course was an entrecôte de Charolais in a sauce béarnaise. The wines were a Meursault and a Côte de Beaune.

It had rained in the night, and Sunday morning was wet and cool and overcast. The rosebud in my cabin had passed from bloom to overblown. My croissant at breakfast turned out to have a chocolate filling. There was an unresolved argument at a table behind me about melons. ("The Persian is the king of melons." "We've always preferred the Colorado Rocky Ford." "Have you ever tasted a Santa Claus?") One of the Texans had found a copy of the *International Herald Tribune* in town the evening before, but by the time it was handed down to me someone had done the crossword puzzle and someone had solved the Jumble word game, and the book review (from the New York *Times)* was one that I had read a week before I left home. And the Saône had changed its character. It looked darker and narrower, and its banks were heavily wooded. It began to drizzle. It seemd a good time to go back to *Maigret Meets a Milord,* but the weather had also changed along the Canal de l'Aisne à la Marne. The sun was shining there. The consensus at noon, when Bernadette opened the bar, was that the ice was again hot ice.

We put in at around two o'clock at a village called Seurre, and a group led by Kirsty debarked for a visit to the ancient fortress of Châteauneuf-en-Auxois and the somewhat less ancient Château de Commarin, somewhere north of Beaune. I was one of several who chose to stay on the boat. We watched the others climb a crumbling ramp to a waiting bus and drive off past a ramshackle building with a sign: "BAR DE L'ESPERANCE." But the place was more than just ramshackle. I looked again: it was boarded up. So much for hope.

Angie cast off, and we were back on the river. We would spend the night at Saint-Jean-de-Losne, at the entrance to the Canal de Bourgogne, and the excursionists would rejoin us there. I stayed on deck. The drizzle had stopped, and the sky had begun to brighten.

Geert came out on deck in his white coat and lighted a cigarette. It was a Marlboro, the cowboy cigarette of Europe. We exchanged a nod, and I said I had much enjoyed our Burgundian dinner last night.

"Ah," he said. "I am happy. Did you know the beef, the Charolais? Good meat. But, you know, it has no fat, no marbling. I lard it to give juice and flavor. This country here is so good for eating. You have heard of the Bresse chicken. It is the best. It comes from near Mâcon. The river has good fish. Fish and crayfish. Burgundy has so much. You have seen the sheep. The goats. Even game. Woodcock."

I was getting hungry again. I asked him about dinner tonight.

"I will tell you," he said. "We start with a pâté—foie de canard. Salad with walnut oil. Very delicate, very good. Then lamb. What you would call chops. With a bouquet of turnips and green cabbage and sautéed potatoes. The finish is sorbet. A variety."

I looked at my watch. It wasn't even three o'clock yet.

The excursionists arrived in Saint-Jean-de-Losne at a little past six. We had been there since five, tied comfortably up below the Café de la Saône, with a view of a dozen freight barges moored two deep along the opposite quay. I asked one of the excursionists about the excursion. He reported that the Châteauneuf-en-Auxois was perched on a great, rocky hill and the Château de Commarin was sinking into a swamp. Talleyrand's mother, he added, had spent her girlhood at the Château de Commarin.

We started early on Monday morning. We were already under way when I came up on deck. We slipped under a bridge, we swung sharply to the right. A narrow canyon loomed: the dark stone mouth of a lock. We had come through half a dozen locks on the Saône, but they were modern locks, of generous size, lined with steel and equipped with great steel sluice gates that were opened and closed by a lockkeeper at a console in a control tower high overhead. The Canal de Bourgogne is a nineteenth-century canal, and its gates are operated by levers and wheels turned entirely by human weight and muscle. We crawled into a slot only inches wider than the Janine and with hardly a foot of clearance fore and aft. We sat for minutes deep down between two walls of dripping stone. There was the sound of rushing water. We began to rise. The earth slopes gently up to Dijon from the Saône at Saint-Jean-de-Losne. This was the first of twenty-two lifts, which would raise us a total of a hundred and ninety feet. We rose slowly, slowly, as slowly as an ancient freight elevator. My eyes came even with the top of the lock wall, with the top of an iron bollard. We kept rising. The lockkeeper's house appeared, a small stone square with a red tile roof and a life preserver in a glass case. Above the door was a sign: "ÉCLUSE ST.-JEAN-DE-LOSNE—DIJON 29.4 KM. ST.-JEAN-DE-LOSNE 0 KM." We came gently to rest. The lockkeeper, a woman, was working a long iron lever. She was a burly figure in a long dress and a thick sweater. The canal stretched straight ahead, a boulevard of shining water lined with poplars, on a kind of causeway ten feet or more above the surrounding countryside. I looked down on fields, on a street, on a Café de la Marine.

I went in to breakfast. By the time I had finished eating (orange juice, coffee, a regular croissant, and a novelty—rhubarb preserves), we were moving into our second lock: Écluse Viranne. When I could, I stepped out on the lockside and walked back to the pilothouse. Halfway there I realized that the pilothouse had become an open cockpit. Its roof and walls were gone.

"It is for the bridges," Captain Malfoy told me. "This is an old canal, and the bridges are low. So we make the pilothouse with hinges to fold back and away. Angie and I did that work this morning. Sometimes with the bridges on this canal there is only one foot of clearance. When you stand on the bow today, watch your head. In bad weather, the low bridges make trouble. The waves can lift the barge too close to the bridge. There is one thing I can do. I accelerate the engine and make lower the stern—and so we get under. You see the towpath along the canal on the right. That goes back to the old times when the barges were pulled by the horse. They had troubles also in those times. Horses don't like to swim. To go under the bridge, they must unhitch the horse and lead him around. Then the men would haul the barge under the bridge. It was the same with the locks. Pretty hard work. The canal is more work than the river even now. But it is pretty. I enjoy the canal." He raised a hand in salute to the lockkeeper. "*Ça va!*"

I could see the next lock in the distance. It looked to be about a mile away. The towpath beckoned. It would be an easy walk. Several of my fellow-travellers had the same impulse. We left the Janine still sitting in the lock, and set off along the path. We walked in the dappled shade of the poplars. It was a countryside of plowed autumn fields and still, green pastures and scattered groves and flocking rocks and, far away, the clustered rooftops of a village. The canal was a deep, oceanic green. Its grassy banks were abloom with wildflowers: something blue that looked like chicory, something pink that looked like thistle, something yellow that looked

like asters, and a delicate lavender flower that I had never seen
before but somehow recognized on sight—an autumn crocus. We
reached the next lock (Écluse Brazey) well before the Janine and
walked on. There were shiny green bunches of foliage growing like
nests in some of the trees. One of the New York women stopped
and pointed.

"Look!"

"What is it?"

"I just noticed. Up there in that tree. It's mistletoe."

"Mistletoe! Alice—give me a kiss."

We were just getting up from lunch. There was a sudden explosion
—a great, thunderous, almost staggering roar. Then another. And
another. We crowded over to the windows. I saw a flash of silver
burst up from beyond a horizon of trees. Another crash of thunder.

Kirsty said, "There's a military airbase just over the way. I'm
sorry. We'll simply have to endure them for a bit. They're practicing takeoffs and landings. They're the fighter plane the French call
the Mirage. A bit frightening, aren't they?"

We waited and watched. It was impossible not to watch. The
terrible thunder roared. It began to fade. It sank to a murmur, to a
mere reminder. The nineteenth century returned. But it had seemed
a long time coming.

We were approaching Écluse Préville. One of the Texans and I were
standing at the rail. The lockkeeper came out of the lock house and
stood watching. Our eyes met. I smiled and waved. She—it was
another thickset woman in a long skirt and a sweater—gazed at me
without expression. But she lifted her hand an inch or maybe two.

"My," the Texan said. "That was a dry wave. That was just
about the *driest* wave I ever saw."

We climbed through Écluse Beauregard, we climbed through
Écluse Longvic. We passed a barge headed down-canal. It was a
family barge—a load of gravel forward, and a cabin with white
curtains at the windows just aft of the pilothouse. Its name was
lettered on the stern: Espérance. We climbed through Écluse Rome-
let. There was a sudden rise of apartment buildings up ahead on the
right. On the left were what looked like warehouses. The canal ran
unchanged between its rows of trees, beside the grassy banks and
the towpath. But the country was giving way. Beyond the apartments was a tract of identical little white houses with identical
geranium gardens. Beyond the warehouses were storage tanks:

"Esso." "Total." "Mobil." "Elf." We climbed through Écluse Colombières. The canal still had its flanking trees, but the grassy banks had become a quay, and the towpath was now a street. Steep-roofed buildings rose up all around us. I became aware of a smell in the air. It was a pleasant smell, and a familiar smell. It was a smell I knew very well. But it was a smell I had never smelled in the open air before. And then I realized. This was Dijon. The smell was the smell of mustard.

[1984]

15. Place Stanislas: Nancy, France

People who think too much about their ancestors are like potatoes
—the best part of them is underground.

—DR. HENRY S. F. COOPER

My wife and I spent the better part of a week in the early autumn of 1984 in northeastern France, in Nancy, the ancient capital of the ancient province of Lorraine. On the little form that visitors are asked to fill out before landing in France, I had declared that the purpose of our visit was tourism. That was only partly true. Our visit to France, to Nancy, was also a kind of pilgrimage, a kind of genealogical quest. Nancy, I had understood from childhood, was the birthplace of the man who founded our family in America—my great-grandfather Henri Constant Roueché. I wanted to see where he, and I, had come from.

But first, before going on to Nancy, we gave ourselves a couple of days in Paris, and were rewarded by more than its usual incomparable pleasures. One afternoon, on an impulse, I opened the Paris telephone directory—and found my name. I found it twice: "Roueche, G.; 21 rue Faidherbe, Paris 11, 371-0649" and "Roueche, F.; 5 Ave. de l'Observatoire, Paris 6, 326-2015." I showed the listings to my wife. My command of French, despite my name, goes little deeper than *"Avez-vous un* Herald-Tribune?" Kay's French is reasonably functional. She sat down on the edge of the hotel bed and dialed F. Roueche. She spoke and listened and spoke, and hung up. I stood at the window and looked down at the Rue du Bac. She dialed again, and talked and listened. She hung up. I turned back from the window.

"Well?"

"I talked to two women. One sounded quite old and the other fairly young. They both married into the family. They don't pro-

nounce the name the way we do. They don't use an accent. When I
said we pronounced our name 'Roo-SHAY,' they sounded puzzled.
One of them called herself 'Roosh,' and the other called herself
'Roo-esch.' They both thought that their husband's family came
from northeastern France. But not recently."

When we checked out of the hotel a day or two later, the concierge, an Austrian, called me "Monsieur Roosh-ah." The cashier,
a Frenchwoman, called me by my given name. She called me
"Monsieur Bérton."

We travelled to Nancy by train, one of the lunchtime trains—two
and a half hours and four courses, with wine and coffee, in a formal
restaurant car—that are understandably popular in France. During
that speedy trip and leisurely meal, between the cold salmon and
the raspberry torte, we reviewed what we knew and what we hoped
to find. The facts, if they were facts, were few: Henri Constant
Roueché was born on February 19, 1813. He came to America in
the early eighteen-thirties. His reason for emigrating, according to
family legend, was to avoid being forced into the priesthood. (That
may explain the fact that I grew up a Presbyterian.) Henri Constant
settled, probably by prearrangement, in western Pennsylvania, in a
predominately French hamlet called Guys Mills, near Meadville,
the seat of Allegheny College. He was, or became, a blacksmith.
There seem to have been other Rouechés of that trade in that area: a
story, or legend, describes a Fourth of July celebration in Guys
Mills in which several Roueché blacksmiths hammered out the
"Anvil Chorus" from Verdi's *Il Trovatore* on "tuned" anvils. He
married on December 1, 1836, one Marie or Victoire (or perhaps,
Marie-Victoire) Richard, a union that produced eleven children, the
sixth of whom, Louis Armand, was my grandfather. Henri Constant died on January 3, 1869. In the early nineteen-twenties, one
of my parents' friends returned from a visit to France to report that
he had noted in Nancy a Confiserie Roueché. Nothing else was
known of the family that Henri Constant left behind in France.

The room clerk at the Grande Hôtel Concorde, into which we
were booked in Nancy, was a young woman. I handed her a letter
confirming our reservation. She gave it a glance and gave me a
welcoming smile. *"Ah, oui,"* she said. *"Bonjour, Monsieur Roo-
esch-uh."*

When the porter had shown us to our room and departed, I
turned to Kay. "'Roosh,'" I said. "'Roo-esch.' 'Roosh-ah.' 'Roo-
esch-uh.' I'm beginning to feel like an imposter."

"No," Kay said. "That's the fascinating part. If your Henri Constant had called himself 'Roosh' or 'Roo-esch' or whatever, that's what we would be calling ourselves. Foreigners coming to America don't complicate their names. If anything, they simplify them— like your friend Stennis, whose great-grandfather's name was Stenhouse. Or they Anglicize them. We can be sure that Henri Constant brought that *accent aigu* with him. He certainly didn't pick it up in western Pennsylvania."

The Grande Hôtel Concorde occupies a square, creamy sandstone building of three lofty stories that has housed a hotel of one name or another since around 1880, but it was built, in the mid-eighteenth century, as a palace. It is one of seven former palaces, of identical rococo design, that face and bound the Place Stanislas, a three-acre rectangle of cobblestones and flowering planters in a checkerboard pattern, which is widely considered to be one of the most beautiful squares in the world. It was conceived by the last Duke of Lorraine—Stanislas Leszczynski (1677-1766), the deposed Stanislas I of Poland—as a home for himself and his court and as a tribute to his benefactor and father-in-law, Louis XV, and it was designed by the architect Emmanuel Heré. Its corners are embellished by gilded wrought-iron grilles and gateways (by Jean Lamour) and by classically figured fountains (by the sculptor Barthelemy Guibal). The Place was originally called the Place Royale, and its center, now marked by a monumental statue of Stanislas, was originally marked by a monumental statue of Louis XV. Four of the former palaces, alike in size and shape and elegance, face each other down the length of the Place, two of them— one the hotel and the other the municipal opera theatre—at the eastern end, and two—one of them the Musée des Beaux-Arts and the other a restaurant—on the west. The former ducal palace, now the Hôtel de Ville, occupies the entire southern side of the Place, and two lesser but still palatial buildings on the north house sidewalk cafés, an Air France office, and a Crédit Lyonnais. A short street (Rue de Heré) between these buildings leads by way of a triumphal arch to a companion square, the Place de la Carrière.

This much, or much of this, I knew, having learned it from reading before we arrived in Nancy. But now I was there. I was seeing it. Our room was a front room, and I opened the windows —a pair of tall French windows that gave on a little gilded wrought-iron balcony—and looked out at its beauty, at its architectural magnificence, at its magnificence of space and serenity. It gave me a curious feeling. It was a magnificence that Henri Constant must also have seen and felt. I wondered if I was feeling the beginning of a link.

It was mid-afternoon, and a Sunday. There was nothing we could do but go out and see the sights. We walked down to the lobby on a wide, winding white-marble staircase with a red carpet under foot and a three-story crystal chandelier overhead. The concierge, a big man with a small, round face and little steel-rimmed glasses, took our key.

"*Bonjour, 'sieur et 'dame,*" he said. "*Merci.* You are American, no?"

We said we were.

"I know many Americans," he said. "Here at the hotel and before. I was attach in the war to the army of General Patton. I was interpreter. But you have, I think, a French name." He looked at a paper on his desk. "ROO-shay. Monsieur ROO-shay. So I am Lucien. I am here to help you if I can."

We went out to the street and crossed to the enormous Place.

"ROO-shay," I said.

"It's an improvement," Kay said.

In the palace next to the Musée des Beaux-Arts, there was a café with tables on the sidewalk. We found a table and ordered coffee. It seemed to be a café for everybody. There were men and women of every age and every language and taste. A German couple two tables away were drinking beer when we sat down. I watched them finish their beers and order a round of cognac. Many of the young men wore narrow yellow neckties, and many of the older men wore sweaters under their jackets, with their neckties hanging outside. Most of the women, and some of the men, had vividly hennaed hair. Everybody seemed to be smoking. We drank our coffee and moved on. We visited the palatial Musée des Beaux-Arts and saw its enormous Rubens *Transfiguration*, its excellent moderns, and, hidden away in a little room on the second floor, its one example of the work of its native son Claude Gelée dit le Lorrain, a tiny pastorale. The palace beyond the Musée was another crowded café. Children were playing a hopping game of some sort on the cobbled checkerboards of the Place. We crossed the Rue de Heré and came to one of Barthelemy Guibal's fountains (cast in lead and depicting an ample Aphrodite and her retinue) and passed through one of Jean Lamour's gilded wrought-iron gateways. (Only, it isn't gilded. The gilt, we later learned, is gold leaf.) We followed a little girl on six-foot stilts into another magnificence of Stanislas—the English park called La Pépinière. We walked the wide aisles of arching chestnuts and lindens and locusts that traverse its fifty immaculate acres. We saw the circular garden of marigolds and begonias and ageratum and sage that resolved itself into a rainbow floral clock, and later learned from Lucien that the clock actually works—"*Il marche.*" We saw, on the knoll just beyond the clock, the three huge floral butterflies—one green, one yellow, one red. We saw the usual *clochard*. We saw the statue of Claude Gelée by Rodin, who gave him the name "Lorrain." We saw two pieces of litter. One was an empty Marlboro package. The other was a red-and-yellow McDonald's wrapper.

We left the Pépinière by way of the classically sculptured and colonnaded Hemicycle du General de Gaulle. ("General de Gaulle is the special hero here," Lucien told me later. "It is the same with Jeanne d'Arc. She was born in this region, in the village of Domremy. General de Gaulle lived in his retirement in Colombey-les-Belles, which is also of this region. The people of Nancy are very patriotic. It is because of so many wars.") The Hemicycle du General de Gaulle, like so much else in Nancy, is new only in name. It is another of the masterpieces that Stanislas commissioned from Heré. From the shadow of de Gaulle we stepped some centuries back, into the gray Gothic loom of the Église St.-Epvre. We stood there looking up at its fragile skyscraper spires—and the heavens opened in a thunder of bells. It was a shuddering, shattering, agony of sound. It was impossible to stand and endure it. There was no escape but the church itself. We ran up the endless steps and through the gray stone portal and into an empty gray stone nave. The bells rang on, but the sound was suddenly different. It was softened now, and humanized, and its thunder had warmed to a jubilation. The nave was furnished in rows of the little rush-bottomed chairs that serve in France as pews. We sat down and caught our breath. The bells rang joyfully on and on, and died away in a dying echo. We sat for a moment longer, and then walked back up the nave and out. Out into sunlight. Out into Sunday peace and quiet. It was like coming out from shelter after a sudden storm.

Before we went out to dinner that night, I had a belated thought. I opened the Nancy telephone directory, and turned to the R's. There were no Roueches in Nancy. I turned to the back of the directory, to a supplement of suburban listings. I went from Agincourt to Laneuville-Devant-Nancy to Saulxures-les-Nancy to Seichamps. I came to Vandoeuvre—and my heart gave a jump: "Rouchy, J. P." It fell back. And then—at Villers-des-Nancy—it jumped again: "Roucheff, A." And fell back even harder.

But that didn't affect my appetite. We dined at the Restaurant

Stanislas on a salad garnished with pâté de foie gras and served
with toasted slices of brioche, on roasted partridge with cabbage,
on cheese (including a strong, earthy Munster, nothing like the
vapid American variety) served with a little dish of ground cumin
for seasoning, on mirabelle-plum sorbet. Our wine was an Alsatian
Riesling, and our mineral water was from the springs at nearby
Vittel. It was my introduction to the cuisine of my ancestors, and I
made the most of it.

I had decided that our search should begin at the Mairie. The
Mairie of Nancy is one of a number of government offices housed
in the Stanislasian splendor of the Hôtel de Ville. We entered (on
Lucien's recommendation) from the Place, the most splendid of the
building's several entrances, and saw and mounted the magnificent
branching stairway (by Heré) and its eighty-foot balustrade and
handrail (cast by Lamour in a single convolution of wrought iron).
We found the Mairie. The clerk on duty informed us with a smile of
bureaucratic satisfaction that we had come to the wrong office. The
appropriate office for our inquiry was the Archives de Meurthe-et-
Moselle. And where would one find the departmental archives? On
the Rue de la Monnaie. Where else?
    We went back to the Place. A passerby directed us to the Rue de
la Monnaie. We found it just off a little square called La Fayette,
inhabited by a towering equestrian statue of Jeanne d'Arc, somewhere behind the Musée des Beaux-Arts. The archives of the Department de Meurthe-et-Moselle were housed in a handsome
building that had the familiar look of Heré. Mademoiselle Bernadette Adam, *secretaire de documentation,* received us in a book-
lined reading room. She was, like me, essentially monolingual. She
and Kay conversed. Mademoiselle Adam looked vague, less vague,
then interested. She gave me a serious look. She left the room and
returned with an armful of books—three big, ledgerlike books
bound in tan linen—and piled them on a vacant table. Beside them
she placed a form: "Nom et Prenoms/Nationalité/Objet des Re-
cherches . . ." I filled out the form, and turned to the books: "Table
Decennale Naissances: 1823-1832." The other two were the birth
records for the decades 1813-1822 and 1802-1813—Mademoiselle
Adam had given Henri Constant a possible birth span of thirty
years. I sat down and opened "1802-1813." The pages were of
heavy, almost parchment, paper, and the names were written in a
sweeping copperplate hand in ink faded to brown. The names were
listed alphabetically by year. I turned to the R's of 1802. Kay
looked over my shoulder. There were many R names, including

many Richards, but no Roueché or Roueche or even Rouche. It was
the same for every other year in volume "1802-1813." It was also
the same for "1813-1822." Also for "1823-1832," but I had given
up hope long before that. I felt puzzled. I felt disappointed. I also
felt somehow cheated. I stacked up the books. Kay and Mademoiselle Adam conversed. I waited.

Kay came back to the table. "Well," she said. "I don't know.
These records don't really prove a whole lot. They only speak for
Nancy. Mademoiselle Adam says our Henri Constant might very
well have been born in one of the neighboring villages in the Nancy
area. And the villages, the communes, all kept their own records.
You remember what your brother said. If somebody in France or
England or wherever asked you where you came from, and you
were actually born in a little place—like, say, Lone Jack—not far
from Kansas City, you would probably say you came from Kansas
City. I think that's what Henri Constant did. He named the nearest
town that somebody might have heard of."

I nodded. That sounded reasonable enough. But I also had a
tempting flicker of hope. "About those villages," I said. "You say
they all kept their own records. Why don't we look into that? Why
don't we check them out?"

"We could," Kay said. "But it might take a little time. Mademoiselle Adam said there are quite a lot of them. Almost six
hundred, in fact."

"Where comes the name of Nancy?" Jean-Pierre Zehnder said.
Monsieur Zehnder is an editor at the Nancy daily *Est Republicain*,
and he has a good command of English. We were gathered in his
office with a group of his colleagues. "The name, I think, is originally Latin. It comes from the name of a farm that was here in
ancient times called *Nanceiensis*."

He turned to his colleagues and repeated in French my question.
There was a moment of silence. Then one of them gave an explosive
laugh. *"Bien sûr,"* he said. *"Pour Nancy Reagan."* I gathered that
Nancy as a woman's name sounds strange to French ears. So, for that
matter, does Lorraine. The French feel much the way an American
would upon hearing of a French girl called Tulsa or Miami.

It began to sprinkle. The Place was only a couple of blocks away.
We began to hurry. We turned into the Rue Stanislas. It began to
rain. We ducked under the awning of a pâtisserie. We looked in the
window at the always dazzling spectacle of cookies and cakes and
breads and rolls and tarts and tortes. Kay went in for a closer, more

professional look. I stayed under the awning and watched the cars splash by and the umbrellas appear. The rain slackened, and then started up again. Kay came out eating a cherry tart and with a chocolate something for me that might have been designed by Cellini.'

"I've just been talking to the nicest woman," she said. "Did you know that Nancy was the home of the macaroon? And that the madeleine was invented in a town not far from here? And another town, the famous Verdun, is where most of the Jordan almonds come from. She said the pretzel is just as French as it is German. Of course, I knew about quiche Lorraine. But guess who brought the brioche to France? His name begins with S."

We climbed the stairs to the second floor of the sixteenth-century palace of the Dukes of Lorraine that is now the Musée Historique Lorrain. We were looking for the room devoted to the work of the first of Nancy's native artists, Georges de La Tour. We passed a guard, and a reek of garlic and sweat and cigarette smoke. We came into a long room displaying the household artifacts, the costumes, the weapons, the trophies of the chase, the portraits, and the emphatic depictions of the military triumphs of the pre-Stanislas dukes. A stocky couple of late middle age were standing before a massive wall tapestry that showed in still rich colors a battle scene of rearing horses and waving banners and flashing swords and headless bodies. As we approached, the woman said, "Ian! Please! The guard is watching. Do try to look interested."

The military are well served, well remembered, in Nancy. Lucien was right. I had this thrust upon me one day while studying a municipal street map. There is not only the Hemicycle du General de Gaulle and the giant statue of Jeanne d'Arc—as well as the Avenue Jeanne d'Arc, the Rue Jeanne d'Arc, and the Lycée Jeanne d'Arc—there is also the Avenue Foch, the Rue du Maréchal Oudinot, the Boulevard Joffre, the Rue Maréchal Michel Ney, the Avenue du General Mangin, the Avenue du General Leclerc, the Rue General Hoche, the Rue de General Lyautey, the Place General Giraud, and the Rue de General Drouot. There is also a statue (with campaign citations) of General Drouot, a native son, in the Cours Léopold. There is a Rue Vauban, in celebration of the seventeenth-century military engineer whose chief fortress, Landau, was a disaster, and a Place Maginot, in memory of another military engineer. There is even another homage to Stanislas—the Porte Stanislas. I was pleased to find that General de Gaulle and Jeanne d'Arc are not the only saviors of France that Nancy had chosen to honor. There is also the Rue de l'Armée Patton.

* * *

We shared a table at lunch at the Restaurant Muller ("Taverne Alsa-cienne") with a young French couple in jeans and an older French-man of indeterminate age in the ubiquitous navy-blue blazer. The couple were eating their first course—an hors d'oeuvre that in-cluded tiny buttered radishes and slices of cold boiled ham thickly spread with butter—and the older man was drinking his *apéritif*. We sat and waited for a menu. The couple finished their hors d'oeuvres. The older man finished his Ricard. We still waited to order. The four of us sat and waited. And waited. The older man caught my eye. He rocked his head from side to side. He smiled an ironic smile. He nodded toward a distant waiter. He walked two fingers across the tablecloth—slowly, then slower, then even slower than that. He rolled his eyes toward Heaven. He said, *"Oh là là."*

"You are learning about Stanislas?" Lucien said. I had stopped at his desk to leave a postcard (a view of the Place Stanislas) for mailing. "You have seen him in the Place, his statue? And the portraits in the Musée Historique Lorrain? You have seen how fat is his face, his chins, his *bedon*. He was a patron of the arts. Oh, yes. He gave us so much beauty. But he was also a patron of the plea-sures. You cannot imagine how much Stanislas was eating—the meat, the chicken, the fish, everything. There is a square behind the hotel that you have maybe seen. It has now trees and flowers. It is a park. In the time of Stanislas it was the garden for his vegeta-bles. His weight? One hundred fifty kilos! Maybe more. He liked all good things. The women, the girls. You know his statue, how his finger is pointing? It is correct to say that he is pointing his finger to the Arc de Triomphe and the portrait there of Louis XV. But there is another story. This story tells that he is pointing to the Old Town, where those who wished found prostitutes."

I opened the door to the floor maid. She had my laundry. It was three shirts—perfectly laundered and faultlessly ironed—each wrapped like a gift in white tissue paper, and the three of them precisely stacked in a flat little brown wicker basket.

"I am thinking since we talk before," Didier Hemardinquer said to me. "I am thinking about your ancestor." Hemardinquer—young, slight, blond, immaculate—is an English-speaking writer on the staff of the *Est Republicain* whom Kay and I had met through the editor, Jean-Pierre Zehnder. We were standing under the Arc de

Triomphe, looking down the Place de la Carrière—a wide allée of over-arching linden trees flanked by two rows of palatial three-story row houses by Heré. "I am thinking," Hemardinquer said, "if he lived in Nancy in the time you say, he would live in what we call the Old Town. I am thinking we will go there, and you will be seeing what he saw. Nancy in that time was not a big city. It was maybe thirty thousand people—one fourth the size of now. The Old Town is here before Stanislas, and it is here the same today. This square, this Place de la Carrière, was here before Stanislas. It was first the jousting field of the early dukes. The name means 'pit.' The Old Town goes back to the beginning. It is where Nancy began, in the eleventh century. We go this way, to behind the Arc. And here we are already in *la Ville-Vieille*. This street is now the beginning. It is the Grand Rue, the main street of the Old Town. It goes from here to the ancient city wall, to the Porte de la Craffe, five hundred fifty meters in distance."

We turned into a cobbled street just wide enough for two cars to pass. The sidewalks were hardly four feet wide, and the people walking there were walking single file. To walk abreast, the three of us walked with the traffic in the street. The buildings, too, were narrow, and they seemed to arch overhead. We passed a sign on a door: "Societé Canine de l'Est." We passed a shop called Cactus, with a window full of granny dresses and faded Levis and cowboy boots. The side streets were no more than alleys. We came out into a familiar square and the Gothic rise of the Église St.-Epvre.

"Here is the Place de St.-Epvre," Hemardinquer said. "Your ancestor would have known it well. It was in the Middle Ages the farmers' marketplace. But also there has always been here a church. The name is Latin. There is never such a word in French. There is never a P and a V together. We cross now to the palace of the first dukes of Lorraine. Notice there are gargoyles. The palace is built for the Duke René II. René II is a big hero of Nancy. There was a big battle here with Charles le Téméraire, the duke of Burgundy, in 1477. 'Téméraire' means reckless. He was killed by René II, and his body thrown into a field where is now the Pépinière and was eaten by the wolves. Do you know the flower of Lorraine? It is the thistle. It was chosen by René II after the battle that saved Lorraine, and it has also a motto. It says in English: 'Touch me not, I scratch.' The Old Town has known much war. Look across the street—that building on the Rue St.-Michel. Look to the little tower on the corner. In the wall below the window—a cannonball. It is let stay there as a souvenir of the Thirty Years War."

We passed "Antiquités." We passed "Blanc-Neige Blanchis-
serie." We passed "Centre Video—Toutes Cartes de Credit." We
passed a street-cleaner in orange overalls sweeping the street with a
broom made out of a bundle of twigs. The Grand Rue came to an
end at two tall conical towers with a passageway between them
blazoned with the double-barred Cross of Lorraine. Hemardinquer
raised a hand in the manner of Stanislas.

"You are seeing the Porte de la Craffe," he said. "It is of the
fourteenth century, and it is here that René II saved Lorraine. We
turn now on the Rue Haut-Bourgeois. There are here many beautiful houses of the early eighteenth century. They were built for the
nobles by Boffrand, the teacher of Heré."

I said I supposed that was why it was called the Rue Haut-Bourgeois.

Hemardinquer smiled. "No," he said. "It is true that 'haut-
bourgeois' means a social class. But there is also a different meaning, an older meaning, maybe. It means a river that runs down the
center of the street to carry away the sewage, like a gutter. 'Haut' is
a big gutter. Around the corner here is a street called Rue Petit-
Bourgeois. It was made with a little gutter. And there is a beautiful
house—the one with the open courtyard and the sculpture wolves
on the gateposts. We are now on the Rue de Loup, and that is the
Hôtel de Loup. It was the house of the Master of the Hunt under the
Duke Léopold, the duke before Stanislas. It is by the great Boffrand. The next street now is the Rue de Guise. The Rue de Guise
is where I live. I wish you to come now and see my wife and son.
And for tea. My house is also of the eighteenth century." He smiled
and shook his head. "It is amusing. In the beginning, the Old Town
was where everybody lived. Then came the nobles. Then, in the
time of your ancestor, the Old Town was where the ordinary people
lived. Then for maybe one hundred years it was the place where
nobody wanted to live. Any place was better. Now it is again the
place to live. It is fashionable."

On our last night in Nancy, we dined at Le Capucin Gourmand. It
was a celebration of a sort, and Le Capucin Gourmand is the most
celebrated of Nancy's several celebrated restaurants. We hadn't
found what had brought us to Nancy. We had only found Nancy
itself. But that was something, that was enough. Le Capucin Gourmand is richly Nancienne. Its decor reflects the inspirations of such
artists as Emile Gallé, who made l'École de Nancy the leader in
France of the Art Nouveau movement. It takes no credit cards, its
patrons are urged (in a menu note) not to smoke before they are

served their coffee, and its most celebrated, and practically obliga-
tory, dish is fresh foie gras au natural. Its kitchen understands
potée, the complicated Lorrainean version of choucroute. Its wine
list is a hefty leather-bound book. The wines of Lorraine (red and
white and "gray") are of local reputation only, but Nancy has
neighbors of the highest distinction—Champagne, Alsace, and
Burgundy. The glasses at Le Capucin Gourmand are exquisitely of
the region. They come from the crystal manufactory at the nearby
village of Baccarat. Our dessert was also local. It was a rhubarb
sorbet.

The night was bright with a waxing moon. We walked back to
the hotel, and strolled for one last time around the Place Stanislas.
The corner fountains splashed. There were rows of lighted windows in the reception rooms of the Hôtel de Ville. The opera
theatre was alight and alive. I heard a whisper of music. I knew I
had never seen a more beautiful square, and I thought it had never
looked more beautiful. And I felt a kind of pride that it was here in
Nancy.

                                                              [1985]

16. The Steeple: *Sag Harbor, Long Island*

One early autumn afternoon, on a day of wild winds and sudden silences, I drove out to the village of Sag Harbor to make a pilgrimage to the Whalers' Presbyterian Church there. Sag Harbor is on the north shore of the southeastern fluke of Long Island and covers a secluded point on Shelter Island Sound, near the head of Gardiners Bay. It was settled around the beginning of the eighteenth century. For a few years just before the Revolution, it was a busier port than New York; it once had as rich and restless a whaling fleet as New Bedford or Nantucket; it has been almost motionless since the Civil War; and it is full of big, splendid, creaky old houses and intimations of mortality. The Whalers' Church, although little more than a hundred years old, is its noblest and most disquieting structure. It would be arresting anywhere. Except for a mean and slovenly copy in Essex, Connecticut, it is the only building of its kind in the world.

The Whalers' Church was designed by Minard Lafever, a gifted and expensive New York architect, whose more accessible works include the Church of St. James, near Chatham Square, and the Church of the Holy Trinity, in Brooklyn, and it was put together by local shipbuilders and ships' carpenters. The foundation was laid in the spring of 1843 and the church was dedicated on May 16, 1844. It cost seventeen thousand dollars. That was an immense sum in the eighteen-forties (carpenters were paid a dollar and a half for a twelve-hour day, the finest St. Croix rum sold for three cents a glass, and clear Havana stogies were two cents each), but it was not considered excessive by Sag Harbor Presbyterians. Most of the parishioners who made substantial contributions to the building fund were whaling officers, shipyard owners, shipowners, or ship chandlers and outfitters, and several were among the wealthiest men on Long Island; practically all the members of the congregation, including farmers and shopkeepers, held rewarding shares in at least one whaler. The first

Sag Harbor whaling voyage on record was made in 1775, by a brig called the *Lucy;* she returned home with some three hundred barrels of oil on that occasion. The last Sag Harbor whaler was the *Myra;* she put out in July, 1871, and never returned.

In the intervening years, Sag Harbor whalers made more than five hundred successful voyages, many of which lasted three or four years, and brought back between twenty-five and thirty million dollars' worth of whale oil, sperm oil, and whalebone. The first ship to sail through the Bering Strait was the *Superior,* a Sag Harbor whaler, in 1848. The first American ship to enter a Japanese port was the *Manhattan,* in 1845, commanded by Mercator Cooper, a Sag Harbor whaling captain; Commodore Matthew C. Perry, who is commonly celebrated for this feat, turned up off Japan eight years later. Between 1820 and 1850, Sag Harbor's richest period, the local fleet brought in a total of 83,102 barrels of sperm oil, 812,595 barrels of whale oil, and 6,728,809 pounds of bone, with an aggregate value of more than fifteen million dollars. The industry began to decline in the eighteen-fifties, and it collapsed in the sixties; an abundance of petroleum, which had just been discovered in western Pennsylvania, had all but put an end to the demand for whale oil. The Whalers' Church was completed in Sag Harbor's most vigorous year; the town's fleet in 1844 numbered sixty-three vessels, and its population was 3,621. Sag Harbor no longer has even the semblance of a fleet, its harbor is deserted except for a few pleasure craft in summer, its railroad station has been boarded up since 1939, and its population is 2,373.

Sag Harbor is surrounded on the north and east by the waters of Shelter Island Sound and a sandy cove hems it in on the west. Above it, to the south rises a wilderness of scrub oak and jack pine that stretches almost to the ocean, seven miles away. Three or four rambling, humpbacked roads, cut through the woods, link the village to the Montauk Highway, which skirts the seacoast. On the day of my visit I turned into one of these roads at about two o'clock. After a couple of miles, I passed a woman on a wobbly bicycle. Farther on, I passed a weathered sign: "Good Luck and Safe Return—Welcome to Sag Harbor." Just beyond it was a cemetery. Then the road curved, and I emerged abruptly into a wide, angular downhill street of arching elms and peeling white clapboard houses. The houses sat close to the sidewalk, behind rickety picket fences; there were leaded fanlights over most of their doorways, and one had a widow's walk on the roof. An elderly man in a blue serge suit and an Army sweater was puttering around in one of the yards. He was the only human being in sight. I pulled up and asked him if he could direct me to the Whalers' Church: He leaned on the fence and gazed at me.

"Want to have a look at it, eh?" he said. "Well, it's a sight. Should have come down here ten years ago, though, before the hurricane carried off the steeple. Wouldn't of been any need to ask your way then. You'd of seen it for yourself from here, downstreet, or anywhere. Far as that goes, you could see it from Montauk. That steeple was two hundred feet high, more or less, and there wasn't two parts of it alike. They were every one different. That steeple really tickled me. I enjoyed looking at it. Religion aside, of course. I run with the Methodists, when I go." The old man fished a package of chewing gum from his pocket, popped a stick into his mouth, and jerked his thumb in the direction I was headed. "Two blocks down, turn left at the blinker, and you'll see it," he said. "I guess there's enough of it left to hold you."

I thanked him and drove on down the windy, deserted street. The air smelled wet and salty. As I made the turn at the blinker, a ragged army of gulls wheeled overhead. Then I saw the church. It came hulking up through the heaving treetops—big and baleful and as white as an old clamshell. Set on a wooded knoll, well back from the street, between a row of splayed early-eighteenth-century cottages and a crumbling graveyard, it looked larger than Grand Central Station, and it held me. I parked my car and got out and stared at it. It is a numbing blend of the chaste, the finical, and the stolid. Its facade is predominantly Babylonian and Theban Egyptian in style. The auditorium—of clapboard, slate-roofed, boxy, and severe—is pure meeting-house Colonial. A kind of annex jutting out in back is mid-Victorian. From where I stood, at one end of a semicircular walk leading up to the church, only a corner of the main body of the building was visible. The auditorium is a hundred and thirty feet long, sixty-five feet wide, and the equivalent of three considerable stories in height, but the façade obscured it. A massive, shingle-sided, hundred-foot truncated pyramidal wooden tower, some forty feet square at the base and tapering to almost half that at the top, forms the center of the façade. It is flanked by two similar, though broader and slightly lower, wing pylons. Surmounting each of the pylons and the tower is a fragile parapet. The cornices are decorated with a complicated Corinthian frosting. A toothy row of antefixes conceals the eaves. Just below this is a banding of classic-Grecian verticals. An uncovered porch, with an iron-pipe railing, runs the width of the facade. Opening onto it are three narrow, story-high, white, panelled doors, one in the tower and one in each pylon. The antefixes are repeated on their cornices, and the center door is crowned by another parapet. Above each door, and rising almost to the roof line, is a tall window of opaque and faintly lavender small-paned glass. I stood there for a minute or two gazing up at the church, and then I started up the walk leading to the porch. It was hard to imagine a mighty steeple rearing above that vast, chalky face. The building didn't look at all incomplete. It didn't even look old. It looked like a brand-new mausoleum.

I tried all three doors and found them locked. As I turned uncertainly away from the last one, I heard voices approaching, and then a sudden shriek of laughter. I almost jumped. Then an unshaven old man in work clothes and a hunting cap came around the side of the building. With him was a somewhat younger woman. She had on a pink dress, a grass-green coat, and golden slippers, and there was a red patent-leather pocketbook under her arm. I went over to them. They were laughing and chattering, but they broke off when they saw me, and stopped dead. I said I had come out from New York to see the church and asked if the pastor was around.

"Here?" the man said, studying me closely. "Ain't he down to the Manse?"

His companion giggled. "If Reverend Crawford was here," she said, "he'd have me down on my knees. He's been praying for me to find a job. I'm praying right along with him, too."

"He's down to the Manse," the man said. "Either that or he's out preaching a funeral."

"Probably a funeral," the woman said cheerfully. "There's nothing likelier in this town. How many did you say he had last week, Mr. Cleveland?"

"Four " Mr. Cleveland said. "I doubt there's one today, though."

The woman turned to me. "Mr. Cleveland, here, is sexton of the church," she said. "He knows everything that's going on. That's why I come by and see him—to learn the news."

"Sexton, janitor, superintendent, and a little bit of everything else," Mr. Cleveland said. "You might say I've got more jobs here than there is congregation. We had eighty turn up last Sunday. There's room in there for a thousand, spread out just four to the pew. I guess they used to fill her up—sides, center, and gallery—but not in my time. Nor in my dad's, neither. In the old days, most everybody in town was Presbyterian. The R.C.'s got the edge now."

"I wonder why that is," the woman said. "Unless it's those Poles and Italians at the watch factory."

"Times change," Mr. Cleveland said. "I remember when there was steamboats running down to New York from here and over to New London, and Sag Harbor was the end of the main line of the Long Island Railroad. That was in the nineties, before they built on out to Montauk and stuck us off on a branch. Now we ain't even on that. You must of drove out here—you don't look like you walked. Well, I've got the time and the right to open her up and let you in—done it before for visitors. But maybe you'd better get Crawford to take you through. Since you come all the way out from New York, he'd be sorry to miss you. You see that gray house with a fence around it down there at the end of the block—where that old dog is laying in the drive? That's the Manse. I'll show you one thing, though. You've heard about the famous steeple we had, I guess, and how it went down in the hurricane. September 21, 1938, at three-thirty in the afternoon, was the date. Well, see that patch of new-looking concrete in the walk there, alongside the burying-ground wall? That's where the butt of the steeple hit. I live just the other side of the burying ground, and I was looking out the window and I saw it go. I couldn't hardly believe my eyes. Why, that steeple had been there all my life. What happened was the wind caught under the louvers in the Sir Christopher Wren section. It lifted the whole shebang straight up in the air—the whole hundred and fifty-or-more feet of it—swung it clear of the building, and dropped it on the walk there. Then it toppled over into the burying ground and smashed to smithereens. All except the bell. That didn't get a scratch on it. We've got it set up inside now, in the lobby. I won't say I heard the bell ring because I didn't. I was inside, and the wind was too loud. But I know people that did. It rang once, hanging up there in midair, just before it hit. And that patch there is the exact spot where the steeple come down."

"I've got a piece of it at home for a souvenir," the woman said. "I guess everybody in town has. Mine's part of the Chinese part."

I left Mr. Cleveland and his friend on the church steps and walked down to the Manse. The sidewalk tilted every which way, and there were tree roots as big as my arm pushing up through the cracks. Most of the houses in the block were so old that moss was growing on their roofs. The dog in the driveway made a halfhearted attempt to rise as I pushed through the front gate, and then slumped somnolently back. Before I could knock at the door, it swung open and a sleek, bald, broad-shouldered man of about forty looked out. He wore metal-rimmed glasses and had on a red flannel shirt, faded dungarees, and dirty white sneakers, and he was eating an apple. "Heard you at the gate," he said, a bit indistinctly. Then he swallowed, grinned, and added, "It's as good as a bell." I introduced myself and explained why I was there. "That's fine," he said. "I'm Donald Crawford. Excuse me." He tossed the core of his apple over my head, out into the street. "Come right in. You picked a good day for your visit. For me, anyway. This is my day off— hence these clothes. I've been burning some trash." I stepped into a dim hall. From upstairs came the sound of running water and an occasional wail. "That's my little helper," Mr. Crawford remarked. "Douglas, aged four. He's enduring a bath. Our other treasure is at school. Mary Alice is seven. Let's go in the parlor." I followed him into a small, high-ceilinged room gently ravaged by time and children. A tall, lanky, white-haired man in a sombre suit and a high collar was leaning against the mantel of a handsome white marble fireplace. In an ashtray at his elbow lay an elaborate spiral of apple peel. "This is Dr. Charles H. Tillinghast," Mr. Crawford said to me. "He hasn't got a care in the world. He's just retired after forty-nine years of dentistry, and he recently ended a long term as president of our church board of trustees. You're not interrupting anything. He just dropped by for a chat. How about it, Doctor? Would you like to go up to the church with us?"

Dr. Tillinghast extended me a bony hand. "My boy," he said, "it would be a privilege to show you through. Historic Sag Harbor and its proudest monument, the Whalers' Church, are the chief interests of my declining years. As you may know, we have here the second-largest number of authentic Colonial buildings of any community in the United States. We are exceeded only by Nantucket. But even Nantucket, if I may say so, has no such church as ours. My one regret is that our glorious steeple is gone. You've read of it, I'm sure. Perhaps you have seen pictures of it. A work of art." He shook his head. "It was the crowning glory of Minard Lafever's ecclesiastical masterpiece. I miss it as I would an old and cherished friend."

"I'll go get my coat," Mr. Crawford said.

Dr. Tillinghast nodded, cleared his throat, and continued, "It was a loss that everyone felt deeply. One of our local poetesses, the late Annie Cooper Boyd, wrote very movingly about it. I believe I have a copy of her poem here. You might care to glance at it." He drew a wallet from his pocket, extracted a tousled clipping, and handed it to me. The poem, eleven stanzas long, was entitled "The Steeple." It began:

> *The Steeple—what!—the Steeple—*
> *Don't say that it has gone!*
> *Thus spoke the village people*
> *With voice and face forlorn.*

Another stanza read:

> *Oh, lovely, lofty steeple,*
> *We loved thee from the heart—*
> *Thy curious construction,*
> *Thy myriad types of art!*

"Of course " said Dr. Tillinghast as I returned the clipping, "we must be thankful that the church itself was spared."

Mr. Crawford, wearing an elegant covert-cloth topcoat, appeared in the hall doorway. I helped Dr. Tillinghast into his coat, he placed a floppy hat on his head, and we filed out to the street. Just outside the gate, Dr. Tillinghast halted. "Perhaps," he said, "we should call our young friend's attention to some of the historic points of interest adjacent to this particular corner. The magnificent Greek Revival edifice that you have undoubtedly noticed directly across the street is the old Benjamin Huntting place. Its architect was none other than Minard Lafever. I see that surprises you. I'll admit that the resemblance between Sag Harbor's two examples of the great Lafever's art is not pronounced. The answer lies in the fact that he was a man of great versatility. Captain Huntting was one of our whaling princes and, I'm proud to say, a prominent member of our church. In fact, like myself, he served as president of our board of trustees. His home was built in 1846. It was later purchased by Mrs. Russell Sage, whom we claim as a fellow-citizen and esteem as a generous civic benefactor."

"She put a new coat of paint on the church once," Mr. Crawford said.

"At least once," Dr. Tillinghast said. "Including the steeple. The old Huntting place is now our Whaling Museum. That large white clapboard structure over there on the right is the old Hannibal French mansion, built around 1800. And behind those trees in the distance is the old Customs House, built in 1790. In its yard is a boxwood bush that there is every reason to believe was grown from a slip presented to our first Collector of Port by Martha Washington herself. Our port, unfortunately, was discontinued in 1905, but the old Customs House, quite properly, has been preserved."

"Don't forget the Manse, Doctor," Mr. Crawford said. He grinned at me and began to move on up the street. "Built in eighteen-twenty-something and never restored. It's a good thing I'm handy."

"I know, Donald," Dr. Tillinghast said mildly. "As I recall, Mr. Barrett often said the same."

"My predecessor," Mr. Crawford explained. "I'm number nineteen in the line. The ministry here goes back to 1794. It gives me a funny feeling sometimes to realize that this church had already gone through four generations of ministers before my home town was even founded."

"You're not from around here?" I asked.

"Hardly," Mr. Crawford said. "I'm from Chicago—Winnetka, to be exact. If you'll forgive me, Doctor, I'm not sure that I'd ever even heard of Sag Harbor until I received my call. That was only back in 1940. I must say it seems like a lifetime ago, though. Time sags along pretty slowly in Sag Harbor."

Dr. Tillinghast smiled a thin smile. "The name of Sag Harbor, as Donald knows, does not refer to that, however," he said. "It derives from a Shinnecock Indian word, *sagaponack,* which means 'place of the groundnuts.' Groundnuts are an edible root, something like a potato."

"Actually," Mr. Crawford said, "my call to Sag Harbor wasn't much more unexpected than my call to the ministry. My mother has never really got over that. Selling stocks and bonds was more the custom in our family. I may not look it, but I used to be a bond salesman. As soon as I got out of Yale—I was class of '28—I went right into a brokerage house back home. Sold bonds all day and danced all night. Then the market crashed. That did something to me. It wasn't simply a matter of economics. I can't explain it—I walked around in a daze. Then, one Sunday night in November, 1929, I wandered into the old Moody Church, on North LaSalle Street. That evening changed my entire life. I came out converted. I went on selling bonds, of course. I had to. But I spent my nights at the Moody Bible Institute, studying the Bible and making up for lost time. When I was ready—in 1936—I quit my job and came East and started all over again, at Princeton Theological Seminary. My family—well, one of my aunts—helped put me through. I was ordained in 1940. That was an eventful year for me. I was ordained, I got married, and I got this call. My wife is a Philadelphian. We were on our honeymoon when the call came, and she cried for hours." He shrugged. "She likes it here now—we both do. Sag Harbor's a little off the beaten trail, but there's a tremendous spiritual challenge here. When a whole town lives in the past . . . I mean there are some extraordinary problems."

"Youth is always restless," Dr. Tillinghast said comfortably. He turned to me. "It might interest you to know that the Long Island

Herald, founded in Sag Harbor in 1791, was the first newspaper published on Long Island. No one would have called this off the beaten path a hundred years ago. One of America's greatest preachers, Edward Hopper, served our church from 1852 to 1863, and it was the daring seamen of Sag Harbor who inspired him to write his immortal hymn 'Jesus, Saviour, Pilot Me.' James Fenimore Cooper lived here for some years, before he established himself as a writer. *The Pioneers* and *The Sea Lions* are both full of Sag Harbor. Why, this very street has known the tread of half the races of mankind. It was nothing in the old days to see Fiji Islanders, Malayans, Kanakas, Chinamen, Portuguese, Shinnecocks, and Montauks, and heaven only knows what else, roaming all over town. I imagine you've read *Moby Dick.* Old Melville knew what he was doing when he had his pagan harpooner Queequeg brought to America on a Sag Harbor whaler."

"Well," Mr. Crawford said, with a wave of his hand, "there she blows—the church that whale oil built. I sometimes think that God placed me in Sag Harbor to humble me, but He certainly gave me a beautiful church."

The sight of the church was momentarily silencing. Familiarity didn't seem to diminish it. Even Dr. Tillinghast gazed at it without comment. There was no sign of Mr. Cleveland or his friend. Nobody spoke until we were halfway up the walk. Then Dr. Tillinghast gave a short puzzled laugh. "In all fairness," he said, "I should point out that our church has attracted a few—a very few—unfavorable criticisms. We had an architect visiting here one summer who called it a hodgepodge. The unconventionality of its parts apparently blinded him to the beauty of the whole. He was from one of the newer settlements in the Middle West."

I remarked that Lafever must have been an extremely imaginative man.

"Lafever scorned the commonplace," Dr. Tillinghast said. "The old Benjamin Huntting place, though traditional, has many unusual touches. But I'm not sure that the style of our church was entirely Lafever's idea. His was the guiding hand, of course, but it must be remembered that he was dealing here with men who sailed the Seven Seas and had absorbed the flavor of foreign lands. They had their own ideas. What Lafever did was combine their impressions with his own. I think he was also inspired to suggest something of their courageous way of life. Look at the curious design of the railings up there on the tower and the pylons and over the center door. One of our less appreciative visitors said they looked like a row of lollipops." A trace of pain crossed Dr. Tillinghast's face. "Of course," he went on, "that motif is a stylized version, in what I take to be the Gothic manner, of the whaler's blubber spade. That would be obvious to anyone who had examined the fine collection of old Sag Harbor whaling implements at the Museum. Ridicule comes easy to some people. It may surprise you to hear that even our steeple was not completely immune to criticism. The Sag Harbor *Corrector*, now defunct, once called it 'fantastic' and Lafever 'bewildered.' If you could only have seen that glorious steeple! Perhaps I can describe it to you. It rose, naturally, from the top of the tower, and the height of it was truly majestic—one hundred and eighty-seven feet. Its height was another seafaring note. Our mariners wanted their church spire to serve as a landmark, visible to the returning ship as it rounded Montauk Point. For many years, a whale-oil beacon lamp at the pinnacle was lighted every night."

"I've read somewhere that it used to be noted on the U.S. Coast and Geodetic Survey maps," Mr. Crawford said.

"Very likely," Dr. Tillinghast said. "Our steeple was composed in three tapering sections, each smaller in diameter than the one beneath it. I don't think it was accidental that it resembled somewhat the sea captain's spyglass in use at that time. I doubt, too, if anyone but a shipwright could have raised it. It was raised by ox power, each section pulled up through the inside of the preceding one. The lowest section, in which the bell was installed, was in the seventeenth-century English style of Sir Christopher Wren, and extremely decorative. The main feature of it was an octagonal colonnade. In its pediment were four beautiful clocks. The derivation of the second section is uncertain. It was probably either Greek or as some experts have suggested, Phoenician. Its chief ornamentation, at any rate, was a series of long panels, in which were cut the ancient Phoenician swastika. That was a symbol, I understand, of good luck. The topmost section was a replica of a Chinese pagoda. Needless to say, the entire structure was made of the finest Suffolk County white pine, chosen and seasoned by our own shipbuilders, and every inch of it was hand-carved." Dr. Tillinghast shook his head. "No," he said, "I hardly think that you or any person with a feeling for beauty would have called our steeple 'fantastic.'"

"Is there any prospect of restoring it?" I asked.

"We talk about it," Mr. Crawford said. "A year or two ago, we even had an architect out from New York to look into it. He said it could be done. There are plenty of good photographs of the old steeple around that an expert could go by. There hasn't been so much talk of it since we got his estimate, though. It was a little

over seventy-five thousand dollars." Mr. Crawford unlocked the
center door, pushed it open, and waved us in. "That's just about
five times the original cost of the whole church."

We entered the lobby, big and square and gloomy. Opening off it
were three panelled oak doors leading to the auditorium and the
flanking pylons. The walls were dark and hung with marble memorial plaques, one of which read:

REV. SAMUEL KING,

A Native of England,
who departed this life Nov. 29th 1833;
after having ministered to this
congregation
one year and three months,
in the 42 year of his life.

THIS TABLET

as a token of respect
is devoted to the memory of a stranger
and a good man.
"The memory of the just is blessed."

Mounted on a low wooden frame in the middle of the lobby was a
mighty bell. Dr. Tillinghast caught up a knotted end of rope attached to
it as we passed. "Listen to this tone," he said, and struck the bell a
savage whack. It gave an exhausted moan. "Sound as a dollar," he
said. "I venture to say not many bells could survive such a fall."

"God spared what He deemed essential," Mr. Crawford said. "If
you like, I'll take you up on the bell deck—what used to be the
bell deck—before we leave. But right now..." He opened the
auditorium door and took me by the arm. The three of us stepped
into a silent immensity of whiteness. At the foot of a long center
aisle, carpeted in faded green and lined with boxed pews, was a
high rostrum. It was set in a *trompe-l'oeil* circular arcade, flanked
on either side by a door, and framed by a pair of round, fluted
Corinthian columns and two square pilasters that rose, well over
fifty feet, to a coffered ceiling. Two steeply inclined overhanging
galleries, faced with an intricate frieze of carved volutes and ro-
settes, ran the length of the side walls. Behind each of them was a
row of tall, tinted windows, ablaze with frosty lavender light. Ex-

cept for the carpet, three tortuous black chairs on the rostrum, and a narrow trimming of rich, red mahogany along the sides and backs of the pews, the entire chamber was salt-white, and they made it look even whiter. For an instant, it was as dazzling as sun on snow.

Mr. Crawford dropped his hand from my arm. "It's beautiful, isn't it?" he said. "I don't mean to seem proud." I said, quite truthfully, that I'd never seen a more handsome room. "No," he said. "Of course, it's a few sizes too big for us now. I guess it always was. The sad thing is that it was built for the future. A hundred years ago, you know, there was a tremendous religious revival sweeping the country, and at the same time Sag Harbor was getting more prosperous every year. We had the main floor pretty well filled for our centennial celebration. Maybe someday..." He sighed and smiled. "Those doors on either side of the platform go into the Sunday School. That's a good, big room, too."

"The Sunday-school annex is a later addition," Dr. Tillinghast said, without interest. Moving briskly down the aisle, he continued, "Let me call your attention to the fine Cuban-mahogany trimming on these pews—a very unusual touch. One of our whaling captains selected the wood himself in Cuba and brought it home in his own ship. The workmanship is that of shipwrights. You may have seen some photographs of old ships, railings that resembled it. And notice the little silver nameplates and numerals on the pew doors. That's another pretty touch. Up to about the Civil War, I understand, every pew was also furnished with a fine brass spittoon. Those old Sag Harbor whalers were a rough lot." He shook his head with a kind of admiration and pointed up at the wall. "I mentioned the Phoenician-swastika motif," he went on. "Well, there it is again, in that frieze just under the ceiling. Also, the columns supporting the galleries are exactly like those that formed the colonnade in the Sir Christopher Wren section of the steeple. You see how perfectly Lafever tied everything together?"

"There's another example of it, up there in the choir loft," Mr. Crawford said, turning back toward the lobby. He nodded in the direction of a third, and smaller, gallery, which linked the two side ones just above the door to the lobby. In a niche in the wall behind it stood what appeared to be a replica in miniature of the church's towering facade. I could even make out a row of tiny blubber spades around the parapets. "Our organ," he said. "You can see the pipes through those vents in the casing." He glanced at his watch. "If we're going up on the bell deck, we'd better get started. It's a good climb. How about you, Doctor?"

"You flatter me, Donald," Dr. Tillinghast said. "I'll try to content myself here below. I think, in fact, I'll sit down."

We left Dr. Tillinghast, looking wistfully after us, among the melancholy plaques in the vestibule. A circular staircase in the pylon to the right led us up to a bare anteroom on the gallery level. We went through a door into the choir loft, where there was another door, about the size of a transom, leading into the base of the tower. Mr. Crawford squirmed through this one. "I don't know who designed this," he said, "but he must have been thinking of a porthole." I followed him into a cobwebby cubicle behind the organ niche. It was not quite pitch-dark. "Watch yourself, now," he said. "These steps are steep." We went up two angular flights to a twilit landing, where Mr. Crawford directed my hand to the rail of an almost perpendicular stepladder. Then he disappeared overhead, breathing hard. I felt my way slowly after him to another landing and another ladder. We were well up in the tower now, and I could hear the sound of the wind outside. Light appeared above, and broadened into a tinted window, extending a foot or two above the level of a third landing, where we found ourselves in a forest of bare joists, beams, and uprights. On one of the uprights was painstakingly carved "J. M. F., Sept. 27, 1862." Mr. Crawford leaned limply against a foot-square, hand-hewn pillar. It was anchored, like a mast, in a thick, cast-iron shoe bolted to a wooden girder. "This was one of the steeple supports," he said, giving it an indifferent pat. "The only one that held. It snapped off higher up. The others sailed away with the steeple. Listen to that wind up there. They tell me the steeple used to shake like a tree on a day like this. One more climb and we'll be in the middle of that gale." He moved off along a catwalk of teetering planks. It ended at the foot of a runged ladder, which rose some twenty feet to a trapdoor in the ceiling. The ladder was as unsteady as a rope as I followed him up. "Hold your hat," he said, and heaved back the trap. We stepped out, coattails flying and trousers flapping, onto a creaking tin roof. It seemed like the top of the world.

We gazed down, over roofs and treetops and the spires of three humbler churches at the deserted harbor. Beyond it lay the gray-green plain of the sea and the hazy gray sand bluffs of faraway points and islands. "That's Shelter Island, straight ahead," Mr. Crawford said, hunching deeper into his coat. "Over there to the left of it is Noyack Bay. This smudge in the distance is the north fluke of Long Island—we're about on a line here with Greenport.

That's another old whaling ruin. Off to the right, there, you can see the Rhode Island shore on a good, bright day."

I said it was quite a view. "It must have been magnificent from the top of the old steeple," I added.

"I suppose so," Mr. Crawford said. He turned and looked at me. "I suppose," he went on, "you noticed that our organ casing hasn't got a steeple. It was made that way. Prophetic, wasn't it?" There was an odd expression on his face. "I'll tell you what I think," he said. "Our steeple wasn't blown down by accident. These people here had got so they were worshiping the steeple more than they did God. So He took it away."

AUTHOR'S NOTE:

Sag Harbor has long since emerged from the long sleep in which I first saw it. It is now, like the rest of the area known to visitors from New York City as the Hamptons, fully awake. It has a year-round population of about 2,700. But in summer its population is several times that, and its once deserted waterfront is now, in season, crowded with pleasure craft. Its many fine old houses have been rescued from decay and are among the glories of the area. The Whalers' Church has survived unharmed and "unimproved."

[1948]

17. Shore Whaler: *East Hampton, Long Island*

Shore whaling, the pursuit and capture of whales by a small company of oarsmen in a boat launched from the beach, is a harsh and perilous form of fishery that was evolved by the Puritan settlers of southeastern Long Island in the middle of the seventeenth century and carried on there by their descendants, with an almost ritualistic ferocity, until around 1910. By then, the North Atlantic right whale, to which they were partial, had nearly vanished from the North Atlantic. Shore whaling had ceased some years before that to be very profitable. A generation has now passed since the last chase, and there will probably never be another, but about a dozen Long Island whalemen are still alive. They are all in their seventies or eighties, they are all more or less cousins, they all reside in either East Hampton or Amagansett, and they are the only surviving shore whalers in the world. One of the spryest and unquestionably the most experienced of them is a calm, soft-spoken patriarch named Everett Joshua Edwards, who lives in East Hampton. During his shore-whaling career, he participated in fifteen successful hunts, including one in February 1907, that resulted in the capture of the fifty-four-foot right whale whose skeleton dominates the Hall of Ocean Life at the American Museum of Natural History; and it was he who killed the last right whale ever taken on the Eastern seaboard. That was six miles off the Amagansett beach, in the summer of 1918.

Most of the few remaining shore whalers have been in retirement for years. Edwards is still gainfully active. He could have dropped comfortably into a rocking chair long ago, but he despises idleness. "I enjoy laying hold," he says. His principal hold is on the presidency and managership of the Home Water Company, in East Hampton, which supplies the village with drinking water, and he also has a good grip on much of its stock. He has headed the company since 1931, succeeding his father-in-law, the late Jeremiah Huntting, who was one of its organizers. Edwards's duties at the water company take up most of his time, but he has other rewarding interests. He is secretary-treasurer of Edwards Brothers & Co., a fraternal partnership that operates a fish dock, three gasoline draggers, and a ship chandlery at Promised Land, a snug cove some five miles northeast of East Hampton, on Gardiners Bay. The business was established by Edwards and two of his three brothers, Herbert and Samuel, in 1916. Samuel, who lives in Amagansett, is president of the firm. Herbert, the eldest of the brothers and Everett's senior by two years, died in 1941. The fourth brother, David, is an East Hampton physician. Edwards also has money in the H. W. Sweet Shipyard & Machine Works, in Greenport, and he is a director of the Osborne Trust Company, the East Hampton bank. His activities have always been numerous. From 1904 to 1908 and from 1910 to 1918, he was clerk of the Town of East Hampton, which includes East Hampton, Amagansett, Montauk, and part of Sag Harbor. For a couple of years in the late nineties, he ran a grocery store in Amagansett, and between 1901 and 1917 he was the proprietor of a drugstore in East Hampton.

Despite this abundance of circumstantial evidence, Edwards does not consider himself a businessman and never has. In some humors, it riles him to be taken for one. He explains that he drifted into business by accident and was swept helplessly and unwillingly away. "I've got a head for figures, and I'm not mortally afraid of the work," he says, "but I'm not a real businessman. For one thing, I lack the constitution. I'm bothered by desk pains." Edwards prefers to think of himself as, and in fact he is, a retired fisherman. "I've fished for the table since," he says, "but I really come ashore in 1930. The fishing turned poor. Up to then, no matter what, I was generally on the water. I pulled seine in the surf, I handlined for cod, and I set ocean traps. When there was whaling, I whaled. I had my master's-and-pilot's license at twenty-one, and from beginning to end I went bunkering in season." Bunkers, or menhaden, are a species of inedible fish, being intolerably bony and oily, but they are commercially useful in the manufacture of fertilizer and medicinal oils. They are caught with capacious drawstring nets known as purse seines. In the course of Edwards's nearly fifty years on the water, he was captain of a succession of bunker-fishingboats —among them a hundred-and-seventy-six-foot steamer, the *Amagansett*—that worked out of Promised Land. One June day in 1910, the *Amagansett*, with Edwards and a crew of thirteen aboard, wallowed into port with a load of nearly two million bunkers—the

largest haul ever made by a Long Island bunker boat. "We were
mainly awash all the way from Boston Bay," he says, "but I was
young and greedy then, and bunkering paid. The fact of the matter
is the only clear money I ever made came out of the ocean. 'Twas
all fish money, one way or another."

Edwards is seventy-eight years old. He stands six feet one in his
stocking feet and weighs close to two hundred pounds. He is big-
boned and broad-shouldered, his step is firm, and, unlike many tall
men, he holds his head high. His gaze is serene but a trifle intimi-
dating. He has a hard jaw, a straight and thin-lipped mouth, and
prominent cheekbones, and his eyes are cold and gray and shad-
owed by an unruly lock of glacially white hair that falls across his
forehead. He has been formally designated a handsome man. This
unusual distinction was conferred upon him by Arnold Genthe, the
photographer. It was recorded in the February 1, 1937, issue of
Vogue, in an article entitled "The Handsomest Man I Have Ever
Photographed," to which Genthe and each of several other notable
cameramen contributed a study in male beauty. Genthe encountered
Edwards during a weekend visit to East Hampton in the summer of
1933 and within an hour of their meeting had wheedled him into
sitting for a portrait. Genthe was so persuasive that he even induced
Edwards to change from a business suit to a set of greasy oilskins.
"I didn't much care for having my picture taken in my old work
clothes," Edwards says, "but I obliged him." His expression in the
portrait is stern and somewhat dazed. This look was interpreted by
Genthe and the editors of *Vogue* as evincing a "fearlessness and
pride of race [that] can give the classical mold cards and spades."
The classical mold was adequately represented by the other nomi-
nees, who included Ronald Colman, Gary Cooper, Jack Whiting, and
the Duke of Kent. Edwards was not annoyed by Genthe's tribute, but
he is disinclined to dwell upon the incident. "It surprised me a little,"
he says. "Yes, it did. The others were all young fellows. Mr. Genthe
must have looked at me cross-eyed."

Neither Edwards's good looks nor the state of his health has
been noticeably impaired by time. His appearance has not altered
since the day it first excited Genthe's admiration, and he says he
still feels as nimble as ever. He is, however, a diabetic. He has
been afflicted with this ailment for five years, but he insists that it
rarely inconveniences him. "It's like the desk pains," he says.
"When the desk pains come on, I stand up for a spell. I ward off the
diabetes by standing up when there's pie or pudding put on the
table. That way, and with insulin. I leave my diabetes mostly to my

wife and my brother Dr. Dave." Edwards's confidence in his continuing physical powers is not misplaced. Just before his seventy-seventh birthday, he almost succeeded in tipping and emptying a sixteen-foot dory, beached in his daughter's backyard, that was three-quarters full of rain water. He had wrestled with the boat for an hour and was beginning to ease it over when a couple of neighbors came along and, ignoring his protests, gave him a hand. "I guess we hurt the old man's pride," one of them said later, "but there was a ton of water in that boat. He might have busted himself wide open." A few months later Edwards snatched a spade from a trench digger for his water company who, he decided, was idling, and finished the job himself. He attributes his undiminished strength to the will of God, an unusually happy marriage, and five lifelong precautions. "I don't toy with my food," he explains, "I won't carouse, I've never drunk rum except to keep out the cold, I go to bed when night comes, and I keep my head covered outdoors." On Sunday, when Edwards and his wife, Florence, emerge from their house only for church (like most deeply rooted eastern Long Islanders, they are Presbyterians), he covers his head with a sedate fedora. Every other day of the year, he wears a black, high-crowned, turn-of-the-century pilot's cap. Caps of this sort are no longer on the market; his are made for him by a marine-outfitting firm near Fulton Fish Market. His dress is otherwise conventionally inconspicuous. He favors gray suits, blue shirts with unconstricting collars, and sensible, hump-toed tan shoes. A thick gold chain hangs across his vest, anchored at one end by a heavy gold watch and at the other by a heavier, bone-handled jackknife. He wears a Masonic emblem in his buttonhole.

Mrs. Edwards, a small, bustling, bright-eyed woman of seventy-four, shares her husband's conviction that their marriage has been an extraordinarily happy one. She was seventeen when they were married in 1892. Edwards was twenty-one and had seven hundred and forty-three dollars, all clear fish money, in the Sag Harbor Savings Bank. "I don't recall that we ever had but one little difference," Mrs. Edwards said the other day, "and that was long ago. What happened was Everett grew a mustache. It came in red, and it was big and prickly. Oh, I didn't care for it at all. We had words about that mustache off and on for weeks, until one night I ended it. I waited until Everett fell asleep and then I got up and fetched a pair of scissors and snipped it off. I saved his good looks. With that awful mustache, I'm sure Everett would never have got his picture in *Vogue*." Edwards often feels that he owes his wife an even greater debt of gratitude. He likes to claim that it is possible

that by marrying him she saved his life. "Around the time we met,"
he says, "I was aiming to try and ship on a deep-sea whaler. There
were still a few old whalers putting out. Miss Florence Huntting
changed my mind. I had too much sense to turn my back on a
pretty girl like that for forty-four months. If it hadn't been for her,
though, I'd have gone. Then, the chances are, I'd have been lost
among the icebergs, like my mother's Uncle Rance Conkling. Last
seen, he was on a bull whale's back, heading for the South Pole."

Edwards and his wife make their home in a substantial two-story
faded brown shingle house on David's Lane. He built the place
shortly before his retirement from the sea. It is neither the smallest
nor the largest house on the block, but it is somewhat less humble
than the cottages inhabited by most retired fishermen. They live
comfortably but modestly. Edwards drives to and from his several
offices in a creaky old Dodge coupé, and his wife has always done
all her own housework. They have two children, both married
—Clifford Conkling Edwards and Mrs. Arnold E. Rattray—who
reside in East Hampton, and six grandchildren and one great-
grandchild, and there are nieces and nephews of various generations. Mrs. Rattray is the wife of the editor-and-publisher of the
East Hampton weekly *Star,* and she reports and writes much of the
news in the paper. She also found time, some years ago, to write,
in collaboration with her father, a history of American shore whaling, entitled *Whale Off!,* which was published by Stokes in 1932
and favorably received. Clifford Edwards is a lawyer. With the
exception of Dr. Edwards, he is the first male Edwards in eleven
generations who hasn't fished, clammed, or whaled for a living.
"Clifford is a fine boy and a fine lawyer," his father has said, "but
I'd just as soon he hadn't stayed ashore. He surprised me. The
Edwardses have always been as fishy as could be."

Edwards has lived in East Hampton the better part of his life, but he
is not a native of the village. He was born in Amagansett, which his
ancestors helped settle in the sixteen-eighties, on August 10, 1871,
and he grew up there. "I rarely set foot here in town till I was
full-grown," he says. "Never much cared to. Us 'Gansett boys
liked it where we were." Amagansett is three miles east of East
Hampton and a hundred and ten miles east of New York. Except for
the straggling hamlet of Montauk, which emerged from the wilderness just before the First World War, it is the most easterly village
in the state. It is situated on the scrawny neck of the Montauk
Peninsula. It overlooks the ocean, half a mile to the south, across a

windswept expanse of dunes and beach. There is a desolation of moorland just to the east. To the west and north are potato fields and a low wooded ridge that shelters it only slightly from Gardiners Bay. In spite of its exposed position, it is a snug and peaceful place. Its wandering main street is a hundred and fifty feet wide and lined with picket fences, weathered elms and maples, and comfortable, stooped old houses in deep and shadowy lawns. Several of these houses were built in the seventeenth century. Its population is about a thousand. East Hampton is a little larger than Amagansett, a little older, and a little less withdrawn, but the two are much alike and they have always been closely linked. Both are traditionally oriented toward New England rather than New York, both remained almost motionless throughout the eighteenth and nineteenth centuries, and both within the last generation have more than doubled in size.

The spirited growth of East Hampton and Amagansett vexes Edwards. He cannot reconcile himself to it. In his opinion, they have become unwieldy. He is even more rigidly persuaded that their growth has been accompanied by an abysmal decline in manners, morals, and economic stability. "'Up-to-date' don't mean a thing to me," he says. "I'm old-fashioned. I believe in long drawers and keeping the Sabbath and the best good for all hands. I've seen a lot of changes around here, but I can't say I've noticed much improvement. There's more rich and there's more poor. There's less working and there's more worrying. If I was a few years younger, I might feel some different. I wouldn't remember so well how things used to be out here on the East End. I was twenty-four years of age before the railroad arrived. All the time I was growing up, Sag Harbor was the end of the line. That was an hour or more away by stage. We were out of touch and glad of it, especially us 'Gansetters. Nobody ever had it better than we did. We lived off the land and the sea. There were few drunkards and no roadhouses, and plenty to eat and a good bed to sleep in for all. Everybody was fishy. Wasn't a boy I knew wouldn't rather be a whaleman than the President of the United States. Then the summer people come. There had been a few before, off and on, and mostly in East Hampton, but 'twasn't till 1895, when we got the railroad, that anybody paid much attention to them. Ever since, it's been mortgage the farm and easy money and fall in step with the boarders. In the old days, New York City was Fulton Fish Market. Now it's Wall Street. I don't put the blame here or there. Good or bad, it can't be helped. But, by the gods, I'd like to see things back the way they were when I was a boy. Yes, I would."

* * *

Edwards is haunted happily by the past. Reminiscence rejuvenates him. His voice quickens when he speaks of his youth, and his face softens and his eyes warm and widen. All his early years are wonderfully vivid to him, but it is of whaling and his father, Joshua Edwards, that he most often talks. They dominate his memory and they are inseparable in his mind. "Pop was a whaleman," he says. "I guess he was about the best they ever had around here. The reason us 'Gansetters whaled harder and longer than anybody else was mainly my father. He led all the chases. There were close to fifty whales taken off this stretch of beach in his time, and he killed all but one. It wasn't just the money. A fifty-footer—what we called a big one—would bring better than two thousand dollars in bone and oil back then, but it was more than that to him. He loved whaling. Never got enough. Always wild to go. I remember once, when I was little, asking him wasn't he afraid of a whale. 'Yes, yes,' he said. 'I generally try to keep clear of him.' Pop was really rank. He was eighty-five years of age when he died, in 1915, and he went off the beach almost to the end. He saw it all. The first part of his life, he was a deep-sea whaler, around the Horn and up in the arctic. I remember him telling how they were chased through the Bering Strait, during the Civil War, by the Rebel privateer the *Shenandoah*. He started in at twenty, as soon as a chance made, as a harpooner on the *Ontario*, out of Sag Harbor. Nobody had to show him how. He was a 'Gansett boy, so he knew. Altogether, he made five deep-sea voyages, ending up on the *Jireh Perry*, out of New Bedford, as first mate. When he come home for good, in 1868, deep-sea whaling was mostly over. He and Mother got married that year, and they built a house on a twenty-five-acre farm he had from his father. It was just off Main Street, on Whippoorwill Lane, and that's where I was born and raised. It's still there, but we had to let it go after Mother died, in 1929. City people own it now. There isn't any Whippoorwill Lane any more. They call it Atlantic Avenue. Even our old house has got a name to it—I forget what. I generally look the other way when I go by.

"Pop didn't farm much. I guess he was too fishy. He whaled when he could, and when he couldn't whale, he fished. At one time, he went after sturgeon. Used to be plenty of them right off the coast here. He was in the Russian-caviar trade. What they did was ship the roe to New York, and there was somebody there who shipped it to Russia, and the Russians put their fancy labels on it and shipped it back to New York. There was many an American millionaire ate Long Island caviar and thought he was living high.

Most summers, Pop bunkered. He was captain of the *Amagansett* before me. And he did a good deal of codfishing in the fall. He usually handlined off the beach or set small trawls. We lived on salt cod in the winter—that and samp. During the cod run, our ham and eggs tasted like fish. We salted and dried our cod out in the pightle—what they call the back yard now—and the stock ate the scraps. One hog we slaughtered, you couldn't tell the meat from fresh cod. Samp is a kind of porridge made out of hulled corn cooked up with dried beans and salt pork. The white men got it from the Indians. Our Sunday dinner was always samp and pie and a big pitcher of milk. The reason was samp was one thing that could be cooked the day before. We didn't break the Sabbath on any account, even to cook. That was one day when the whales were safe. The 'Gansett beach could be alive with them, but if 'twas Sunday, Pop wouldn't do no more than look. He was a good, God-fearing man. I've seen him some riled, but I never heard him profane. The worst he'd ever come out with was 'cod dum.'

I can see Pop still, as plain as day, walking the beach or sitting on the stern sheets of a whaleboat, in his old sealskin cap and his old pea jacket that he'd patched himself in a hundred different colors, and his beard tucked in his vest, and his white hair down to his shoulders and blowing in the breeze. He was a big man, as big and strong as me. When he sung out, somebody jumped. It was the same at home or afloat. He was the captain. Mother and us boys and my sister Rosa, who's dead now—we were the crew. I guess Mother was first mate. They saw to it together that the morning sun never shone on any of us in bed. I was doing a boy's work by the time I was five, and a man's work at ten. All of our fun was work. If we wanted to go swimming, we had to take along a clam rake. The place we went to for a picnic was a cranberry bog or a blackberry patch. Pop was stern and he hated idleness, but I never knew him mean. When there was a compliment due, he gave it. He had his own ideas and he was generally right. The first time I ever saw New York City was in 1885, when Pop took me in to Fulton Market with him to sell some whalebone and oil. We stayed at the United States Hotel, on Pearl Street, and I remember the dressed-up people in the lobby staring at those seven-foot slabs of bone that we had under our arms for samples. Pop stared right back. Anybody didn't like the way he travelled could look the other way. He was one man that wouldn't mimic.

"All I ever wanted was to do things the way my father did, and as good. He taught me just about everything I was able to learn. I had pretty slim schooling after the age of ten. Never went when it interfered with fishing or farming. Until I was fourteen, though, I'd sometimes go back to school in the middle of winter if there was nothing else doing. As soon as I could handle my hands, Pop had me sewing a good sailmaker's herringbone stitch. I mended my clothes and I pieced quilts. The best quilt I made is still in use. There were a good many wrecks in those days. Every so often, a coasting vessel would get in trouble on the bar a quarter mile off here, or on the rocks this side of Montauk Point. Salvage meant a lot to us. After a storm, you could find whatever you needed on the beach. The *George Appold*, a freighter out of Providence and bound for Newport News, is one wreck I remember. Pop and I helped bring the crew off. She went down with a load of calico and copper-toed work shoes in 1889. The quilt I still use is mostly brown-and-white calico from the *George Appold*. Another wreck, in 1890, was the *Elsie Fay*. She carried coconuts. I never cared much for coconut anything after the *Elsie Fay* went down. A good while later, in the winter of 1922, the *Madonna* foundered. She was carrying nothing but liquor. Just about everybody risked pneumonia in the surf that day.

"Pop learned to pull teeth on his voyages, and for some years he was the closest thing to a dentist we had in 'Gansett. He even pulled his own. I can see him twisting and scolding now. He taught me that trade, too. Something else I learned from him was how to make a lop fence. You never hear about lop fences any more. They're out of date, like everything else. I understand they never were made anywhere in the world except here on the East End and in some parts of England. The way we did it was this. We picked out a row of young trees in the right place, cut each trunk halfway through about two or three feet from the ground, and then pulled the trees over. The upright part made the post, and the rest of the tree was the bar. It didn't kill the tree, so it kept on growing, but on the horizontal. There never was a better fence to keep cattle out of a wood lot, or one that needed less mending. Over in the Northwest Woods, between here and Sag Harbor, there are still a few lop fences left. They're as old as I am and still going just as strong.

"I learned the most from Pop down on the beach. When I was five, he put me in the surf and told me to come ashore. That's the way all us boys learned to swim. A little later, he began to teach me how to handle an oar, and then how to throw a harpoon. I practiced darting with a wagon stake that was about the heft of a whale iron. That and launching a boat in the surf are two things you can't pick up from a book. You've got to absorb them when you're young. The only grown man I ever knew who got hold of the surf quick was a fellow from Connecticut, a codfisherman. He married a 'Gansett girl, and a brother of hers who had been around surf a lot helped him. To be a surfman and do business right, you've got to know when you can get off and when you can't, and you've got to have oarsmen who have confidence in you. If there's a wind sea—a lot of chop—and the surf is breaking much over eight or nine feet, my advice is stay ashore. You can get off in a heavy sea if it's a ground swell and steady. There is generally three heavy seas and then will come a slatch—two or three smaller seas behind them. You follow as near you dare after a heavy sea, and if it's smooth behind, let her go. The crew's confidence in the judgment of the boat header, the man at the tiller, is important. And they've got to have discipline. They're rowing, so they're all facing aft. They don't know what's ahead. The boat header is the only one can see, and he gives the orders accordingly. Pop was always boat header when we whaled. Oh, I can hear him now. 'Shove her in!' he'd sing out, and we'd shove her in and each grab an oar. Then 'Pull ahead! Hold water! Stern! Pull ahead!'—and we'd be off and clear.

"That's the one big difference between shore whaling and deep-sea whaling—the surf. In deep-sea whaling, you launch the whaleboat from the ship. When you go off the beach, you've got the surf to contend with. Otherwise, the two are the same, or were. The whaleboat is the same, the tools are the same, and the methods are the same. I've got my father's whaleboat and all our old gear put away in my daughter's barn. I like to go over there sometimes and just sit down for a while. Pop's boat was built in New London in 1877, when they still knew how, and she's regulation size. She's twenty-eight feet long, six feet wide at the center thwart, and sharp at both ends, with oak ribs and half-inch cedar planks. She's big but light—lighter than some dories. You want a whaleboat that will stand some weather and hold up when you make fast to a whale, but you don't want one so heavy you can't get her off the beach in a hurry. The regulation crew is six, counting all hands. Going off and up till you fasten, every man except the boat header pulls an oar. The boat header steers. On a whaleboat, his tiller a twenty-eight-foot oar. The harpooner is called boat steerer, but he don't steer till after you're fast. He pulls the forward oar, a little fourteen-footer, till you're right on the whale. Then the boat header sings out 'Give it to him!' and the boat steerer ships his oar, gets up his iron, and darts it quick as he can. He's got a second harpoon handy, and he'll hurl it if there's time or need. Soon as he makes fast, he moves aft to take over the steering oar and to tend the towline. Our towline was generally a hundred fathom. It's fixed to the harpoon shank and threaded through a chock in the bow. It runs into a tub about midship, where it's coiled so it won't foul, and then on aft to an upright post—what we call the loggerhead—in the stern. The boat header looks after the line, taking a hitch around the loggerhead, till the boat steerer relieves him. Then the boat header goes forward to kill the whale. He's got two lances there, and he'll throw both. A good man, like Pop, could dart a lance fifty or sixty feet and sink five feet of iron into the whale.

"There's some difference between a harpoon and a lance. People talk as if the harpooner does the killing. He don't. He just makes fast. That's all a harpoon is made for. We used an eleven-foot harpoon—eight foot of hickory shaft and a three-foot iron shank, tempered so it could bend double and not break. The way a harpoon works is this. There is an iron pin that goes through the center of the barbed head to make a hinge and fix it to the shank. Another pin, made of soft wood, holds the head in line with the shaft till it's into the blubber. When the whale sounds, that wooden pin snaps and the head toggles around on the iron pin at a right angle to the rest of the iron. It can't pull out, so you're fast as long as the line holds and the boat don't get stove. A lance is a spear. It's got a ten-foot shaft and a five-foot shank and a razor-edged head. I've seen my father shave with his lance. The other men in the boat mainly just row, but by golly, they earn their passage. When I went off with Pop, I pulled leading oar, just forward of the boat header. Here in town, though, nobody knew as much as I did about whaling. I generally went boat header then.

"The only whale we ever hunted was the right whale. Finbacks were common, but we didn't try for them. The reason was they're too fast, they don't make much oil, and their bone is short and brittle. Any 'Gansett boy could tell a right whale from a finback just by watching the spout. A whale comes up to breathe and blow every twenty minutes or so. The air he lets out makes the spout. The right whale has two blowholes in the tip of his head, so he'll send up a crotched spout, maybe eight feet high. A finback spouts a single stream. He blows quicker than the right whale and he blows higher. Another way to tell is to watch a whale round out his bilge to go down. The right whale will bring his flukes out of water, but all you'll see of a finback when he rounds to sound is the fin on the afterpart of his bilge.

"The right whale got his name from the old whalemen because he was the right one for oil and bone, especially bone. Whalebone —baleen, to give it its proper name—isn't really bone. Instead of teeth, most whales have a row of long, flat, black, hairy slabs of something like horn set close together in both sides of the upper jaw. That's baleen. A whale lives on a tiny little animal, no bigger than a bug, called brit. When he feeds, he throws back his lips and the brit floats in. The baleen hair acts like a sieve. It lets the water out, but it holds the brit. I've seen slabs of whalebone fourteen feet long and it comes longer than that. I remember Pop telling of some he got on his voyages that measured nineteen feet. There could be close to three thousand pounds of baleen alone in a whale with bone that long. Toward the end of whaling, baleen is what mainly interested us. It generally brought around four dollars a pound. Don't let anybody tell you the whale couldn't swallow Jonah. I remember one we pulled up to. He had his mouth open and his lips laid off. He was feeding. We came up fast, and I just happened to cast my eye around and I looked right down his throat. It must have been fourteen feet deep, and better than a third as wide. I kept pulling, but my blood started to circulate."

Altogether, Edwards estimates, he took part in some thirty chases. Most of his fifteen successful hunts occurred in the eighteen-eighties and nineties. He went off for the first time on a raw and windy day in March, 1887. He was then fifteen and a half. "I was young to whale," he says, "but my father decided I was ready. I was big for my age, almost full-grown, and I pulled an oar as good as a man. He figured I'd watched enough chases and heard enough talk to know. I agreed with him. My recollection is that the weft went out in the forenoon. What we called the weft was an old American flag. It was raised for a signal on a rooftop near the beach when a whale was sighted. Soon as we'd see the weft, everybody would sing out 'Whale off!' and make for the beach. Three boats rallied for the hunt that day, every one headed by an Edwards. My Uncle Jonathan headed one, with David Barnes for boat steerer. Another was headed by my Uncle Charles, who was in his sixties then, with Charles Mulford going boat steerer. I went with Pop as leading oar, and my Uncle Gabe Edwards was his boat steerer. Uncle Gabe was as rank as Pop—ranker, if anything. Oh, he was callous. Nothing fazed him.

"The whale was laying to the east, about a mile and a half offshore, when we shoved in. He breached three times and sounded. We sprung ahead, aiming to get to him by the next rising, and, pulling hard, with Pop nagging us, we just made it. Pop sung out 'Give it to him, Gabe!' and Uncle Gabe got fast, right in the back of the neck, with all his might and main, and his teeth set.

Then Uncle Jonathan come up, and David Barnes put both his irons in. Pop shifted with Uncle Gabe, but before he could dart his lance, the whale went into his flurry, head out of water and running in circles. Running like that meant he was liable to sink. About that moment, Uncle Charles come up, and Charles Mulford darted. The lances shot right across the whale's nose, and that last iron riled him. He lifted his nose right through the middle of their boat. I guess my eyes were popping out of my head. She rolled over, bottom up, and all hands went in the air—all except Uncle Charles. He was an old man, but he scrambled like a monkey, rolling right over with the boat and ending up sitting astraddle of her keel. There wasn't a drop of water on him. The whale was dead by then. Pop and Uncle Jonathan had lanced him plenty. We began to get the men out of the water. Charles Mulford was the last to come up. He'd gone deep and he come up pale. While he was down there, he told us later, he saw something close by and he put out a hand to shove it away. He shoved, but it didn't budge. Turned out to be the whale's mouth. That whale was a big one, a bull, mostly black but with some white on him. Took us a good while rowing and towing to get him ashore.

"A good many of the whales we raised in those days were that limber. There's one I remember come along around Easter in 1894. Pop had Charles Mulford for boat steerer, and my brother Dave, who was home from medical school for the holiday, was pulling his leading oar. I went off as boat steerer for my Uncle Jess Edwards. Charles Mulford got fast with both irons without much trouble. That's when the fun began. Instead of turning to fight and giving Pop a chance to sicken him quick, the whale settled right down to run. He headed for East Hampton with Pop and them in tow, and then he headed back to 'Gansett, and then he dodged around and made for East Hampton again. He gave them a regular sleigh ride. I guess he hit twenty-five miles an hour. He was some fast whale, and he never slackened. He had them in tow, bow all out of water and the stern sheets near awash, from morning till mid-afternoon. The rest of us couldn't do anything but just lay around and watch while three and a half hours went by. Toward the end, he cut all of a sudden right across our bow. Without waiting for Uncle Jess to call me up—I shouldn't have done it, but I did—I peaked my oar and got around and threw my harpoon. The whale was rounding to go down, and I missed. My iron went about a foot under his small. I never got another chance, but Pop had him at the next rising. He must have lanced him seventy-five times without letting go of the pole. Dave told me afterward that from where he sat aft, all he could see through the spray of thick blood was the top of Pop's head. The whale went into his flurry soon after, and we gave some cheer when he was dead. Charles Mulford did more than yell. He hopped right out and danced a jig on the whale's back.

"Pop got his last whale in 1907, on George Washington's Birthday, when he was seventy-seven years of age. He whaled after that, but he never fastened again. Uncle Gabe was his boat steerer that day, and there were four boats went off—three from 'Gansett and one from East Hampton. I headed the East Hampton boat, with Felix Dominy, who owned her, as boat steerer. We got the first chance—the whale broke water three boat lengths ahead of us. But when I sung out 'Spring ahead!' Charles Baker pulled so hard and quick his oar broke. That put us out. I minded some, but I'd really hoped the chance would fall to Pop. He hadn't had a whale in a good while, and he wanted one. Next rising, Uncle Gabe got fast. Then Pop shifted with him and lanced the whale as pretty as you please, and 'twas soon over. That whale wasn't as limber as some, but she was a good-sized cow. She's the whale they've got in the Museum of Natural History, in New York. Roy Chapman Andrews was just starting in at the Museum back then, and my father's last whale was his first job. The Museum heard about that whale somehow, and they sent him out here to buy her from us. My father figured we did all right. We got a hundred dollars for the skeleton and five percent over the market for the baleen, and we kept the blubber. I think it made around two thousand gallons of oil.

"Whaling began to fall off after that chase. The last whale I, or anybody, got didn't amount to much. 'Twas only a calf and couldn't have measured over twenty feet. The old cow that was with him got away. We were rusty by that time—hadn't been off in three or four years—and then, toward twilight, a squall come up. Started in to blow feathers. We were twelve miles offshore when we had to let the old cow go. As 'twas, it took fifteen hours of rowing and towing to get the baby ashore. He didn't make but about thirty gallons of oil, and we never sold a drop. Nobody cared to buy. All we really got out of that rally was old times' sake."

The right whale, though rare, is not yet wholly extinct. They are still observed from time to time along the eastern Long Island coast. One, a fifty-foot cow, turned up just off East Hampton not long after I first met Mr. Edwards. She was raised toward noon by the caretaker of the village bathing pavilion, William Talmage. Talmage is a retired whaler, a robust man of eighty, and he at once telephoned Edwards, who is one of his closest friends. Edwards joined him on the beach a few minutes later. The whale had sounded just as he drove up, and Talmage pointed out where he thought she would be at her next rising. She came up there, blowing lazily, in deep water less than a mile beyond the bar. The two old men stood just off the road on the soft, frosty sand and watched her in silence until she rounded to go down. Then Talmage cleared his throat. "Good-sized," he remarked. "Yes, yes," Edwards said, and turned back to his car.

[1950]

18. Storm: Amagansett, Long Island

When my wife and I went to bed in our house, about a mile inland from the coastal village of Amagansett, on eastern Long Island, on Wednesday night, March 28, it was raining hard, and a wild north wind was blowing the rain against the windows. I woke up for a moment around three o'clock, and the sound at the windows had changed. The rain had turned to sleet. When we came down to breakfast on Thursday morning, it was snowing—a dense, driving snow. We live on a hilltop in a countryside of potato fields and woods, and the treetops were twisting and thrashing and bending low. It looked like a blizzard. I let our current dog, a black cocker spaniel named Sam, out the kitchen door, but he took one look and came back in.

We ate breakfast and listened to the news on the radio. A series of tornadoes in the Carolinas had killed at least fifty people, injured hundreds, and left thousands homeless. High tides and twenty-foot waves were ripping the New Jersey shore. There were maritime warnings as far north as Boston. Winds had reached gale force, and higher gusts—hurricane gusts—were predicted. Many highways were flooded, and all highways were treacherous. More than a foot of snow had fallen in the Poconos. Schools and colleges throughout the metropolitan area were closing. All metropolitan airports were—The radio went dead and the lights went out. The furnace stopped. We sat and waited. Like all people who live in the country, Kay and I had been through this before—many times before. We waited, and hoped, for the lights to flicker on again. But nothing happened. The worst of it was that we were one of the Long Island Lighting Company's up-to-the-minute all-electric homes. Everything was electric—the oil-fired furnace, the kitchen range, the hot-water heater, the pump that drew water from our well, even my razor. I finished what was left of my breakfast and went to the telephone and called 727-8400, the emergency number of the Long

269

Island Lighting Company. I got the busy signal. So we were not alone. I put on a sweater and made a fire in the living-room fireplace. The barometer in my office registered 28.9—the lowest I could remember in recent years. The thermometer outside my office window registered 30 degrees. The three of us—Kay and Sam and I—sat by the fire and listened to the roar of the wind. Every four or five minutes, either Kay or I would go to the telephone and call 727-8400. And would get the busy signal.

Around ten o'clock, I put on boots and a down jacket and went out to the woodshed and brought in an armful of cordwood. Then, such is habit, I drove in to the village for the morning *Times* and the mail. There was an inch or two of snow on the ground, and the air was full of driving snow and flying litter. I could hear a heavy roaring, and thought of the twenty-foot waves along the New Jersey shore. But I listened again, and it wasn't the boom of the surf that I was hearing. What I heard was the wind, only the wind. I saw a big elm down—one of the last of the turn-of-the-century elms—near the fire station on Amagansett's Main Street. There were broken branches everywhere. Both the store and the post office were without lights, but the *Times* and the mail had both been delivered. The electric clock on the post office wall read nine-forty. I could hardly get back to my car against the wind. I watched an abandoned shopping cart wobble across the parking lot and overturn. I thought of driving on to the ocean for a look at the surf, and then remembered a friend who had had the same thought several years before and had lost most of the paint on one side of his car in a blast of blowing sand. I drove directly home. I turned up my driveway and parked in the turnaround and got out and happened to glance at the verge of woods that marks our north property line—and saw the cause of our trouble. The top of a sixty-foot oak had broken off and was hanging, bouncing in the wind, on what was left of our power line. I went in the house and told Kay the bad news. A general power outage, even a neighborhood power outage, was one thing; it would be attended to without an individual complaint from every affected Lilco customer. The hanging treetop meant that our outage was ours alone; it would have to be specifically reported. Kay told me her news. The Lilco emergency number was still busy.

I sat down by the fire with the *Times*. But I couldn't comfortably see to read. I got up and went over to the big front window. There wasn't much light even there. I looked at the front page and scanned a few headlines. The cold seeped through the window like a draft. The furnace had been off for a good two hours. I gave up, and went back to the fire to get warm. It was more, though, than the growing cold in the room. I felt too restless to read. There is an excitement about a big storm. It dominates the mind and trivializes everything else. I knew there was no cause for alarm. We would, however uncomfortably, endure. But there was a pressing sense of survival. I went to the telephone and called 727-8400 again. It was still busy. I came back and piled some more wood on the fire, and made an inventory of our assets. We had plenty of firewood: I'd been cutting wood all winter. There was water—warm, tepid, or cool—in the hot-water tank. There was bound to be some water in the water tank in the pump room. We had two tank toilets: two flushes. We had plenty of candles and plenty of candlesticks, including some hurricane globes. We had a flashlight. And somewhere up in the attic there was a little two-burner butane picnic stove. I went and got it. It turned out that one of the burners was broken. There were, however, two cylinders of gas. Kay said one burner was enough, at least for some kind of lunch. She could manage. The fire was getting low. It was astonishing how much wood it took to keep it going strong. I went out to the shed and brought in three big armloads. I checked the barometer. It had fallen a fraction, to 28.8. The temperature reading was 29 degrees. I hadn't noticed before, but when I came back from my office there was a thin haze of smoke along the living-room ceiling.

Lunch was canned chili, heated on the little picnic stove, and soda crackers. With it we drank, in the rationed absence of water, a bottle of beer. Sam had his usual dog biscuits. My hands were inky from the *Times* and grimy from tending the fire, and I would have liked to have a wash, but I thought I'd better save that amenity until just before dinner. There was nothing I could do about shaving. Kay cleared away the dishes and glasses and silverware, and added them to the breakfast things in the paralyzed dishwasher. I tried the Lilco number again. I went out and started the car and turned on the radio and found a local station. I listened to an endless list of cancellations—schools, meetings, club activities, sports events, exercise classes, little-theatre rehearsals, trains, buses. I had no idea we were such a busy community. The snow was expected to end this evening. Strong winds were expected to continue through tonight. A fishing boat was missing off Montauk Point. Then came the thump and screech of rock music. I took another look at the broken treetop. It was still hanging there. I went back to the woodshed and brought in another load of wood. Kay said a friend in our neighboring village of East Hampton had called. We were dining there on Saturday night. No, their power had only flickered. I would have to do something about shaving by Saturday. The telephone rang. My foolish heart leaped. Could it be Lilco? No. It could not. And it wasn't. It was our son, calling from his home in south-central Massachusetts. He was at home because of the storm. So was his little daughter. He guessed they had had almost fifteen inches of snow. Their power had gone off, but only for about twenty minutes. He wished us well. He was sure we would have power in time for dinner. A moment later, I thought he might just possibly be right. I called Lilco again—and this time it rang. It rang and rang and rang, and finally a man answered. I told him my name and address and the nature of my complaint.

He said, "What street is that near?"

I told him.

"Can you give me the grid number there?"

"Grid number?"

"It's on your bill. Down near the bottom, under the red line."

Kay was standing in rapture at my side. I turned to her.

"Do we have a bill?"

"Yes—it came yesterday. Why? Is something wrong?"

"It has our grid number on it."

She came running, racing, back triumphantly with our bill. I found a red line. I found a number. I read it off. It was three digits, two digits, four digits—like a Social Security number.

"Can you give me your pole number?"

I did know that, from experience. "It's three point five. When do you think your people might be here?"

"I can't say, sir. This is a bad storm. We've got a whole lot of complaints. But I'll make a report of your call. We'll get to you as soon as we can."

I thanked him warmly and hung up. "Well!"

"I just can't believe it," Kay said. "Oh, I feel so much better. Now that they know about us, all we have to do is wait."

"I doubt if they'll get here today. It'll be tomorrow. Probably tomorrow morning."

We dined that night by candlelight on a card table in front of the fire. But first we celebrated. I opened the freezer long enough to snatch out a tray of ice, and mixed a round of Martinis. Kay put a carefully minimal pot of water—tepid water from the hot-water faucet—on the picnic stove to boil for cooking pasta for fettuccine Alfredo, and fixed some boiled shrimp (also snatched from the freezer) in Russian dressing for a first course. She made a green salad to go with the pasta. Sam had his usual dinner of dog food and table scraps. We drank our drinks and told each other that this was kind of fun, that we were really pretty comfortable, even cozy.

The water had not yet boiled by the time we finished our drinks. I made another round. By the time we finished that, the water had come to a feeble boil. Kay dropped in the pasta, and I got out a bottle of wine—a bottle of Fleurie. We dined, as I say, by candle-light—by the light of a varied symphony of dinner-table candles, votive candles, plumbers' candles, candles in hurricane globes. There were more than a dozen of them in all, but the light by which we dined was a soft, romantic twilight. We finished dinner a little after seven. At eight o'clock, we went to bed.

It was a long night, and I woke up several times. The wind was still blowing. I woke up for the last time just after seven. Sam was barking his head off in the kitchen. I listened, and between barks I could hear what sounded like a heavy truck coming up the road. I strained my ears. The sound came louder and louder—and then faded slowly away.

Kay said, "What is it?"

"I heard a truck on the road. I thought it might be Lilco. But it didn't stop."

"Maybe there's some trouble up the road. Maybe it'll stop on the way back."

"Maybe."

"I don't know what to do about breakfast. I guess I could make some oatmeal. When the power goes on, we can have a good lunch."

We jumped into our clothes—our warmest clothes. The snow had stopped—it was only raining now—but it was still cold. In the gray morning light I could see my breath. We went downstairs, Kay to the kitchen and I to the fireplace. Yesterday's day-long fire had left a mountain of ashes. I cleaned them out, and got a new fire going. The living room smelled of smoke. It was a good smell. It made me hungry: it smelled like country-cured ham or bacon cooking. We had a breakfast of oatmeal and instant coffee. Last night's euphoria had dimmed to an anxious hope. I ate with one ear cocked for the truck. I heard only the wind and the rain. Kay cleared away the breakfast things. The dishwasher was getting close to full. The barometer had risen a point, to 28.9. The temperature reading was 32 degrees. I went to the telephone and called 727-8400. I thought they might be able to give me an approximate time of relief. I got the busy signal. I went out and brought in some more wood.

I went out again at ten o'clock and got in the car and headed for the village. There were puddles, almost ponds, everywhere. A fold in a big potato field at the foot of the hill was white with gulls squatting down out of the wind. The lights were on in the store and also in the post office. The *Times* had a page-one story with a three-column headline: "STORM BATTERS EAST WITH SNOW, WIND AND WAVES." I learned that more than three hundred and thirty thousand homes were without power, from south Jersey to Boston. These included some thirty-six thousand customers of the Long Island Lighting Company. I thought that over gloomily as I drove back home. Of course, I told myself, that was yesterday's figure. Still, I wondered how many repair trucks the company had. The treetop was still in place on our power line. Kay was sitting hunched by the fire. Sam was curled at her feet, grinning in his sleep.

"I tried Lilco again," she said. "I got a recording. The man gave a number to call if your problem was gas. If your problem was electricity, he said to hold on and somebody would be with you in a minute. I held on for twelve minutes by my watch. Then I hung up. My ear was beginning to hurt."

We lunched in front of the fireplace on the reheated remains of last night's fettuccine Alfredo and what was left of last night's wine. The rain stopped and the wind dropped. We called Lilco four more times. We got the busy signal three times, and the fourth time it simply rang and rang and rang. I called a fifth time, and was answered by a live voice. I gave my name and address and my grid number and my pole number.

"Just when did your power go off?" the man asked.

I told him yesterday morning.

"Then," he said, "you should have reported it yesterday."

"I did," I said.

"Oh," he said. "Well, we're doing the best we can. I'll see that your report goes into the file."

I hung up, and Kay said, "What did they say? Did they give you any idea when?"

I told her what the man had said. Or hadn't said. We sat by the fire. I thought, A roaring fire in the fireplace. I thought, A good fire blazing on the hearth. They were images of comfort and well-being that were beginning to lose their resonance. The weather had begun to clear. I could see patches of open sky. The storm was over. That should have made me feel better, but it didn't. It made me feel worse. The storm wasn't over for us. We were still stormbound here in the house.

Kay said, "I think we're going to have to do something. This isn't any fun anymore. It's getting impossible. I can't do anything about dinner. There isn't anything I can cook on the stove. We're practically out of water. I feel dirty. And I'm cold."

"You think we should call somebody—ask somebody to take us in?"

"No. I don't think I want to do that. I think we should go to that motel in East Hampton. That East Hampton House. I've always thought it looked very nice. And Sam could go to Crooked Pond."

"You don't think we'll be seeing Lilco today?"

"I think this could go on forever."

"Well . . ." I thought of a clean, well-lighted room. I thought of a warm room. I thought of a hot bath. "I could give them a call and see how they're fixed."

I went to the telephone and called. The East Hampton House had plenty of room (this wasn't July), and we could come in any time we liked.

We sat by the fire for another hour, listening for the sound of a heavy truck. Then we packed a bag and put Sam on his leash and put out the fire with the last of our water. We went out to the car.

"Isn't it funny?" Kay said. "I mean, that we've still got our telephone. The telephone never seems to go out."

We dropped Sam off at the Crooked Pond Kennel, where he was known and liked, and checked in at the East Hampton House around five o'clock. We had a second-floor room with a view in front of Pantigo Road, the highway link between East Hampton and Amagansett, and a view in back of the tennis courts and swimming pool of summer—and, surprisingly, of a barnyard. I turned up the heat. We had long, hot baths. I shaved. We put on clean clothes. We drove back to Amagansett to a restaurant there called Gordon's, where we were taken hospitably in and given a satisfying dinner. We went back to the East Hampton House and looked at television and went to bed. I woke up on Saturday morning to the sound of a rooster crowing.

I bought a copy of the *Times* on the way to breakfast. The storm had been retired from page one to page twenty-five, and the headline had shrunk from three columns to one: "AFTER STORM, THE CLEANUP GETS STARTED." The fishing boat off Montauk Point was presumed lost with all hands. Twelve thousand homes on Long Island remained without electricity. We had breakfast at a place in East Hampton (recommended by the East Hampton House) locally called the Buttery. There were photographs on the walls of Elizabeth II, of Prince Charles and Princess Diana, and of the English countryside. The breakfast offerings included scones and sausage rolls. The Buttery was crowded with men and women of all ages and in all manner of costumes. Everybody seemed to know everybody else, and the customers all seemed to be known to the waitresses. We had lived in East Hampton Township for thirty years and had never seen any of them before. This was a different East

Hampton. It gave me an odd feeling. I was a stranger among regulars. I was a stranger in what had become my home town.

We drove back to our house after breakfast. It was a cool morning, a gray morning, but the wind was only a breeze. It was hard not to feel a little hopeful, a little expectant. We turned up the driveway, and nothing had changed. The treetop still lay across the power line. But the house no longer smelled like country-cured ham. It smelled like the scene of a fire. I called the Lilco number, and after eight or ten rings a man answered. I gave him my regular report. He promised to add it to the file. I asked about our prospects.

"We're beginning to see light at the end of the tunnel," he said.

I reported that curious metaphor to Kay. She was in the kitchen cleaning perished perishables out of the refrigerator. They made an unattractive parcel—yogurt, cottage cheese, milk, cream, butter, mayonnaise. The refrigerator was warmer than the kitchen. We decided to leave the freezer alone and hope for the best. I carried the perishables out to the garbage can, and took a walk around the place. The storm had touched only that treetop. Wispy locusts, rigid hickories, ancient beeches, tortured chokecherries, even a big dead red oak pitted with woodpecker holes had come through undamaged. I went back to the house, and Kay told me that another friend in East Hampton had called and invited us to Sunday lunch.

"I've got an idea," she said. "Let's get in the car and drive around. There's bound to be Lilco trucks working around here somewhere. We might get some satisfaction from somebody actually on the job."

So we cruised. I thought, What if we had lost the telephone? What if something had happened to the car? We cruised. Up the road, down the street, along the lane—and, sure enough, around eleven-thirty we came upon a Lilco pickup and a Lilco van and a big yellow Lilco truck with a cherry picker angled into the sky and a man in the crow's nest cutting a big oak free from an entanglement of power lines. I parked and got out and asked around among a crowd of neighbors and rubberneckers and men in work clothes, and was directed to a young man in a plum-colored windbreaker. I introduced myself and gave him my report. He looked through a sheaf of papers on a clipboard. He shook his head.

"I don't see your name on my list," he said. He got out a map and studied it. "But where you live isn't too far from here. I'll tell you what I'll do. When we get finished up here, I'll radio in to the office. If they say go, I'll go."

We lunched at Gordon's, where we had dined the night before. It was a tense and tentative occasion. But there did seem to be some